*Peasant Society and Marxist
Intellectuals in China*

Peasant Society and Marxist Intellectuals in China

Fang Zhimin and the Origin of a Revolutionary Movement in the Xinjiang Region

KAMAL SHEEL

Princeton University Press

Princeton, New Jersey

Copyright © 1989 by Princeton University Press
Published by Princeton University Press,
41 William Street, Princeton, New Jersey   08540
In the United Kingdom:
Princeton University Press, Oxford

Library of Congress Cataloging-in-Publication Data
Sheel, Kamal, 1950–
    Peasant society and Marxist intellectuals in China : Fang Zhimin and the origin of a
revolutionary movement in the Xinjiang region / Kamal Sheel.
    p.   cm.
    Bibliography: p.
    Includes index.
    ISBN 0–691–05571–8
    1. Communism—China—Kiangsi Province—History. 2. Fang, Chih-min, 1900–1935. 3.
Communists—China—Biography. 4. Peasant uprisings—China—Kiangsi Province—History.
I. Title.
HX420.K5S47   1989
335.43′45′0951222—dc19   88–37476
                                                                                                       CIP

This book has been composed in Linotron Janson

Clothbound editions of Princeton University Press books
are printed on acid-free paper, and binding materials are
chosen for strength and durability. Paperbacks, although satisfactory
for personal collections, are not usually suitable for library rebinding

Printed in the United States of America
by Princeton University Press,
Princeton, New Jersey

To my parents

Contents

Tables

Preface

In the late 1920s, a large revolutionary movement engulfed the Xinjiang region of Jiangxi province. It was led by one of the most remarkable Marxist intellectuals of China, Fang Zhimin. The present study deals with the historical origin of this movement. Its central theme concerns specific features of the peasant society in the Xinjiang region and the role of Marxist intellectuals in the making of a revolutionary movement. It raises and offers answers to the questions: What made precapitalist peasants march forward and forge revolutionary bonds with Marxist intellectuals? Why did the Chinese Communist Party, with a belief in the revolutionary potential of the proletariat, move backward to embrace peasantry? And, finally, how did this sociohistorically eventuate?

Peasants, not the proletariat, were the major force of the Chinese Communist revolution. This revolution was rooted in the material conditions of the rural society. It succeeded when Marxist intellectuals besieged the political power-structure riding high on the support of peasantry. Yet this truth has not emerged as the central theme in most of the scholarly writings on the Chinese revolution.[1] More often than not, peasants have been portrayed as participants in, not as makers of, modern revolutionary history.

The emphasis on the Party and its leaders, while enlightening, fails to

---

[1] In his pioneering work on Chinese communism, Schwartz (1958: 199) aptly concludes that in China "an elite of professional revolutionaries has risen to power by basing itself on *the dynamic of peasant discontent* [emphasis mine]." In his review of peasant revolution in China, Bianco (1976: 313), however, writes: "Studies done so far have concerned themselves less with the peasant movement as such than with the Communist movement in the countryside. Even when special emphasis has been placed on the peasant phases in the history of the Communist movement (the Kiangsi [Jiangxi] Soviets and Yenan) the rural masses are not often discussed in any great detail." While Chinese peasants have been the focus of some recent studies, Bianco's remarks are still, to a large extent, valid.

satisfactorily illuminate the dynamics of the Chinese revolution. This is particularly true of scholarly contributions on the Jiangxi era, which are concerned only with the CCP's history in this period and completely ignore the region itself.[2] Instead of either overlooking peasants or viewing them as passive pawns in the making of history, it is necessary to ask why and how peasants utilized Marxist intellectuals for their own end. Such a task naturally requires comprehension of the historical origins of those crucial factors in the rural society of the Xinjiang region which precipitated a revolutionary movement and which afforded opportunities to Marxist intellectuals for playing a significant role in it.

Only recently have scholars begun to take the peasant perspective seriously in their studies of revolution. The current focus on what Wolf terms, "the people without history" has succeeded in unveiling many aspects of the Chinese revolution.[3] Scholarly contributions of Professors Elizabeth Perry, Ralph Thaxton, and Bob Marks illuminate the growth of revolutionary movements and the critical nexus between peasants and Marxist intellectuals in different regions of rural China.[4] Placing Xinjiang peasants and their society in the forefront, this study hopes to contribute to a better understanding of the dynamics of rural revolution in China.

The Xinjiang peasant movement began in a region that was neither traditionally backward nor ecologically unstable. Commercially active, it was located on an ancient trade route linking north with south China and was well connected with larger market towns. Agriculturally dynamic, it produced a wide variety of both subsistence and cash crops for local consumption and export. Socioculturally rich, its diverse and entrenched rural traditions were characteristic of the Chinese countryside. Moreover, in this relatively prosperous region, the first center of revolutionary activity was located not in a peripheral area but in three central districts of northeastern Jiangxi. It conforms to William Skinner's model of outer periphery only in the sense of an abundance of hilly terrain, rather than in terms of a generally

[2] For example, works on the Jiangxi era by Rue (1966), Swarup (1966), Kim (1973), Lotveit (1973), and others are concerned with either the structure of the Provincial Soviet Government or the developments within the CCP organization during this period. The relationship between the peasants and Communists in Jiangxi has been discussed in a short study by Huang, Bell, and Walker (1978). Averill (1982) provides the first in-depth study of the development of the political movement at the provincial level, though with more emphasis on southern Jiangxi. There is, however, no detailed study of the Xinjiang region and the growth of a revolutionary movement there.

[3] See Wolf 1982.

[4] See Perry 1980; Thaxton 1983; Marks 1984; Galbiati 1985; and others.

depressed socioeconomic unit.[5] It was thus among the few regions of China where the origin of a strong and effective peasant movement transcends explanations based predominantly on traditional backwardness, ecological instabilities, or geographic periphery. These regions indicate the importance of understanding the historical development of those people, classes or forces which mattered as crucially, if not more, in peasants' lives as the larger environment.

This movement emanated from below. Several local peasant forces, coming together, laid the foundation in Xinjiang for one of the largest and most successful soviets. They were unlike Mao Zedong's Red Army, which came from the outside to prepare a base for precipitating a revolutionary movement from below and for establishing soviets in the Jingangshan, central Jiangxi, and Shenxi regions. Admiring the activities of Fang Zhimin in the Xinjiang region, Mao once commented that "the policy that merely calls for roving guerilla actions cannot accomplish the task of accelerating this nationwide revolutionary high tide, while the kind of policy adopted by Zhu De and Mao Zedong and also by Fang Zhimin is undoubtedly correct."[6] Elsewhere, he remarked that "comrades in Northeastern Jiangxi have done good work and are also model workers. By linking the problem of the well-being of the masses with that of revolutionary war, the comrades . . . are simultaneously solving the problem of revolutionary methods of work and of accomplishing their revolutionary task."[7] In this sense, we have thus an example from one more region of China where a local agrarian crisis manifested itself in a successful revolutionary movement. How did this happen?

Finally, in the history of Chinese Communist revolution, a group of

[5] Skinner 1977: 275–351. These special characteristics of the Gandongbei, or Min-Zhe-Wan-Gan, soviet have been highlighted by Li Liuru in an article on different origins of soviets in different areas (Li Liuru 1944, in Kuang 1983: 40–42). Mao also discusses the development of soviets in three distinct types of areas, namely, mountainous, lowland, and river-lake regions, in his strategies for the guerrilla war against the Japanese (see Mao 1965, 1:147–248). The location of most of the better-studied soviets in the peripheral mountainous and ecologically unstable areas has led some scholars to overemphasize this factor in the growth of a peasant or a peasant-based Communist movement. This tendency is apparent in an otherwise very illuminating work by Perry (1980). Works of Thaxton (1983) and Marks (1984), however, provide a useful corrective. "The significant point," Thaxton correctly argues, "is that the mobilization potentiality of the peasantry was determined as much by the geo-political locations to be taken advantage of by the CCP revolutionary army as by the social structure or eco-system of rural society" (Thaxton 1983: 225).

[6] Mao 1965, 1:118.

[7] Ibid., 1:151.

Marxist intellectuals acted as catalysts of revolution from the countryside. In spite of urban education and commitment to Marxist ideology, they were not totally alienated from their traditional rural environment. The leader of this movement, Fang Zhimin, was one such Marxist intellectual. He thus stands in line with Mao Zedong and Peng Pai. This study's focus on Fang's revolutionary beliefs and practices will, I hope, enrich knowledge of those leaders who contributed to the revolution from below.

A revolution, however, cannot be understood in terms of the wisdom of intellectuals only. "Intellectuals," Barrington Moore perceptively notes, "as such can do little unless they attach themselves to a massive form of discontent . . . it is a particularly misleading trick to deny that a revolution stems from peasant grievances because its leaders happen to be professional men or intellectuals."[8] How then did Fang Zhimin and other similar-minded Marxist intellectuals match their revolutionary expectations with peasants' demands to project an ideology for rural revolution?

A focus on rural society does not mean that it should be viewed in isolation—as a closed or completely autonomous community. It is a society within the society. What sets it apart is its independence within the larger artifacts of the state, economy, and culture, which influences the nature of its absorption of external reality and designates its specific characteristic and tendencies.[9] A study of the internal dynamics of the rural society is necessary to comprehend peasants' sociopolitical actions.

A useful concept in analyzing the precapitalist agrarian order is what Scott terms the "subsistence ethic." Rooted in peasants' existential needs, this ethic provides the framework for the social and economic arrangements to minimize risks. It is as much formed by, as it serves to shape, the prevailing cultural and moral values within the village. Embedded in it are demands for the right to subsistence and the maintenance of norms of reciprocity. "Reciprocity," Scott argues, "serves as a central moral formula for impersonal conduct. The right to subsistence, in effect, defines the minimal needs that must be met for members of the community within the context of reciprocity."[10]

To the extent that these moral rights or expectations continue to define social, economic, and political situations to peasants, they serve as a reliable

[8] Moore 1966: 480.

[9] See the works of E. P. Thompson and James C. Scott listed in the References and also Marx 1969; Tilly 1975, 1978; Cobb 1972; Wolf 1969; Hobsbawm and Rude 1968; Hobsbawm 1959, 1973.

[10] Scott 1976: 167.

guide to understanding their sentiments and behavior. Their violation by local or outside forces leads to rural crisis and precipitates social protests. "A study of moral economy of peasants," Scott writes, "can tell us what makes them angry and what is likely, other things being equal, to generate an explosive situation."[11] Thus, rural class relations as well as class struggles need to be viewed in terms of moral economy.

The first chapter thus describes the characteristic features of the rural world in the Xinjiang region, and the second examines its structural form immediately after the Taiping Rebellion. I have chosen the Taiping Rebellion as the starting point not because the Taiping rebels altered the rural social, political, and economic conditions—in fact, they failed to bring about any significant change—but because a decade-long civil war significantly modified the land tenure pattern in the region and provided opportunities for the predominance of small rural cultivators. It is in subsequent constraints on the development of these cultivators that the origins of the twentieth-century agrarian crisis and the revolutionary movement can be traced.

As indicated earlier, however, the rural society existed within the overarching structure of a larger society. It is, therefore, imperative that historical changes within it should be viewed within a similarly moving structural framework. This task has been undertaken in the next three chapters. Without emphasizing the priority of one over the other, I believe that the larger structural framework was as much a part of the state system and world market system as it was of the cultural system.[12] The third chapter thus examines pressures on the rural society that emanated particularly from the characteristic features of the existing larger structure. To be more precise, this analyzes disruptions wrought not only by the closer integration of rural society with the world economy but also by the new demands of a state-in-crisis. The fourth chapter deals with the landed upper class—the closest social and political link between peasants and the outside world—the actions of which considerably influenced the rural reality. The questions discussed are how, why, and to what extent a shift in landed-upper-class domination of the rural society ought about concomitant changes in rural social relationships and created conditions for class struggles and a revolution in the Xinjiang region. The socioeconomic consequences of these disruptions have been analyzed in chapter 5. In the perspective of the post-Taiping rural society, this chapter indicates the nature of the transformation in peasants' liv-

[11] Ibid., 4.
[12] See Skocpol 1979; Wallerstein 1974, 1979; Geertz 1973.

ing conditions. It analyzes exploitation in rural areas and examines the way in which peasants sociopolitically reacted to changes in the social relations of their production. What do their riots and uprisings suggest?

The final three chapters describe the origin of a revolutionary movement under the leadership of Fang Zhimin in the Xinjiang region. The life and revolutionary ideology of Fang Zhimin is described in the sixth chapter. He provides an example of urban-educated Marxist intellectuals in China who had never abandoned their rural roots and whose revolutionary ideology was strongly influenced by their deeply entrenched rural experiences. In the history of Chinese revolution, these revolutionary intellectuals played the most significant role. The next chapter examines the emergence of peasant associations from the top and the tenuous existence of peasants within the framework of politically changing stances of the United Front government. The final chapter describes the characteristic ways in which the revolutionary movement arose and grew in the Xinjiang region.

Finally, a point must be made about the source materials. Compared with that of the rich coastal regions of China, the regional history of Jiangxi has thus far not been taken seriously either in Western or Chinese scholarship. Moreover, due to the (until recently) prevalent tradition of basing written history on the ruling class and its achievements, there is a paucity of historical materials on peasants and their society in Jiangxi. As Barrington Moore writes: "The discontented intellectual with his soul searchings has attracted attention wholly out of proportion to his political importance, partly because these searchings leave behind them written records and also because those who write history are themselves intellectuals."[13] I have, therefore, attempted to construct the history of rural society in the Xinjiang region from diverse available sources and have filled gaps, wherever necessary, through examples from neighboring regions. This study is thus, at best, an attempt to place the Xinjiang revolutionary movement in proper historical perspective. I am hopeful that the recent resurgence of history-writing activity in China will provide more and better material on the role of peasants.

In the process of bringing this book to completion, so many persons generously gave me so much of their time and energy that my deepest gratitude to them cannot be adequately expressed in an acknowledgment. I am, first of all, greatly indebted to my teacher and supervisor, Professor Maurice Meisner, whose intellectual guidance helped me to comprehend modern

[13] Moore 1966: 480.

China and to get hooked on history. Without his unfailing support, this project would not have been completed in its present form. Professor Edward Friedman encouraged and advised me in each and every stage of the research both as a friend and a teacher. His constant faith in my work and his remarkable understanding of China helped me immensely in improving my presentation. For furthering my comprehension of peasants and rural society, I am thankful to Professor Jim Scott, whose excellent works have provided the basis for this study. Besides them, I owe a major debt to John Dower, Chow Tse-tung, Manoranjan Mohanty, Tan Chung, Lin Yu-sheng, Clara Sun, R. C. Jauhri, Jerome Chen, Iqbal Narain, Li Wenzhi, and Shinkichi Eto for their help and suggestions. Bob Marks, Henny Sender, Brenda Sansom, Steve Davidson, Katie Lynch, Abid Kureshi, Lynn Lubekman, Ted Laves, Hiroko Oikawa, Jerry Brennig, and Lee Feigon assisted me in numerous ways during my research at the University of Wisconsin, Madison.

I am also thankful to the Graduate School, University of Wisconsin, and the Indian Council of Historical Research, New Delhi, for granting me necessary funds to pursue research for this study.

Ms. Margaret Case of the Princeton University Press merits special thanks for not only considering this work for publication but also painstakingly helping me to put the manuscript in a better order. I also greatly appreciate thoughtful suggestions from the two anonymous readers of the Press that benefited me greatly in preparing the final draft.

Finally, my greatest debt goes to my parents, Professor and Mrs. A. K. Narain; my wife, Ranjana; and my kids, Siddharth and Aditi, who have waited longer than anybody else to see the completion of this work. Needless to say, I alone am responsible for any errors.

The Xinjiang Region and the Min-Zhe-Wan-Gan Soviet

● Soviet Area
□ Non-Soviet Area

Guangde

Jingxian

Taiping

Yixian

Xiuning

Qimen

Dongliu

Qiubo

Pengze

Hukou

Ruichang

Jiujiang

Dean

Yongxiu

Nanchang

ANHUI

HUBEI

JIANGXI

Wuyuan

Jingdezhen

Fouliang

Dexing

Leping

Wannian

Yugan

Xin

Yujiang (Anren)

Yingtan

Jinxian

Dongxiang

Dong

Linchuan (Fuzhou)

Chongren

Yihuang

Duchang

Poyang Lake

Boyang (Raozhou)

River

Yushan

Hengfeng (Xingan)

Shangrao (Guangxin)

Hekou

Yanshan

Guixi

Zixi

Jinxi

Nancheng (Jianchang)

Lichuan (Xincheng)

River

Guangfeng

Jiangshan

Changshan

Quxian

Kaihua

Suichang

Yunhe

Yuhe

Jingning

Qingyuan

Shouning

Taishun

Yunshan

Fuan

Pingnan

Jian'ou

Zhenghe

Jianyang

Shaowu

Chongan

Guangze

Pucheng

ZHEJIANG

FUJIAN

Yangzi River

River

Yangzi River

Qingtian

Yongjia

Ruian

Pingyang

Fuding

Yiyang

Map drawn by V.R. Boscarino

0 10 20 30 40 miles

N

Peasant Society and Marxist
Intellectuals in China

Chapter One

The Xinjiang Region

Site of a highly successful peasant movement and one of the largest and most famous soviets in China, the Xinjiang region lies in the northeast of Jiangxi province.[1] Strictly speaking, it consists of the valley of the Xin River (Xin jiang), from which its name was derived. Originating from high ranges of the Huaiyu Mountains on the boundary of Jiangxi and Zhejiang provinces, the river flows westward and merges with Lake Poyang, the recipient of all rivers in Jiangxi. Administratively, most of the areas of this region belonged to Guangxin and Raozhou prefectures, with a majority of district towns located on the banks of this river. Right in the middle of these two prefectures were three interconnected districts, Yiyang, Guixi, and Hengfeng—the birthplace of the Xinjiang revolutionary movement.

Boundaries of the Xinjiang region, more broadly defined, touched southern Anhui in the north, areas above the Dong River (in east-central Jiangxi) in the south, southwest Zhejiang and northwest Fujian in the east, and Lake Poyang (north-central Jiangxi) in the west. The northern and eastern areas of this region were highlands, consisting respectively of the Wuyu and Huaiyu mountain ranges. The lowland occupied a larger area on the southern and western sides of the valley of the Xin. While physical environment separated high- and lowland areas, both were socially and economically closely intertwined and formed one unit. This whole unit was roughly the area where, in the early 1930s, the Min-Zhe-Wan-Gan (Fujian, Zhejiang, Anhui, and Jiangxi) Soviet was established by Fang Zhimin.

The initial population of this region broadly consisted of the natives (*bendi*) who settled on the low and flat land suitable for human habitation around Lake Poyang and in the Xin River valley. Until the late sixteenth

[1] For the general geographic description of this region see Sun 1958; Toa Dobunkai 1920; Zhou 1928; Kopsch 1878; Li [1931] 1966; Wathe 1926; *Youkehua Jiangxi* 1937; Alley 1962.

century, the mountainous part of this region, like other areas of the Yangzi highlands, were, as Stephen Averill's study indicates, "regular haunts only of hunters and hermits, of Daoist priests and desperate brigands and of a few poor peasants who crept up from the neighboring valleys to cut firewood and dig for medicinal roots."[2] However, the massive increase in population, especially in the southeast region of China, and the introduction of such new subsistence and cash crops as sweet potatoes, maize, jute, indigo, and the like, suitable for cultivation in hilly areas, soon led to a new phase of interregional migration. This brought a large number of people to the highlands. The migration continued, probably in waves, until the end of the eighteenth century. Most of the migrants to the highlands came from the densely populated neighboring provinces of Hunan, Hubei, Fujian, and Guangdong. Composed of groups as they were, they came to be called "shed people," primarily because of their usual practice of first constructing small makeshift sheds or shacks before opening up the land for cultivation purposes.[3] Their numbers increased rapidly, so much so that various imperial edicts from 1723 onward instructed local officials to bring them under the *baojia* administration.

Settlement in the highlands, combined with the relatively peaceful and prosperous reigns of Kangxi (1662–1722), Yongzheng (1723–1735), and Qianlong (1736–1795), stimulated population growth in the whole of Jiangxi province. Between 1393 and 1851, the population total of the area registered what was historically its greatest leap. It almost tripled, rising from roughly 8.9 million in 1393 to about 24.5 million in 1851.[4] In comparison, arable land increased by less than 6 percent, and per capita landholding in this region declined to about 3.5 *mu*, which was well below the national average of about 4.5 mu during that period.[5] The province thus became densely populated by the late eighteenth century.

The massive growth of the population stimulated a reverse trend of movement of people out of the province from the late eighteenth century until the outbreak of the Taiping Rebellion. Confronted with shrinking resources, the Jiangxi people migrated, as Ho Ping-ti's study indicates, to Hunan, Hubei,

[2] Averill 1983: 84.

[3] For an illuminating discussion of the shed people and their settlements see Averill 1983; see also, Ho 1967; Leong 1984; Wan 1985. It was estimated that 20 to 30 percent of the total population in Yushan, Guangfeng, and Shangrao prefectures consisted of the shed people (Wan 1985: 53). For the shed people's struggle in Jiangxi against the Qing state, see Duan 1955; Zheng 1978.

[4] Ho 1967: 10, 56, 283.

[5] *JN* 1936: 76–110.

and Sichuan provinces to find better opportunities. Noting major migration trends in Qing China, Wei Yuan, a well-known nineteenth-century historian and geographer, writes that the "people of Jiangxi poured into Hubei and Hunan, and the people of Hubei and Hunan filled up Sichuan."[6] Local histories of Hunan reveal that most of its aliens were Jiangxi natives. In the Guanhua district of Hubei, for example, immigrants from the Xinjiang region established several guildhalls during the Daoguang reign. As these neighboring provinces began to fill up, Jiangxi people went as far as Sichuan and Shanxi in search of land.[7]

The demographic pressure subjected the province to problems related to wide-scale deforestation. Aliens, settling in increasing numbers in the highlands of Xinjiang and other regions, introduced and cultivated such high-yielding subsistence crops as maize and sweet potatoes and such profitable commercial crops as jute and indigo. Deforestation for cultivation purposes soon brought the usual problem of soil erosion. Peasants dug land deeply to plant various crops, and this resulted in bumper production during the first few years. But the topsoil was in due course washed away by heavy rains, which not only made the land unsuitable for cultivation but also silted up riverbeds and lakebeds, making the whole region flood-prone. The Qing state finally had to issue strict orders forbidding the unsystematic utilization of highlands and promoting the planting of tea and *shan* trees to protect the region against soil erosion.[8]

Thus, although the massive cultivation in the highlands temporarily increased food production and supported a larger population, the consequent erosion of land considerably limited the amount of arable land and frequently caused flooding in many lowland areas. This further increased the pressure of population on available land. By the mid–nineteenth century, the demographic pressure contributed to a serious agrarian crisis. Peasants rebelled throughout the province and the Taiping rebels found many eager supporters. Out of 364 recorded incidents of "social unrest" in the province during 1796–1911, 292 took place in the period between 1846 and 1875.[9]

[6] Cited in Ho 1967: 143.

[7] Ho 1967: 145ff.

[8] Cited in Ho 1967: 148.

[9] Yang 1975: 182. In Yang's statistical data, Jiangxi, together with Guangdong, ranks sixth in the number of uprisings between 1796 and 1911. The following list of uprisings in Jiangxi is based on his data:

Period	Number of Uprisings
1796–1805	2
1806–1815	4

While population explosion was the main reason for the agrarian discontent with which this region was confronted in the mid–nineteenth century, the same cannot be said of the early-twentieth-century rural crisis.

AGRICULTURE

In the Xinjiang region, the high density of population and limited agricultural land naturally promoted intensification of agriculture. Multiple cropping became prevalent. Peasants usually harvested three crops a year on the wetland and two in hilly areas and on dryland. A wide variety of crops was thus produced. For example, according to a survey of the 1920s, peasants in Guangfeng district planted rice, sweet potatoes, soybeans, rapeseed, tobacco, green vegetables, bamboo, and millet as the main crops. In addition, they grew lesser quantities of glutinous grain, maize, sugar cane, beans, tea, and cotton, among other crops.[10]

In total production, however, no crop surpassed rice—the most important crop of the region, cultivated in all the districts. As in other areas of China, dissemination of "Champa" and the introduction of many local early ripening varieties of rice, such as "Jiangxi Early," facilitated the spread of multiple cropping. Early-season rice was sown as the first crop sometime in April and harvested in June; middle-season rice was planted in late June or early July and cut in September. On highlands, only late rice was planted because heavy rainfall in summer made the land unsuitable for repetitive cultivation. The average production of rice was from two to four *dan* per mu, which competed favorably with other top-producing rice regions.

Among other subsistence crops, wheat and millet were planted during the winter. They were followed by early soybean or late sesame crops in the lake area and other low-lying ground. Sweet potatoes and maize were produced in the highlands. Both these crops were introduced during the late

1816–1825	4
1826–1835	13
1836–1845	9
1846–1855	59
1856–1865	205
1866–1875	30
1876–1885	8
1886–1895	9
1896–1911	23

[10] Min 1920: 52–53.

sixteenth century and brought to this region by migrants during the late-Ming and early-Qing periods. Their adaptability to the highlands and pre-servability in diverse weather conditions made them attractive for the shed people settled here.

Cash crops like tea, tobacco, cotton, indigo, and ramie characterized the agriculture of almost all of the districts of this region. According to local gazetteers, in eastern Raozhou and in Guangxin prefecture, the total pro-duction of rice was not sufficient for local consumption for the whole of the year. This was primarily because the high profitability from cash crops and handicraft products—both of which were in greater demand in other areas of China—kept the local population tied to commercial production.[11] Tea was the most extensively grown cash crop. Famous tea regions were Shan-grao, Dexing, Yushan, and Fouliang districts. They produced more than two-thirds of the total output of the province. Leping district was famous for its indigo all over China. Cotton was mostly produced in the western districts. The output of tobacco was high in Guangfeng, Xinfeng, Boyang, and Pengze; and significant amounts of ramie were grown in Jiujiang, Shan-grao, Dean, and Linchuan districts of the region.

The general cropping pattern, as illustrated in a survey of Guangfeng district, indicates that on high-quality wetland, peasants cultivated either one crop each of rice, soybeans, and sesame or two crops of rice and one of sesame. On the medium-quality land, rice and soybeans were planted once. The low-quality wetland was reserved for the cultivation of late rice. Simi-larly, the better-quality highland areas were used for the production of to-bacco leaves once in three years and other crops once in two years. Maize, millet, beans, sweet potatoes, and other crops were cultivated in inferior-quality highland soil. Bamboo, tea, and ramie were grown on the sunny side of the highlands.[12]

In Guangfeng district, agricultural production remained generally good. The convexo-concave shape of the earth created numerous small natural ponds. Filled by rain water, they were extensively used for irrigation during mild droughts. Moreover, because of the comparatively small volume of water and the existence of high hills near the source of the Xin River, there was normally less danger of the river bursting its banks and flooding the land

[11] For a descripton of the general economic situation of this area, see Chen 1983; Fu 1983; Abramson et al. 1935; *Chinese Economic Journal and Bulletin* 1935: 345–359, and 488–505; *JN* 1936; *JJWT* 1934; Toa Dobunkai 1920; and others.

[12] Min 1920: 53–54.

in the district. All this contributed to the reaping of good harvests year after year.

Other districts of the Xinjiang region did not have such a protected geographic location. Areas around Lake Poyang and the valleys of the Xin and Rao rivers frequently suffered from summer floods. In describing the countryside bordering on the Xin River between Yushan and Guangxin fu, Staunton noted in his travel diary that "for a distance of some miles, indeed, on every side of it, the face of the country is one wild and morassy waste, covered with reeds and bushes, and entirely inundated for a part of the year."[13] Midsummer rain frequently flooded a large area of low-lying land. Agricultural production thus, to a large extent, remained dependent upon the natural climate remaining benign.

RURAL INDUSTRY AND COMMERCE

Increasing exploitation of the highlands and the introduction of new hybrid varieties of both subsistence and cash crops enormously raised the total output of agricultural production. Beginning with the late sixteenth century, the "revolution in land utilization," as it was termed by Ho Ping-ti, promoted economic and commercial activities and stimulated the rural handicraft industry in the whole of the Xinjiang region. Location of this region on the main trade route connecting Beijing with Guangdong as well as access to the important route from the north, which went along the Xin to Zhejiang and Fujian, facilitated movement of the locally produced goods to larger markets. Robert Fortune, who visited this area after the Opium War, found these trade routes commercially very active and lively, always full of porters carrying goods for the market. After reaching the district of Yushan through the trade route linking Jiangxi with Zhejiang and Fujian, he noted: "Coolies were now met in great numbers, loaded with tea-chests. Many of them carried only one chest. These I was told were finer teas; the chest was never allowed to touch the ground. . . . Tea grown and manufactured here can of course be conveyed to the great export marts of Shanghai and Canton [Guangzhou] much quicker and more cheaply than those from the southern side of the Bohea mountains."[14]

In 1928, traveling along the Xin River, Zhou Jie found the region to be one of the richest and commercially most active in the province. He wrote

[13] Kopsch 1878: 262.
[14] Fortune 1852: 201–2.

that the region received from Jiangsu, and especially Shanghai, silk and satin, cotton fabrics, kerosene, and white crystal sugar; from Zhejiang, salt and Shao wine; and from Hankou, medicines and cotton. The total volume of trade was estimated to be not less than one million yuan.[15] Expansion of trade, particularly long-distance trade, turned the traditional towns of Jiujiang, Hekou, and Jingdezhen into major industrial and commercial centers. Until the use of foreign and native steam-powered cargo ships and subsequent developments decreased the importance of these traditional trade routes, trade and commerce thrived in the region.

Among the rural handicrafts, the most important was the processing of tea.[16] Primitive tea-processing work was part of the peasant home-industry in almost all the districts of the region. But it was more widespread in the famous tea-producing areas of Shangrao, Dexing, Yushan, and Fouliang. The home-processed black and green tea was usually sold to the tea hongs or merchants in the city who "fired" the tea and sorted it according to its quality for sale in larger internal and external markets. The city of Hekou was the major local tea market. After British occupation of the Jiujiang district, large tea-processing units began to be established there. This, coupled with decreasing demands for Chinese tea in international markets, later led to the decline of the home-based tea industry of this region.

The production of a large quantity of bamboo and other trees on agriculturally unsuitable highlands of the region promoted the growth of timber and paper industries. Booming profits in such activities expanded cultivation of bamboo even on good fertile land and attracted a greater number of peasant households to paper production, including even those whose entire capital comprised the kettle used for preparing paper pulp. Qianshan, Guangfeng, Dexing, and Guixi districts were the major paper producing centers, where more than two hundred varieties of paper were made. There was a great demand for the paper in other provinces, and peasants often sold their home-produced paper to local business agents who dyed and exported it.

Another important rural household industry was connected with the production of textiles. Cotton was produced in all the districts of the region. Almost half of the total output was hand-spun locally, and yarn thus manufactured supplemented the income of the peasants. Spinning and weaving kept peasants, especially women, busy after the end of the agricultural season. Landlords and rich peasants often possessed three to four looms and

[15] Zhou 1928: 59.
[16] The following discussion is based on works cited in note 11 above.

hired labor for the production of textiles. The local *xiabu* (summer linen), made out of ramie, was famous all over China. Its export to different provinces and also to Korea fetched good profits.

Linked to textile manufacturing was the indigo-based rural dyeing industry. The districts of Leping, Boyang, Dean, Wannian, Linchuan, and Dexing produced the finest-quality indigo in China. It was prepared by soaking the liaotan plant overnight in lime water and beating it with wooden rods the next day. Processed indigo usually sold for about twenty Chinese dollars per *tan* and was mainly exported.

Included among other important rural handicrafts of the region was the production of oil. It was prepared by use of different locally grown seeds in home-based wooden oil extractors. Peasants in the districts of Guangfeng, Boyang, and Pengze processed their cultivated tobacco leaves for sale. Prices of such processed goods were usually double the price of raw materials.

Slightly different from the rural handicraft industry was the region's famous and traditional porcelain industry. Located in the town of Jingdezhen, called "the porcelain capital of China" by the Southern Song emperors, the industry greatly prospered during the Ming period. Until the early twentieth century, more than 100,000 workers were employed in local kilns or engaged in porcelain-related activities. This industry was the largest consumer of Xinjiang's timber. Jingdezhen porcelain was in great demand not only in China but also in foreign countries.

Rural handicraft industries thus played a major role in enriching the local economy and in ameliorating the socioeconomic status of peasants. Attracted by the economic prosperity of this region, peasants from neighboring regions flocked here to find jobs. The district gazetteer of Jiangshan (Zhejiang province) noted that in the slack season between harvests local peasants often migrated to the Xinjiang region to work as porters.[17] Until the late nineteenth century, when larger internal and external forces began to disrupt the natural economy all over China, it remained an economically rich area.

THE RURAL WORLD

Both big and small villages dotted the Xinjiang region. A big village usually consisted of about a hundred families, while a small one had ten or more families. Districts close to the western lowland area near Lake Poyang, how-

---

[17] Cited in Chen 1983: 118.

ever, had several very large villages, each with more than a hundred families.[18] Within villages, clan and lineage bound individual families together in
kinship relations. As in many villages of the sub-Yangzi region, as Maurice
Freedman's study demonstrates, single-lineage settlement was not uncommon here. A natural village was often dominated by people having a common surname or ancestors.[19] There were many exceptions, however, especially in larger and administrative villages where the population had multiple
surnames.

In spite of the influx of a large number of shed people in this region, the
continued frequency of single-lineage village settlement was probably due to
the prevalent practice among these migrants of forming fictive lineages. The
shed people, as Averill writes, "often came originally from different areas,
lived in different villages, and may well not really have been related at all,
except through lines of descent artificially contrived to meet at a common
ancestor. Whatever their defects from a genealogical perspective, these lineages were useful for providing and organizing principle-fictive kinship—
around which a large number of people could be gathered in a short time to
defend their economic or political interests."[20] Thus, in the highland region,
opened by shed people having different origins, several single-lineage settlements sprang up.

Most of the villages of the Xinjiang region had lineage and clan land that
was usually located around the local ancestral hall. Such land varied in size
according to the status of lineages and was, more often than not, controlled
by influential and wealthy landlords of the lineage who rented it to tenants.
Rents were customarily equivalent to those charged on the worst-quality
land—that is, one-third of the first crop. The income was used for the up-
keep of ancestral halls and the establishment of schools, granaries, credit
funds, and other social welfare activities. Through such paternalistic activities, leaders of the clan held all members together. In Jiujiang district, members of the clan often gathered together twice a year, on the Qingming and
Dongzhi festival days in spring and fall. Such meetings were occasions for
feasts at which meat was served to all members. Moreover, every ten,
twenty, or thirty years, special meetings were convened to include the
names of new members in the genealogical registers. Servants of civil and
military officials, chair bearers, barbers, actors, yamen runners, and adopted

[18] "Gandongbei Nongcun Kaikuang" 1933: 131.
[19] For an illuminating discussion of lineage organization in villages in central China, see
Freedman 1966.
[20] Averill 1983: 105.

sons were barred from membership. Expulsion from clan or lineage was considered to be the most serious punishment that could be meted out.[21]

Intravillage or intralineage feuds were quite common, since everyone attempted to monopolize the limited resources available. Big villages often dominated the small ones. Disagreements over the right to use water from rivers, streams, canals, or ponds, or to build water-conservancy structures or use hilly grassland, for example, often provoked hostilities. Grounded on such reasons, animosity between villages lasted for years. The intralineage feud between the shed people and the natives became so frequent during the mid-Qing period that district officials were often forced to issue an order to register and account for all the guns to the local baojia organizations.

The relatively weak lineages, especially those of some of the shed people that were unable to compete with well-entrenched and -organized native lineages, often relied for support and survival upon such heterodox organizations as bandit gangs, smuggler bands, and secret societies. Membership in such blood-oath fraternities (baihui) assured a better status. It helped weaker lineages to make their presence felt in competing with strong lineages for land and property. Demographic upheavals and political disruption during the Ming-Qing transition period promoted proliferation of such fraternities in this region. With weak local kinship ties, divorced from their native social and cultural milieu, and competing for scarce economic resources, immigrants welcomed the protection provided by them and became the major force behind them. The fraternity constituency was thus, as Polachek writes, "strongest in the hillside hakka villages and in poorer market towns where a prosperous landlord-merchant elite had not developed. To this constituency, the fraternity offered a vehicle for organization at moments of crisis, such as a sudden natural disaster or famine, and for mutual help while on the trail as seasonal laborers, peddlers, or smugglers."[22]

In the typical hilly terrain of this region, which even before the movement of a large number of immigrants was a favorite hideout for roving bands, bandits and especially salt smugglers abounded. They moved freely to neighboring Zhejiang and Fujian provinces to plunder or smuggle salt.[23] By the late eighteenth century, tangs of the Triad, or Heaven and Earth, secret society had become well entrenched in this region. They played a major role in organizing frequent peasant uprisings and were the major motive force in the expansion of antistate activities during the Boxer Rebellion. They remained a latent but dominant force until the time of liberation.

[21] Brown 1922a: 518–22.
[22] Polachek 1983: 814.
[23] Averill 1983; KYKTL 1979.

Beyond kinship ties and heterodox organizations, popular cult and religious activities strengthened the socioeconomic integrity of local communities. Within villages, religion, as C. K. Yang notes, "came to serve as a symbol of common devotion in bringing people out of their divergent routines and orienting them toward community activities."[24] These periodic activities provided occasions for display of the community's common beliefs and interests. They were also often related to situations over which peasants had no control. Peasants relied on their time-tested skills to produce wealth from land, but forces such as famine, drought, flood, or other natural calamities called for the invocation of a specific popular cult or a particular magico-religious ritual practice. Popular religious deities and rituals more often than not displayed characteristics of the ecology of a particular area. Religion as such was rooted in the process of production and acted as a social-defense mechanism to protect the individual and the community during the period of crisis.

As elsewhere in China, popular cult and religious activities played a dynamic role in the Xinjiang rural society. In the religious calendar of this region, almost every month was designated for the worship of a particular god. The first to twelfth moons were respectively dedicated to such gods as Spring, Money, Rice, Smallpox, Buddha, Medicine, the Eighteen Lohans, Ancestors, Xu Zhenjun, the Moon, and Ru Huang.[25] Some of them were worshiped two or three times a year, depending upon the situation that called for their invocation. All these gods, as their names indicate, were connected with peasants' day-to-day concerns of production, subsistence, and family welfare. Their worship served to uphold the community consciousness of collective interests. Simple children's folk songs sung during these communal religious activities confirm this. For example, in Jiujiang district, a popular song was: "Sing nicely magpie, / Daddy gets rich, / Mother gets me a little brother, / Older brother gets a wife."[26] Simple they might be in expression, but songs like this reflect the vital social function of religious activities in the lives of the peasants.

Of all the gods worshiped, four were specifically related to Jiangxi.[27] They were (1) the Taoist Pope, Zhang Tianshi; (2) Xu Zhenjun, or Xu Zhenyang; (3) Xiao Gong; and (4) Yan Gong. Zhang Tianshi was the living Taoist Pope who resided on the Dragon and Tiger Mountain near Guixi district. He was appointed by the Qing state to prevent expansion of heter-

---

[24] Yang 1967: 81.
[25] Brown 1922b: 497.
[26] See Brown 1922b for several such songs popular in Jiujiang.
[27] Brown 1922a: 520.

odox activities in the empire. Provided with a staff of twenty-six priests and a land grant to perform his functions, he was an agent of temporal power. In local areas, he was reputed to be a magician of irresistible power, and people worshiped him to procure his aid in conquering demons. As a consequence, he wielded great influence in the region.

Xu Zhenjun was a native of Jiangxi and was born in A.D. 239. His successes in water-conservancy works as well as in the control of plague deified him. Reputed to have possessed a magical sword with which he destroyed all evil forces, he was worshiped as the Great Patron Saint. Xiao Gong, according to the legends, was a boatman of extraordinary skill who never had an accident. After his death, a temple was constructed to honor him, and numerous boatmen of the Xinjiang region had great faith in him. Yan Gong was an official who became rich in office. He traveled to foreign lands and never experienced misfortune. Local people worshiped him for protection from all sorts of dangers. All of these gods served the same social purpose as did other deities worshiped in the region.

Each village had at least one temple, and images of all the deities were put up in it. Priests and community leaders controlled the temple, which often had some land attached to it. In some of the districts, temples had large landholdings. For example, in Hengfeng district, between eight hundred and one thousand mu of land belonged to a temple, and about thirty full-time laborers were employed to cultivate it.[28] The Taoist Pope, Zhang Tianshi, had control over several thousand mu of land that was spread over several districts and was rented out to tenants.

The income earned was meant for use in various community activities carried on through the community's temple-fair organization (*saihui*). The main function of this organization was to periodically arrange religious-cum-market fairs. It thus served the vital function of binding the community together through its folk-religious concerns as well as keeping law and order. Noting this, Polachek writes, "The *saihui* provided security against all kinds of lawlessness, from poaching and theft to disowning of rent or loan agreements. This law and order concern of the temple-fair apparatus was revealed symbolically in the form taken by 'welcoming-the-god' processions preceding the fair, which usually wove through the most remote corners of the market town vicinage, clanging gongs, detonating firecrackers, and displaying the massed might of the volunteer militia."[29]

[28] See Abramson et al. 1935: 89–157.
[29] Polachek 1983: 813.

While on the one hand popular cult and communal religious activities acted as a social defense mechanism to provide protection to the individual and the local community, on the other they promoted a world view that legitimized chiliastic actions during the period of an extensive crisis. They thus sometimes acted as an opiate to the point of impeding direct political action on the part of the peasantry, but at other times they redirected peasants' indignation into explicit expressions of social protest. Most of the peasant uprisings thus contained religious elements, expressed through either esoteric initiation rites and rituals or symbolized by the emergence of a new Buddha or other prophets.

In 1803, for example, a large-scale peasant uprising engulfed several districts of the Xinjiang region. It was organized by the Heaven and Earth Society under the leadership of Li Lingkui. Li projected himself as a descendant of the great Tang emperors, fabricated Mahayana Buddhist precepts to make his movement compatible with local needs, and organized *Yangpan* (Sun Bowl) and *Yin-pan* (Moon Bowl) branches of the Heaven and Earth Society to extend his activities to a larger area. *Yang* (sun) and *yin* (moon) symbolized Heaven and Earth characters. After Li's death, his disciple Liao Ganjin continued the movement for several years by shifting it to the southern region of the province.[30]

In the Xinjiang region, like other areas of China, popular religion, combined with various kinship and heterodox organizations, thus provided a framework for social, cultural, and economic unity of the rural society. This framework also prepared the ground for the development of survival and protective strategies that guided peasants' actions during periods of both quietude and crisis. It would therefore be hazardous to ascribe to inbuilt social mechanisms either pro- or antirevolutionary characteristics. In fact, a seemingly cohesive and harmonious structure characterized the rural world within which what peasants did and what they did not do depended upon their selection of a strategy out of those traditionally available to them.

THE RISE OF MODERN LANDLORDISM

Within an outwardly cohesive and harmonious village, families were sharply divided on the basis of their socioeconomic status, which was most often

---

[30] *KYKTL* 1979: 664–65. Perry correctly discusses such activities in the countryside as part of "predatory" and "protective" strategies to survive in a harsh ecological setting (Perry 1980: chap. 3).

determined by their landholdings as well as the nature and extent of their formal or informal control over the rural areas. Perhaps what sharpened the socioeconomic difference most in a village was the emergence of modern landlordism, beginning in the eighteenth century. However, this development did not take place at the cost of the elimination of the small-peasant economy. A major feature of the Chinese rural society was the persistence of the landlord economy side by side with the small-peasant economy. The growth of the latter was, to a large extent, dependent upon the nature of former's strength and control over sociopolitical structure at different historical times.[31]

A brief overview of the origin and growth of modern landlordism before the Taiping Rebellion is necessary to comprehend its role in the post-Taiping rural society, which is the major concern of the first few chapters of this book. Most scholars now associate the rise of modern landlordism with the displacement of the Ming aristocratic landlords by the numerous and massive uprisings of serflike tenants and bond servants during the late-Ming period and the replacement of the Ming by the Qing state. The new state, partly because it suspected the loyalty of the old Ming landlords and also partly because it wanted to expand the tax base enforced several regulations against commendation to the status of official landlord-gentry. Manorialism and serflike tenancy thus disappeared. The state also encouraged settlement on the wasteland, and, more important, abolished the restrictions imposed previously on the sale and purchase of land. The attack on the Ming landlords as well as the elimination of their traditional privileges, which had sustained their domination over the rural area, stimulated the growth of small cultivators. These cultivators either owned small parcels of land as peasant freeholders or had indefinite long-term rights to use land as tenants. They formed the basis of the small-peasant economy, the growth of which characterized the early Qing rural society.[32]

But landlordism, though weakened, did not decline. With the suppression of the Ming aristocratic-official landlords, a new group of landlords emerged from the ranks of the Qing officials consisting of merchants and other rich commoners (largely from the small portion of rural cultivators who had become rich peasants). The commercialization of agriculture provided new opportunities to commoners for upward social mobility. The in-

[31] Li (1981) advances a convincing thesis about the general concentration-dissipation-concentration pattern in landownership, which fluctuated according to the strength of the state and landlords at various times.

[32] For a full discussion see Fang 1984: 129–41.

troduction of high-yielding subsistence and cash crops, the substantial increases in rural handicrafts and commerce, and the chances for Ming bond servants and serflike tenants to use these developments for their own socioeconomic benefit promoted the emergence of a new group of common people who became rich through their mercantile or agricultural activities. As land became a commodity, they purchased it and frequently rented it out, thus turning into the new commoner landlords.[33]

While the return from land was lower than that from commercial activities, it was still the safest and most secure investment. Xu Huaichuan, a Nanjing merchant, succinctly explained, "We use trade to raise our family and agriculture to preserve it."[34] This trend toward investment in land appears to have become dominant in most of the regions by the eighteenth century. In 1740, an official remarked, "Now that merchants have become wealthy, many are buying thousands of mou [mu] of land. Peasants till their land and each year they collect several thousand piculs in rent."[35] In 1748, Yang Xifu, a native of Jiangxi and a long-time governor of Hunan, reported in a memorial that in his area "lately some 50 to 60 percent of the land had passed into the hands of landlords, and small landowners have sunk to the status of tenants."[36]

By the eighteenth century, commoner landlords gradually achieved a predominant status in the rural areas, marking the beginning of, as Mi Chu Wiens aptly remarked, "a new rural order."[37] These commoner landlords continued to be the major factor in Chinese rural society until the revolution in the twentieth century. The unrestricted sale and purchase of land together with the increasing commercialization also promoted closer relations between Qing officials, merchants, and rich commoners. Distinctions between them began to blur as the mobility between these groups increased and as their interest coincided in landownership.

The continued existence of landlordism, in the final analysis, proved to be a major factor in the prolonged stagnation of sprouts of capitalism in agriculture. Li correctly points out:

Because of restrictions within the landlord economic system, while rich peasants often grew to be primitive-capitalist or land-renting landlords, primitive-

[33] Li 1981b: 68–90.
[34] Cited in Elvin 1973: 249. For an excellent discussion of these trends, see Marks 1978: 75–109.
[35] Li 1972: 60–62.
[36] Cited in Ho 1967: 220.
[37] Wiens 1980: 3–39; Wiens 1976.

capitalist landlords who already had a capitalist nature generally reverted to land renting. At the same time, commoner landlords, after having extended their land, always tried to move, by one means or another, towards the status of gentry landlords. All these contradictory movements retarded the development of capitalism in agriculture.[38]

The tenacity of the landlord economic system and its sustenance by the state characterized the rural order from the eighteenth century onward. The absence of a strict hierarchical structure made the Chinese landlord economy more flexible and vigorous than that of Europe.

The paucity of materials makes it difficult to document in detail the increasing trends toward investment in land, concentrated land ownership, and the emergence of a larger number of commoner landlords in the Xinjiang region. However, some very useful data have been gathered by Kang Chao from the fish-scale registers and rent collection records of the landlord families from the Guangxin prefecture of this region and from adjacent areas in southern Anhui and Zhejiang. They are presented in his two illuminating recent studies.[39]

Chao's data reflect a large concentration of tenants in this region, with the total amount of owner-cultivated land reaching as high as 53.4 percent and then declining between 1645 and 1655.[40] This tallies with the general assumption that there was a rise in the number of small cultivators from the late Ming to the early Qing and a decline after that when the rising land acquisition activities by rich commoners gradually began to dispossess the former. While the low percentage of owner-cultivated land in his data for 1581 demonstrates that a larger area was still possessed by the Ming aristocratic-official landlords, their rapid collapse and the gradual emergence of commoner landlords from the late seventeenth century onward once again decreased the percentage of owner-cultivated land, as correctly indicated by Chao's data for 1676 and the later period.[41]

Moreover, from the late seventeenth century onward, the increase in population, the growth of a land market, and the growing commercialization of agriculture provided opportunities for a larger number of people to invest in land and turn into landlords. This limited the amount of land available to each landlord and kept landholdings smaller than the Ming estates. Thus

---

[38] Li 1981b: 88.
[39] See Chao 1981, 1982.
[40] Chao 1981: 721.
[41] Ibid., 721ff.

Chao's data correctly cautions against the assumption that the concentration of land involved an extremely large amount of land in the hands of a few. What characterized the rural area was the emergence of a larger number of landlords who acquired land gradually and in small pieces.

But some broad generalizations about the pattern of the landownership in the region, reached by Chao on the basis of his data, seem unconvincing. These need to be clarified to put the general picture of this region in proper perspective. First, Chao believes that big landlords were absent in the region.[42] But what is meant by big landlords? If these are defined as landlords who possessed more than a thousand mu of land, their number was indeed quite low. However, in each locality there were at least one or two such landlords. For example, Guixi district had the Taoist Pope, with a landholding extending to several thousand mu. Such instances were rare but could be found elsewhere too. This is a fact accepted by Chao in his book and highlighted by Li Wenzhi in several of his articles.[43] But, in a society where the average amount of land per peasant family was less than ten mu, any landlord who owned even a hundred mu was, in fact, quite big. Such landlords, as Chao's data itself indicates, were not rare in the Xinjiang region.

Second, Chao's assumption that these big landlords' rate of land accumulation was low is correct. But it was probably not as low as indicated. He reaches his conclusion by computing a yearly average of land accumulation on the basis of the total landholding acquired by a landlord family in a period spanning more than a hundred, and in some cases several hundred, years.[44] This prevents determining the historical periods when land was purchased at a rapid rate and when it was not. Not all persons in each generation of a landlord family were equally successful economically. There were times in the history of a landlord family when no land could have been purchased due to various socioeconomic problems, and there were times, too, when enterprising landlords could purchase more land than usual. Thus, when the total accumulation is averaged out over a long period, the result is a very low figure of accumulation. In fact, those of Chao's figures which cover a shorter period, usually less than a hundred years, reflect a far higher rate of accumulation. His explanation of this is apt: "Usually land transactions concentrated in the first few years after a family shifted to the rural sector the capital they had accumulated in commerce or government services, but the tempo gradually slowed thereafter. The longer the period cov-

[42] Ibid., 734.
[43] Chao 1982; Li 1972, 1981b.
[44] Chao 1981: 727; see also Chao 1982.

ered by the land purchase records, the lower was the average rate of acquisition."[45]

There were historical periods when the tempo of land acquisition was
much faster than in others. One such period in the rural history of the region
was probably from the beginning of the eighteenth century to just before the
outbreak of the Taiping Rebellion. Thus Li's assumption that, during such
a period in the Yangzi region, "land often changed hands several times
within a decade"[46] seems correct, with Chao's data providing the corrective
that the size of each plot in the average transaction was not big. Moreover,
when viewing such long-term data on landlord families, what impresses one
most is the tenacity of these families in surviving for such a long time.

Finally, Chao's data also reflect that at least a number of tenants of a
particular landlord often defaulted on the payment of rent and were still
permitted to continue cultivation of land. He writes: "There is also an indication that landlord families had no effective control over their tenants,
probably because landlords were merely small landholders lacking monopo-
listic power. Numerous tenants failed to pay their rents in full (*chuan shu*),
yet delinquent tenants were not dismissed. In fact, the turnover rate of tenants was exceedingly low—as if every tenant were protected by permanent
tenancy rights."[47] Such data have also been shown by other scholars studying different regions to reflect the nonexploitative nature of the landlord-
tenant relationship. In fact, any attempt to derive meaning from the cases of
defaulter tenants would be meaningless if these are not seen in historical
perspective.

As indicated earlier, the strength of landlords' socioeconomic power fluctuated according to the historical period, with periods immediately after
peasant uprisings being periods of reassertion of the small-peasant economy
and the slackened authority of landlords. During such times, landlords
found it difficult to dismiss their tenants and in fact maintained a good relationship with them. Further, even when a landlord was able to exercise
greater power, it was better to keep a tenant who frequently defaulted on
rent payment because that provided the landlord with opportunities to
squeeze more profit out of the tenant through such activities as money lending. Moreover, tenants and landlords often belonged to the same lineage or
clan. As the clan leader, the landlord maintained a paternalistic facade by
keeping the defaulting tenant and also squeezing him. Hiring other tenants

[45] Chao 1981: 726.
[46] Li 1981b: 70.
[47] Chao 1981: 733.

in such cases would have reduced his own economic advantage, lowered his social prestige, and made him a target of tenants' indignation. Also, in some cases, landlords purchased surface rights to land from, usually, a socioeconomically declining owner and rented the land in parcels to tenants. While the landlord received rents from his tenants, he himself intentionally defaulted on the payment for surface rights to the weak original owner. Thus, tenants' default on rent payments suggests many possibilities. Without detailed investigation of both the tenants' and landlords' socioeconomic condition, one can at best arrive at mere impressions. A thorough study is a task that, until more local records are available, cannot be adequately carried out.

It thus appears that, beginning with the eighteenth century and just before the Taiping Rebellion, the tremendous growth in population and the rise of landlordism meant greater concentration of land in the hands of numerous commoner landlords. This restricted the availability of land and considerably changed the man-land ratio in the region. A larger percentage of the rural population found themselves increasingly dependent upon landlords for survival and subsistence. An investigative report from Linchuan prefecture, located on the southern boundary of the Xinjiang region, indicated that in the whole of the area "there are nine poor people as against one rich person."[48] It was at this stage that the Taiping rebels struck the region.

[48] Li 1972: 53.

Chapter Two

Impact of the Taiping Rebellion
on Rural Areas in the Xinjiang Region

Taiping rebels wandered frequently in the Xinjiang region during their short ascendancy. But neither the rebels nor their ideology fundamentally altered the rural social, political, and economic structure. In fact, setting out with a belief in a millenarian type of rural egalitarianism, the rebels had no success in implementing any of their revolutionary ideas, let alone in molding the rural reality according to their anachronistic visions. The decade-long civil war between the Taipings and the monarchists, however, considerably devastated the larger Xinjiang region. Its restoration significantly altered the pre-Taiping land-man ratio as well as the land tenure patterns. Consequently, the nature of both state and landed-upper-class authority and control in the countryside was also reshaped. In the long run, disruptions in the newly established post-Taiping rural social and economic patterns would create conditions to which the origin of the twentieth-century agrarian crisis and the growth of the Communist-led peasant movement can be traced. It is in this context that the impact of the Taiping Rebellion on the Xinjiang region is examined.

During the war, which lasted more than a decade, the Xinjiang region was part of a larger battle zone in the lower Yangzi area that included northern and northeastern Jiangxi, southern Anhui, southwestern Zhejiang, and northwestern Fujian.[1] In this zone, from 1853 until the end of the rebellion in 1866, the Taiping and imperial forces fought many of their major battles, each crisscrossing the area either in pursuit or in retreat. Moreover, both forces launched frequent campaigns in the countryside to enlist popular support as well as to procure food and other supplies. Important cities of this

---

[1] For a full description of the warfare in this area, see the monumental works of Li (1982) and Jen (1973). Some specific aspects of the Taipings' activities in Jiangxi are discussed in Hu 1983; Chen 1984; Feng 1984.

region, such as Jiujiang, Hekou, Pengze, and Jingdezhen, remained under the extended control of the Taipings between 1853 and 1858. Making Jiujiang their base, armies of the eminent Taiping general Shi Dakai twice besieged the capital of Jiangxi province, Nanchang. By 1856, more than fifty districts and eight prefectural cities of the province had come under the control of Shi's forces. Zeng Guofan and his famous Xiang Army were forced to retreat to the Xinjiang region before moving again to defeat the Taipings.

After the fall of Nanjing and the consequent weakening of the Taiping forces, it was the central portion of the Xinjiang region that suffered most. Many of the last battles directed by the scattered and retreating Taiping generals were fought here. The Yiyang and Guixi districts where, seventy years later, Fang Zhimin was to organize the famous Xinjiang peasant movement and a soviet, were frequented by forces of both sides. Li Shixian, the Taiping general, encircled Zuo Congtang's headquarters in Jingdezhen and defeated him before finally being wiped out after a series of skirmishes in the Jiangxi, Fujian, and Zhejiang border region. Similarly, Li Xiucheng's retreating Taiping forces fought several of their desperate battles in this region.

The entire Xinjiang region was not only a battle zone; it also supplied men and matériel to both the Taipings and the monarchists. One of the Taiping treatises on the establishment of the heavenly capital in Jinling (Nanjing) stated that "the (Taiping) country's food stuffs are all produced in the south, from such provinces as Jiangxi and Anjing [southern Anhui]. Following river currents, grains can be transported very conveniently."[2] During the Taipings' eastern expedition into Jiangxi, their official proclamation exhorting the rich in rural areas to keep ready stores of provisions was posted in advance in the countryside. Those who resisted or did not heed the notification were warned of serious consequences: "If any family does not come to pay tribute, it is certain that the whole family will be beheaded."[3] In late 1853 and early 1854, various commands were issued by the Taipings calling for the urgent transport of provisions to Nanjing from the Jiangxi and Hubei areas. The ample supply of rice in Jiangxi-Anhui belt led the Taiping generals to request the heavenly king to "order the assistant commanding generals in the garrisons in these places to instruct the good people, according to the ancient practice, to submit rice as tax in kind."[4] Four large armies were sent by the Taipings' Li Xiucheng and Li Shixian to northern Jiangxi,

[2] Michael 1966: 32.
[3] Ibid., 476.
[4] Ibid., 479.

southern Anhui, and southern Jiangsu in early 1864 to search for food for
the starving heavenly capital. Although these armies were defeated within a
year and a half, such campaigns for food indicate the constant depletion of
this region's resources.

While the rich were asked under duress to pay tribute, the poor were
exhorted to join the Taiping forces. For a long time, the Taipings' immense
popularity encouraged a great number of poor peasants of the region to volunteer for the rebel army. Reporting an account by a bookseller of Fuzhou
prefecture (Jiangxi), W.A.P. Martin writes that Taiping recruiting parties,
after arriving in this area in October 1856, received wholehearted support
from the local people and were able to raise speedily a volunteer corps of
nearly ten thousand peasants.[5]

The Taipings were, however, not alone in depleting this region's human
and other resources. The imperial forces, and especially their Xiang Army,
relentlessly pillaged the entire countryside. In Hukou district of this region,
such activities of the Xiang Army provoked retaliation from indignant peasants, and several soldiers were massacred. In spite of Zeng's efforts to discipline his army, the pillaging and frequent hostility between his soldiers
and local peasants continued.[6]

Revenue from Jiangxi, in addition to financing the provincial administration, supported the Jiangxi Army and militia, Zeng Guofan's and Zuo Congtang's mercenaries in Anhui and Jiangsu, and the river fleet of Peng Yulin.
While Hunan and Guangdong after 1862 met a portion of the expenses of
the anti-Taiping armies, Jiangxi remained the major source of income. Zeng
wrote in a memorial dated June 21, 1860, that "both north and south Anhui
are desolated areas. Recently Suzhou and Changzhou have fallen. The rebels
are everywhere and we do not know where to begin. [Under such circum-
stances] it is natural to turn to Hunan and Hubei as recruiting grounds, and
to Jiangxi as the source of military supplies."[7]

David Pong's study of the provincial revenues and military expenditures
of Jiangxi during 1860–1864 indicates that the income of the province,
through *caozhe* (grain tribute), *diding* (land taxes), *changshui* (customs duties),
lijin, and contributions from the gentry and commoners, was 16,465,000
taels. During the same period, the military expenditure, which included
contributions to several anti-Taiping armies outside the province, amounted
to 18,900,000 taels. Pong believes that the amount of the deficit was perhaps

[5] Quoted in Jen 1973: 257. Jen cites several reports from different sources indicating Shi
Dakai's popularity in the region (Jen 1973: 257–59).
[6] Jen 1973: 337.
[7] Pong 1966: 64.

somewhat inflated by the Jiangxi governor Shen Bochen to make a strong case for relief. Even so, these figures reveal a heavy increase in the expenditure of a province whose own civil and military budget was much less.[8]

The drain led to a decline in Jiangxi's economic status from rich to poor. As new necessities demanded larger revenues, the masses had to bear a heavier burden. A large number of changshui and lijin barriers emerged at this time in key areas of the province, and they soon became the most important source of provincial income. Consequently, prices of both food and other items went up sharply. Peasants were pressed for more contributions to the war fund through special levies or forced donations. Adequate information on the amount of money collected by such means is not available. But the gravity of the economic situation can be judged from the fact that while the land-tax quota of Jiangxi was decreased during this period and the intermittent attacks by the Taipings impeded the collection of the land tax in some areas, the overall income of the province did not decline. This indicates the state's ability to procure the much-needed funds through the imposition of various extra levies and through customs and lijin duties. The high wartime taxes and levies, coupled with war-related instabilities, forced many rich peasants and landlords to sell their land cheaply and to move to safer regions elsewhere. As large tracts of agricultural land were abandoned, cultivation suffered and production declined. Thus the rebellion devastated this agriculturally and commercially rich region.

War also greatly reduced the population of the Xinjiang region. The loss in population in the northern Jiangxi and southern Anhui battle zone was only slightly less than what it was in southern Jiangsu and northern Zhejiang, which had suffered most during the rebellion. Unfortunately, there are no reliable population figures for the post-1850 period, thus making it very difficult to ascertain the exact loss of lives in the region. Almost all scholars agree that the population of Jiangxi had reached an all-time high of about 24.5 million in 1851.[9] According to the post-1850 Chinese statistical data, the population of Jiangxi declined to 12.3 million and 9.8 million respectively in 1856 and 1857, but increased to 24.4 million in 1858.[10] Such a massive jump appears to be totally impossible. Moreover, the census investigation carried out during the last three years of the Xuantong emperor estimates that the population of the province was 16.9 million between 1909

---

[8] Ibid., 54–61.

[9] For a detailed examination of the post-Taiping population figures, see Yan 1955; Liu and Yeh 1965; Ho 1967; Perkins 1969; Liang 1980; Xu 1984.

[10] *ZNYS* 1957, 1:10; Xu (1984) cites the adjusted figure of 16.9 million as the total population during 1911–1912.

and 1911. As no major catastrophe took place in the province after the Taiping Rebellion, this low figure probably reflects either that the prerebellion population level had still not been regained or that postrebellion estimates were unreliable.

Ho remarks that post-1850 Chinese statistical figures for Jiangxi are totally useless.[11] In the absence of any fresh census activity after the Taiping Rebellion, the province's official population figures remained static. The mode of their assessmént, as Perkins explains, comprised only simple addition of the 1850 individual district data.[12] Hence, both Ho and Perkins, as well as T. C. Liu and K. C. Yeh, estimate that after the Taiping Rebellion, the population of Jiangxi fell to approximately 17.7 million from 24.4 million in 1850. This figure is close to the census figure of the Xuantong period, which revised the earlier official returns. This also tallies with the People's Republic of China official census of 1953, which puts Jiangxi's total population figure at 16.7 million. The continued downward trend reflects another great loss in population during the Chinese Communist Party–Guomindang civil war in the 1930s.

Contemporary descriptions of the rebellion provide ample circumstantial evidence for the great loss of population in the Xinjiang region. Writing about the conditions in Guangxin prefecture in 1858, Monsignor Danicourt, the vicar apostolic of Jiangxi, noted that for the preceding months the movement of missionaries had been restricted to the prefectural city, which was "in control of neither the insurgents nor the imperialists—the former exterminating everyone that offered them resistance and the latter pillaging everything that came in their way."[13] He further wrote, "For upwards of a month, we had witnessed the burning, first of a portion, and subsequently of the whole, of the suburbs of Kientchang [Jianchang], accompanied by the continual reports of cannon and guns; we had heard the lamentable accounts of the frightful devastations which have converted the flourishing town of Fou-tcheo-fou [Fuzhou Fu] and Ya-tcheou-fou [Raozhou Fu] into piles of ruins, whilst under our own observation, the open country of Kientchang-fou [Jianchang Fu] and the environs of Kienfou (?) were abandoned to pillage."[14]

[11] Ho 1967: 69, 245–46.

[12] Perkins 1969: 204–5, 210–11; see also Ho 1967; Liu and Yeh 1965.

[13] Cited in Clarke and Gregory 1982: 200. Stationed in northeastern Jiangxi, Danicourt wrote: "Never was a country afflicted with greater calamities than those which have befallen China. For instance, in Kiang-si [Jiangxi] alone, there are at present days in this province, upwards of fifteen millions of inhabitants reduced to the most abject misery" (Clarke and Gregory 1982: 201).

[14] Ibid., 200.

Similarly, according to the *Nankang Fu Zhi*, "out of fourteen prefectures and one large departmental county, only two were altogether immune to war ravages."[15] More than one million peasants from Jiangxi and Hubei had joined the Taiping armies. The Taipings' raids from their military and economic base in northern Jiangxi into the Xinjiang region had caused the depopulation of many villages. As counterattacks by the imperial army began, its scorched-earth policy destroyed a large number of areas sympathetic to the Taipings. In the Yining district of northwestern Jiangxi, after a fierce battle lasting twenty-one days, out of a total population of 100,600 less than 10,000 survived. A contemporary account of this battle notes that "for some 100 *li* the Xin river was red and navigation was blocked by corpses. Subsequently dead bodies had to be cremated and buried in a huge tomb which has since been called 'one-hundred-thousand-men tomb.' "[16] The long civil war thus provided a Malthusian solution for the densely populated Xinjiang region. Changes in the population pattern naturally affected the land-man ratio and created opportunities for the reshaping of the nature of land tenure in the rebellion-devastated region.

THE POST-TAIPING LAND TENURE PATTERN

Ho Ping-ti remarks that "by far the most important change in land tenure during the past century took place in the most densely populated lower Yangtze [Yangzi] provinces, where the concentrated landownership was substantially broken up not by the primitive communistic land policies of the Taipings, which were not carried out on a significant scale, but by the result of rebellion and economic forces it engendered."[17] During the long civil war, in most of the affected areas, a large number of landowners were either killed or forced to flee. Their land soon became desolate. After the suppression of the rebellion, the state paid immediate attention to the task of rehabilitation of these war-devastated areas in order to reestablish its traditional sources of revenue through land taxes and to arrest further decline of the rural economy. For these purposes, the state offered liberal incentives to peasants to reclaim the wasteland for agriculture. Ho notes that "the population of southern Kiangsu [Jiangsu] except the Shanghai area, northern Chekiang [Zhejiang], practically the whole province of Anhwei [Anhui], and parts of Kiangsi [Jiangxi] and Hupei [Hubei] were so drastically reduced that every

[15] Cited in Ho 1967: 245; see also *ZNYS* 1957.
[16] Cited in Ho 1967: 245.
[17] Ibid., 221.

effort was made by the provincial governments and surviving landowners to attract immigrants from afar at terms unprecedentedly favourable to the latter."[18]

The northern Jiangxi and southern Anhui belt thus attracted a large number of "guest people" who immigrated from the neighboring densely populated regions. Wang Tianjing mentions that the majority of the "guest people" came from Hubei; their emigration was inspired by their dream of acquiring land of their own and of improving their socioeconomic status.[19] The long war had depressed the price of land in many districts. This attracted a number of landlords from other regions and rich persons and speculators from the villages as well as the cities, who moved in and purchased land for renting purposes. So rapid was the influx of the immigrants, especially in the easily accessible regions, that F. Von Richthofen, who visited southern Anhui in 1871, noted that "it is astonishing what numbers of them [immigrants] have come to southern Nganhwei [Anhui] within the last two or three years. The traveller has often the greatest difficulty in making enquiries regarding the country or the road to some neighboring place. There are instances where only the twentieth man he meets is an old resident. . . . Most of the new men are from Hupe [Hubei], but many are natives of Hunan, Honan [Henan], northern Nganhwei [Anhui], and even Szechwan [Sichaun] and Kweichou [Guizhou]."[20]

Such massive immigration brought about a change in the land tenure pattern that was marked by two significant developments. First, there was an enormous increase in the number of small peasant freeholders, who were not bound by the constraints of earlier socioeconomic relationships characterized by servile dependency. Second, the system of permanent tenancy once again became widely prevalent. The permanent tenants had almost as much freedom in agriculture as that enjoyed by the small peasant freeholders.

THE RISE OF SMALL PEASANT FREEHOLDERS

The rise of small peasant freeholders did not come out of the conscious desire of the state to bring about fundamental changes in land tenure in the wake of numerous mid-nineteenth-century peasant uprisings. In fact, as stated above, the financially bankrupt Qing state was more interested in re-

[18] Ibid., 221.
[19] Wang 1983: 307.
[20] Richthofen 1903: 18.

storing the old agrarian order and widening the cultivation area to obtain much-needed larger tax revenues. This concern predominated the state's views after regions were reconquered and the rebellion was quelled. The state, therefore, pursued a policy aimed at immediate "return of land to its original owner" and "the opening up of wasteland for cultivation purposes."[21] Only when original owners or their family members were not traceable, having been wiped out during the war, were the immigrants to be allowed to take up cultivation under liberal incentives. However, in most of the areas of the northern Jiangxi and southern Anhui belt, the state completely failed in its policy of reestablishing the earlier pattern of land tenure.

The immigrants, who came to dominate the rural areas immediately after the rebellion, vigorously resisted the state's policy of uprooting them at the expense of original owners. In northern Jiangxi and southern Anhui, a large number of immigrants consisted of disbanded soldiers of the Anhui and Jiangxi armies raised by Zeng Guofan and Li Hongzhang for the suppression of the rebellion. The state had relied upon their loyal support in the internecine warfare and was unwilling to let these soldiers become disgruntled and join the counterstate secret societies and brigands after their disbandment. It had, therefore, offered them incentives to live in and cultivate wasteland areas. It proved to be difficult later to take back the land in order to resettle the original owners.

Moreover, attracted by liberal incentives offered by the state, a large number of peasants, especially from Hubei, had also settled on unclaimed wasteland. These settlers devised means to guarantee the possession of abandoned land. Often, in spite of the fact that the state provided land free to immigrants, the latter paid about eight hundred to four thousand cash per mu to the surviving distant relatives of the killed or runaway landowners to deter them from making any claim on the basis of their clan connections. Writing about strong clan villages in the southern Anhui area, Richthofen noted, "It appears that it is tacitly convened, to consider the survivors in each village as the lawful heirs of the abandoned fields, and to hold them entitled to an indemnity, perhaps because many a village was indeed inhabited by a single family or clan." However, "the settlers agreed equally in the statement that they pay nothing whatever to the mandarins, and that they enjoy great liberty such as they were not accustomed to in their native province."[22] These immigrants, once settled, formed their own powerful organi-

---

[21] Much of the ensuing discussion is based on Liu 1981: 32–48; Liu 1982: 105–20; Li 1981: 81–96; Li 1961; ZNYS 1957, 1:115–72; Lin 1979

[22] Richthofen 1903: 18.

zations to defend vigorously their claims on land and prevent the intrusion of either clan associations or the state on their landed property. Many branches of the prominent secret societies rapidly appeared in local areas, where the membership of most was composed entirely of new immigrants.[23] The latter had thus become powerful enough to oppose strongly the state's policy of returning land to the original owners.

The original owners, who had begun to return to their native places by 1871, found to their dismay that their land had been occupied or claimed by new and powerful aliens. The politically weak state was unable to hand over these lands to the original owners. In fact, it was unable to do anything more than confirm the property rights of the latter. In such a situation the original owners suggested several remedial measures in order to get at least some return out of their land. In Dingguo and Guangde prefectures of southern Anhui, they offered their land exclusively to immigrants for purchase or hire. In other areas of this belt, they were even ready to relinquish control over half of their land by granting outright ownership rights to immigrants in return for possession of the other half. Moreover, they proposed to the local authorities that all "ownerless land" should be confiscated by the state and rented out to immigrants. These compromise measures were, however, unacceptable to the new settlers, who ruefully remarked to a reporter from the *Shanghai Xinbao* that "we came alone when the land was desolate and there was no owner. We spent capital and labor and opened up the area for settlement after making it productive. You aliens have come only today and are desirous to promptly get back the land."[24]

In the wake of such strong resistance to the state's policy as well as to the remedial measures suggested by the original owners, local authorities were forced to provide preferential treatment to the new settlers. It was finally decided that the latter would be granted ownership rights to all "ownerless wasteland" cultivated by them. In return, they were to pay to the state a nominal price for the land, which was well below the prevailing market rate. Moreover, they were also authorized to assume control over those lands which were not personally reclaimed by the original owners within a short, stipulated time. Agents and representatives of the latter were denied any right to negotiate on their behalf and were prevented from making any claim to their land. Such restrictions resulted in the transfer of a large amount of land from the control of the original owners to the immigrants.

[23] Wang 1983: 225–33.
[24] Cited in Li 1981: 92.

According to one estimate, these stipulations prevented eight out of ten original owners from reclaiming their land. In Guangde prefecture alone, ownership rights to about 24,000 mu of land were transferred to immigrants.[25] Some members of the old landlord families, however, repurchased their own land at the low prices fixed by the state after the land had been declared ownerless. But their number was small compared with that of the new settlers who had priority in land purchases.[26]

A small number of original owners who successfully reclaimed their land were prevented by various regulations from operating their leasing businesses as in the past. The state forbade them to fix rents according to their own economic interests. In order to protect the rights of immigrants who had originally opened up the land, a lower grain rent amounting to eighty jin per mu was fixed. Moreover, the practice of requiring a security deposit from a tenant was abolished. But in spite of these incentives, the immigrants resisted and refused to pay even the fixed low rents. In such a hostile rural atmosphere, the original owners found it difficult to continue using their land in a financially profitable manner. Consequently, many of them preferred to sell the land to immigrants at the low state prices.[27] Such terms attracted immigrants to the region.

These post-Taiping developments resulted in breaking up the concentrated landownership in traditional domains of the great landlords. The number of small peasant freeholders, who were mostly new settlers, enormously increased. For example, by 1875 in Guangde prefecture, out of 353,822 mu of cultivated land, about 240,000 mu were owned by immigrants. They had acquired ownership rights over more than 67 percent of the total land area. Moreover, by 1880, they constituted 80 percent of the total population of that area.[28] There were similar changes after the rebellion in other Taiping-affected regions. This indicates not only an enormous influx of immigrants due to the massive loss of population but also a significant increase in the number of small peasant freeholders. Various data about population and cultivated land in the northern Jiangxi and southern Anhui belt disclose that these small peasant freeholders owned, on average, ten to twelve mu of land per family.[29]

It is not surprising, therefore, that George Jamieson, who visited the Xin-

---

[25] Ibid., 92.
[26] Ibid., 92.
[27] Ibid., 92–93.
[28] Ibid., 93.
[29] See note 21 above.

jiang region between 1883 and 1884 to study the condition of the peasantry, noted the existence of a large number of economically-better-off small peasant freeholders. He found a few big landowners in this area, but only in exceptional cases did they possess more than fifty mu of land. Of his fifteen case studies, the smallest landowner had three mu of land and the biggest, twenty-six mu. Eighty percent of the peasant families owned fifteen or fewer mu of land. The landholding of an average peasant family was approximately eight mu. He writes that "a family of five or six persons owning eight *mu* of land can manage to get along with tolerable comfort in good years but there is nothing left over for luxuries."[30] If eight mu can be considered the minimum requisite for survival, it is safe to assume that most of the peasants were able to provide for their daily requirements from the land, and no grave subsistence crisis existed. The peasants who owned more than eight mu were definitely a little better off. Moreover, the relative absence of big landowners possessing more than fifty mu of land suggests that the distribution of land in northern Jiangxi after the Taiping Rebellion was not inequitable. While Jamieson does not name the districts involved in his case studies on which the above data are based, he mentions that cotton was an important summer crop of this region. This suggests that his portrayal of the rural situation specifically relates to major cotton-producing northern and western districts of the Xinjiang region, such as Jiujiang, Leping, Boyang, Pengze, and Hukou. This was the area that was also most affected by the rebellion.

Examples from other Taiping-affected provinces present a similar picture. In his study of the impact of the Taiping Rebellion on Jiangsu, Wang Yeh-ch'ien notes that in the western region of this province "the war left in its wake not only a great amount of waste land, but also much land without owners. Moreover, the government's attitude towards the settlement of immigrants in this area generally favored their ownership of the unclaimed land they brought back to production. It is therefore not surprising that there were many independent peasants in the west in the latter part of the nineteenth century."[31] While neither in the case of Jiangxi nor of Jiangsu is there complete information about the number of peasant freeholders, given the gravity of the pre-Taiping agrarian crisis as well as the loss of population and economic hardships during the period of rebellion, it can be safely assumed that there was a significant increase in their number in the late nineteenth century.

[30] Jamieson 1888: 97–98.
[31] Wang 1965: 143; see also Chang 1975.

THE PREVALENCE
OF PERMANENT TENANCY

Permanent tenancy was not a new phenomenon in rural China. Guaranteeing tenants permanent rights to land similar to those of independent owners, it reappeared after the Taiping Rebellion as the predominant tenancy system. To comprehend the prevalence of permanent tenancy immediately after the rebellion, it is necessary first to trace its historical evolution. This will also help in better understanding its significance in comparison with other systems of tenancy that developed later in Jiangxi.

The origin of permanent tenancy can be traced to the demise of the Ming aristocratic-official landlords in the late seventeenth century. During that period, a large number of tenant and tenant-serf uprisings demanding the end of servile, dependent relationships broke out, not only in Jiangxi but in the whole of central and south China. Self-proclaimed "leveling kings" fought to eliminate the distinction between the master and the serf, the rich and the poor. In an uprising in the Zhizhou district of Jiangxi during 1644–1645, thousands of tenant-serfs in every village of the district rebelled under the leadership of "leveling kings."[32] Another serf uprising of this period, which began among the indignant serfs of the Qu family in Jiangdong (in the lower Yangzi valley) and spread to Zhujiagu in Jiangxi, is described by the Baoshan gazetteer as one "which has not been seen for a millennium."[33] The antilandlord peasant movement soon spread like a wildfire in the region.

Serfs and serf-tenants coined slogans in support of equal rights and free status. They often destroyed such explicit symbols of lords' power as clothes, mansions, and granaries and forced the lords to act like servants. Resistance to payment of rent was widespread, and the lords' right to collect it was vigorously challenged. The declining Ming state, further weakened by these peasant uprisings and the rebellions of Li Zecheng and Zheng Zhongxian, was unable to control rebellious serfs and thereby protect the lords' traditional claims on their tenants. Serfs exerted real power in rural areas, and the lords were forced to endorse their demands for a free status.

The victory of the Manchus over the Mings brought about the final collapse of the feudal manorial system. In order to maintain stability in rural areas, increase its tax base, and completely control the loyalist Ming lords, the Qing emperor Kangxi legally prohibited the serf system. He approved

[32] Fu 1961: 109, translated in Elvin 1973: 245–46. Elvin's discussion of the late Ming uprisings is most illuminating.

[33] Fu 1961: 95.

a memorial from the governor of Anhui that stated: "Henceforth, when landlords are buying and selling land they must allow their tenants to do as they please. They may not sell them along with their fields or compel them to perform services."[34] By the beginning of eighteenth century, various other proclamations had severely restricted the lords' traditional power.

The widespread peasant uprisings and the antifeudal policies of the new Qing state debilitated the lords' control over land and labor to the extent that many of them preferred to move to urban areas. Drawn by luxuries of urban living and profitable commercial opportunities available in the cities, they entered into such paying business as pawnbroking and real estate. Landowning thus became a less attractive source of income. Although land still was a source of social prestige, capital investment in agricultural enterprise was significantly reduced. This reduction promoted fragmentation of large landholdings and the growth of absentee landlordism. Unable to maintain their customary power, the landlords found it more profitable to turn their serfs into tenants and receive rent. A seventeenth-century treatise on agriculture mentions that in the lower Yangzi region, "all land is rented out, and the owners peacefully enjoy the profit of idleness. Isn't that excellent? Here (probably Lien-ch'uan [Lianchuan] in Chekiang [Zhejiang] province), however, there is no custom of letting land. If one owns land, one must have it cultivated; and if one is to have it cultivated, one must engage long term laborers and toil diligently all year around—this is simply unavoidable."[35]

Thus, during the early Qing period, as the force of the landlord in the countryside weakened and absentee landlordism became prevalent, permanent tenancy and multiple landownership were introduced. These innovations emerged as a compromise solution that, on the one hand, guaranteed tenants permanent rights on the land and the security of subsistence while, on the other, it enabled landlords to maintain some control over their tenants and land. A tenant was now free to use land and cultivate his crops as he wished. Since the rent was low and fixed permanently, the tenant had an incentive to raise production by fertilizing and double cropping. Furthermore, the landlord was legally allowed to evict a tenant only when the latter continuously failed to pay his rent.

Fei Xiaotong [Hsiao-t'ung] remarked that "the system of permanent tenancy seems to be a protection of the peasant against loss of land rights owing to the financial needs of rural industry. It should be studied not as an histor-

---

[34] Wei 1972: 157; see also Elvin 1973: 236–46; Fu 1977.
[35] Cited in Elvin 1973: 252–53.

ical survival but as an adjustment of the interests of cultivator and financier, an integral part of the absentee landlord system."[36] While Fei's obvious preference for a functional rather than a historical study emphasizes the practical aspect of permanent tenancy, it cannot be denied that this system also contributed to the survival of landlordism. Landlords were soon able to dominate the tenants with renewed vigor by restricting their customary permanent tenancy rights under various pretexts. The continued existence of landlordism thus had grave implications for the historical development of the rural socioeconomic structure. However, in the transitional period of the seventeenth century as well as in the extraordinary situation after the rebellion, permanent tenancy was a favorable arrangement for the tenants, one that strengthened their status in rural society.

How did the system of permanent tenancy function? Two levels of landownership were defined by which the rights to the subsoil were kept by the landlord and the rights to the surface were possessed by the tenant. To understand the nature and scope of these rights under permanent tenancy, Peter Hoang's description is worth quoting at length:

> The field bottom [*tiandi*] is distinguished from the field surface [*tianmian*]. The possessor of the bottom is called a tributary, for he pays the impost on land. The possessor of the surface, to whom consequently the right to rent the bottom for cultivation is attached, is called a tenant, the same as simple lessees of the land who have not the above right. Registration of title and validation of deed concern only the owner of the bottom and not the owner of the surface, since the latter is not called on to pay taxes.
>
> The field bottom is commonly worth from three to six times as much as the surface. If the bottom and the surface belong to two different owners, neither . . . has the right to construct a house or build a tomb on the land. The one who possesses the bottom only cannot cultivate it himself; he must rent it to others who possess the surface and who have the right to farm it permanently. The owner of the bottom cannot eject the tenant at will save in the case where the sum total of rent unpaid is equal to the value of the surface. When the owner of the surface has contracted this debt, the cultivation is taken from him, and the surface goes to the owner of the bottom, who can then either sell the surface to another person, or rent it out with the bottom.
>
> When the tributary sells his field bottom to another, besides the deed of sale he commonly signs a testimony of the transfer which is shown to the tenant through the "district warden" [*dibao*], that the tenant may thereby be warned of the change of the bottom ownership and may sign a new lease.

[36] Fei 1939: 184n.

Likewise, when the tenant sells his field surface, he is required to introduce the new tenant to the bottom owner in order that he may sign a new lease. If the owner of the bottom doubts the good faith of the new tenant he may require the former tenant to guarantee the rent of his successor. The tenant who possesses the surface may lease to another his right to cultivate the land, then the lessee pays rent to the owners of the bottom and the surface as may be due.[37]

Permanent tenancy thus entitled the landlord to a steady income from rent. The tenant, on the other hand, had almost the same right to land as property owners. He could transfer, mortgage, and sell his rights. Since the overriding concern of the tenant was to meet the subsistence demands of his family, for which he would even pay the self-exploitative fees that are generally called "hunger rents," the usufructuary right on land that guaranteed him and his family security of subsistence was a relatively advantageous tenancy arrangement for him. Indeed, the emergence and prevalence of permanent tenancy could be interpreted as a victory of tenants over landlords.

Motonosuke has explained the four most common ways a tenant acquired the right to permanent tenancy.[38] First, a tenant could claim permanent right by cultivating and improving the wasteland of a landlord by his labor and capital. The recurring term "old land reborn" refers to the reclamation of an alluvial deposit. "Ash-fertilized land" or land under "fertilizer-compensation lease" in the lower Yangzi provinces are other examples of improved land that became subject to the permanent tenancy system. Second, a considerable sum could be paid to a landlord as a rent deposit to purchase the surface rights on land. Third, during times of financial crisis many independent landowners could become permanent tenants by selling the rights to bottom soil and retaining only the rights to the surface. Fourth, tenants cultivating land owned by the state or clan could acquire permanent tilling rights by agreement. Such a situation generally arose when agrarian unrest, war, or a major dislocation destroyed a region and reduced the population, leaving large areas of unclaimed land to be rehabilitated. The state then strove to recolonize such waste areas by granting permanent tenancy rights to new immigrant tenants. In such cases, if the original landowner returned after a certain fixed time following the catastrophe, he was not allowed to collect rent and deprive tenants of their rights. Moreover, both the state and

---

[37] Hoang 1920: 29–30; see also Watson 1977.
[38] Amano 1940: 485–87.

the clan also granted permanent tenancy rights on new land created by changes in the course of a river or stream.

Frequently, means of gaining permanent tenancy were indicated by different names in different regions. For example, *Daye* (greater business) and *xiaoye* (smaller business) in northern Jiangxi and *gutian* (bone land) and *pitian* (skin land) in southern Jiangxi denote a form of permanent tenancy originating from the above-mentioned second or third method.[39] The "ash-fertilized tenancy" indicates that the tenant acquired permanent right to the land by improving wastelands of a landlord through fertilizers. In Shanghobei village of Leping district, land on which permanent tenancy was granted was called *fan-wan-tian* (rice bowl land, or one's job land). The name suggests that many small rural cultivators had become permanent tenants by selling their bottom-soil rights to land in exchange for rice, thus preserving their occupation as cultivators to ensure subsistence. The permanent tenancy agreement in Jiangxi was guaranteed by a document called a *pitie* (surface rights agreement). The loss of these rights was known as *guoye* or *bietie*, meaning loss of business.[40]

There is not much information available about the development of permanent tenancy in rural Jiangxi before the Taiping Rebellion. However, the bursary records recently found in Yixian of southern Anhui (adjoining the Xinjiang region) and exposited by Zhang Youyi provide an example of its nature and growth in the pre-Taiping period.[41] In Anhui, the rights to land under permanent tenancy were known as *damai* (greater purchase, or subsoil, rights) and *xiaomai* (smaller purchase, or surface, rights), slightly different from the titles *daye* (greater business) and *xiaoye* (smaller business) in northern Jiangxi. According to the bursary records, the landlord initially granted the "smaller purchase" rights to those tenants, who, by their labor, reclaimed his wasteland. While the "greater purchase" rights were alienable, by the late eighteenth century many permanent tenants had also begun to either sell, mortgage, or buy the "smaller purchase" rights like private property. Thus, on some portions of Landlord Jiang's land, the rights to "smaller purchase" were transferred at least four times within a few years. The agrarian crisis, growing since the beginning of the nineteenth century, appears to have forced a large number of tenants to sell their "smaller purchase" rights, and many small peasant freeholders sold their "greater purchase" rights. In the early nineteenth century, Landlord Jiang's family thus expanded its

[39] Wang 1935: 8–9.
[40] Ibid., 8–9; *ZNYS* 1957, 1:252.
[41] For the ensuing description, see Zhang 1975: 34–36.

landholding by acquiring the rights to "greater purchase" on land belonging to a number of small peasant freeholders, and by buying the "smaller purchase" rights on land belonging to permanent tenants.

While permanent tenancy existed in Jiangxi before the Taiping Rebellion, its prevalence following the rebellion was the result of an increase in the area of wasteland and acute labor shortages. Moreover, the Taiping onslaughts on landlords swelled the number of absentee landowners who found it safer to control land from the cities. The imperative to reclaim wasteland and to maintain control over their surplus land forced landlords to grant many concessions to tenants. The imperial state also promoted immigration on excellent terms.

Various forms of permanent tenancy were thus introduced. The *Economic Yearbook of China* for 1934 mentions that because of the ravages of both Taiping and imperial forces, much of the land in northern Jiangxi was deserted by its owners. Hence, many newcomers occupied land and distributed it to tenants for cultivation. Those who occupied land collected rent, and those who cultivated it were granted permanent tenancy rights. In other cases, many small peasant freeholders, economically devastated by the civil war, sold off either the bottom or surface rights of their land and became permanent tenants.[42] Although there is a lack of definite and detailed information on the total number of permanent tenants in the northern region of Jiangxi, it appears most likely that a large number of such tenants emerged in the areas along the Xin River and Lake Poyang, especially in the districts of Jiujiang, Hukou, and Pengze. It should be noted that the prevalence of permanent tenancy in northern Jiangxi was not a unique phenomenon. Similar developments also took place in other regions where the civil war raged, such as in Anhui, Zhejiang, and Jiangsu.[43]

The growth of small peasant freeholders and the prevalence of permanent tenancy can be seen as the most significant developments in land tenure patterns after the great seventeenth-century uprisings. Exacting a heavy toll in human lives, the Taiping Rebellion provided a Malthusian solution to the mid-nineteenth-century agrarian crisis and restored the old population and land balance. In the Xinjiang region, small rural cultivators once again dominated the countryside.

Many regions reported a return of general prosperity and an improvement in the living conditions of the masses. According to a European eyewitness

---

[42] *Zhongguo jingji nianqian* 1934: G.78; see also *ZNYS* 1957, 2:252.
[43] For such developments in other provinces, see Li 1981.

account, "Within the year the settlement of the districts lately disturbed by the rebellion has proceeded. Accounts from Soochow [Suzhou] and Hangchow [Hangzhou] as well as from the provinces of Cheh-kiang [Zhejiang], Anhwei [Anhui], and Kiang-si [Jiangxi] speak of returning prosperity."[44] In a report about southern Anhui, Hu Chuan mentioned: "I personally witnessed in 1866–67 that within the several hundred *li* stretch between Hui-chou [Huizhou] and Ning-kuo [Ningguo] and T'ai-p'ing [Taiping] the survivors had surplus grains in their storerooms, meat in their kitchens, and wine in their pitchers. They were well fed, occasionally got drunk, and enjoyed to the full what a restored peace could offer."[45] Hu's statement may be slightly exaggerated but it is safe to assume that the general condition of the rural masses improved immediately after the rebellion.

Li Wenzhi remarks that post-Taiping changes in land tenure considerably weakened the feudal patriarchal clan system. The growth of small peasant freeholders and permanent tenants not only enervated the structural basis for feudal landlordism but also created favorable conditions for the beginning of the capitalist economy.[46] Liu Yao notes that a qualitative shift in the rural economy took place immediately after the Taiping Rebellion. It was marked by a new stimulus to the commercialization of agriculture, the market economy, and the capitalist wage-labor system.[47]

It should be noted, however, that these changes took place in a unique Chinese context in which both the imperial state and landlordism continued to exist. Their continued existence, and especially the rapid growth of the power of the landlords soon after the rebellion, placed major barriers in the way of the independent development of the small rural cultivators. Post-Taiping changes in land tenure thus proved to be transient and failed to make any lasting impact on the historical development of the rural socio-economic structure. Freeholding peasants progressively lost their land, and tenancy conditions worsened. Within less than fifty years, rapid deterioration in the living conditions of the masses once again led to massive peasant movements and finally to a Communist revolution. Naturally, the question arises: Why, despite such significant changes in land tenure, did a serious agrarian crisis again confront rural Xinjiang and other regions? Why did the

[44] Cited in Wright 1957: 62.
[45] Cited in Ho 1967: 275–76.
[46] Li 1981: 45.
[47] Lin 1979: 32–48; see also Liu 1982: 105–20; Wen and Wang 1985: 64–72; Liu 1978: 547–76.

Malthusian solution fail to ameliorate rural socioeconomic conditions in the long run?

In this context, Jean Chesneaux reflects that "a new crisis of rural economy, *the precise causes of which are no better understood*, seems to have developed around the end of the nineteenth century and led to countless peasant riots in the years 1909–1911 [emphasis mine]."[48] To be sure, the notion about the growth of a new agrarian crisis indicates a contradiction between the extent of the post-Taiping amelioration of the rural situation arising out of changes in land tenure and the fierce class struggle between landlords and peasants due to deterioration in rural socioeconomic conditions by the end of the nineteenth century. It is precisely because of this contradiction that some Chinese scholars have rejected the contention of Li Wenzhi and others that the feudal system of landownership suffered a great setback after the Taiping Rebellion. They have instead either disputed or underestimated the antilandlord nature of the post-Taiping changes in land tenure. Without denying the increase in the number of small peasant freeholders, Mao Jiaqi argues that, as the families of great landlords still existed, there was no question of any fundamental change in land tenure leading to the "postfeudal" relationship in the rebellion-affected regions. The promotion of reclamation of wasteland by the state was for tenancy purposes, not for the grant of ownership to the immigrants. It was not the decline of landlords but the purchase of land—the price of which had drastically fallen after the rebellion—by immigrants that led to an increase in the number of small peasant freeholders. Moreover, their number did not rise to the extent of destroying the earlier land tenure pattern.[49] Similarly, Shao Xunzheng remarks that changes in land tenure did not bring about any major shift in the rural socioeconomic pattern, mainly because the feudal system remained deeply entrenched in rural areas. The restoration of the earlier pattern of land tenure and of landlordism within a short period after the rebellion confirms this.[50]

I think these assumptions are primarily the result of a failure to examine the above-mentioned contradiction in the proper perspective. Within the context of the historical significance of the post-Taiping changes, one should ask: How and why did a new agrarian crisis confront rural areas within such a short period? What was it that inhibited the socioeconomic development of the post-Taiping small peasant freeholders and permanent tenants? What were the causes for the further strengthening of the landed-upper-class po-

[48] Chesneaux 1973: 66.
[49] Mao Jiaqi 1961: 49–56.
[50] Shao 1961: 3–4.

sition in the countryside? Answers to these questions, as I will discuss later, can be primarily found, on the one hand, in the failure of the Taiping rebels to completely destroy the old order and, on the other, in the growth of several constraints inhibiting the independent development of the social, political, and economic power of the post-Taiping small rural cultivators. These generated newer pressures on both the small rural cultivators and the small-peasant economy. Also, the landed upper class survived the Taiping holocaust and, backed by a dependent state, soon emerged in a markedly stronger position to dominate the rural scene.

Chapter Three

New Pressures on Small Rural Cultivators: Imperialism, the State, and the Small-Peasant Economy

After the Taiping Rebellion, the small rural cultivator predominated in rural areas of the Xinjiang region. This consequently stimulated a reassertion of the small-peasant economy. The post-Taiping cultivators, as indicated by Rawski and others, were free to indulge in such agricultural innovations and economic rationalizations as related to the selection, rotation, and production of crops as well as to the accumulation of capital through independent participation in regional and international markets.[1] This freedom, however, did not turn them into "autonomous simple commodity producers." In reality, their socioeconomic survival and mobility depended to a large extent upon the nature of their interplay with dynamic forces outside their society.

In this context, the major concern of this chapter is a comprehension of the nature of the relationship between the wider economic system and the small-peasant economy in the Xinjiang region. The attempt here is to examine the constraints imposed and dislocations wrought by the gradual subsumption of the small-peasant economy under an expanding commodity economy and the long-distance trade stimulated by the deeper penetration of world market forces in the late nineteenth and early twentieth centuries. Moreover, as the state was also dependent upon the small-peasant economy for the generation of its financial resources, an analysis of its economic linkages with the rural areas also becomes imperative to get a fuller and more accurate picture of new pressures on the small rural cultivators.

IMPERIALISM AND THE SMALL-PEASANT ECONOMY

How did the small-peasant economy respond to the growing penetration of world market forces in the post-Taiping Xinjiang region? Soon after the

[1] See, Rawski 1972; Myers 1970, 1972; see also Feuerwerker 1969.

Taiping Rebellion, two developments in the already commercially active Xinjiang region firmly linked the small-peasant economy with larger national and international markets. The first was the emergence of Jiujiang, one of the four traditional commercial towns of Jiangxi, as the largest market center of the province after it was forced to become a foreign treaty port under the Treaty of Nanjing in 1861. The second was the appearance of steamship traffic in Lake Poyang in 1896 and its gradual replacement of the native junks as commercial transport. These developments considerably reduced the commercial importance of this region's traditionally active market towns and trade routes.

As trade activities began to be concentrated in Jiujiang, the fame and prosperity of Hekou, also among one of the four largest and oldest market towns of Jiangxi, rapidly declined. Surrounded by the famous tea-producing districts of northern Jiangxi, northern Fujian, and southern Zhejiang, Hekou was the leading tea market town of the Xinjiang region. Almost all the tea produced in this region was collected here through numerous commission agents of the large business concerns. It was then processed in local factories and repacked in cases for sale in the Shanghai and Guangzhou markets. Robert Fortune, who visited this town in the 1850s, found it to be the center of a great deal of commercial activity with a very large volume of trade being carried out.[2] During the early 1870s, it was estimated that more than 100,000 cases of tea were exported every year. However, by the late 1870s, the competition from Jiujiang and Hankou, the newly emerged tea export centers, greatly diminished the commercial activities of this town. In 1904, Kopsch found that Hekou "does not seem to be such an important place as one is led to suppose from the description given by Fortune and Milne [in the 1850s]. The trade doubtless has very much fallen off, as formerly Fukien [Fujian] tea were packed here for both Canton [Guangzhou] and Shanghai markets."[3]

The appearance of foreign-owned steamships in Lake Poyang and the consequent growing commercial importance of the Yangzi River route to Shanghai dealt a further blow to the traditional trade route passing through the Xinjiang region to the eastern and southern provinces of China. The steamships carrying cargo, in addition to passengers, were introduced in the Lake Poyang area in 1896. By 1901, about eleven of them had begun plying the lake area. In 1909, a regular steam-cargo service, managed by the foreign firm Messers. Butterfield and Swire, started its operation from the lake. The

[2] Fortune 1852: 201–2.
[3] Kopsch 1878: 263.

Japanese firm Nishin Kisen Kaisha also entered this region in 1907 and captured a portion of the carrying trade. By 1917, more than forty-nine steamboats were regularly plying this area.[4] Stanley Wright remarked in 1920 that

> a little over twenty years ago, the entire carrying trade of Poyang lake was in the hands of the junks; but today steam launch, cargo boat, and railway competition have caused whole classes of these boats to disappear and others are fast following suit. Even in far distant Kanchow [Ganzhou], the host of the steam launch whistle is now heard and this, taken with the steady development of the shallow drought cargo-boat traffic with its exemption from native customs charges, augurs ill for the junkmen . . . so far as can be seen its [junk traffic's] gradual extinction in the routes open to steam traffic is inevitable.[5]

Both these developments altered the traditional trade pattern in the Xinjiang region. They displaced a large number of people customarily associated with trade and commercial activities in traditional market towns and disrupted the enormous flow of goods through the old and active trade route passing along the Xin River to Zhejiang, Fujian, and Guangdong through Yushan Pass. Thus, many junkmen and other boatmen rapidly lost their source of income. Numerous coolies carrying goods on the traditional trade route and workers engaged in various commercial activities in the town of Hekou and Yushan district were also left unemployed. Some Hekou tea workers went out to other areas to find employment: "Formerly they did not have the necessity to seek their livelihood in distant places, but they are now obliged to work in Anhui. They secure barely sufficient to cover living expenses and with the deduction of travelling expenses almost nothing is left."[6]

On the other hand, however, the closer integration of the small-peasant economy of the Xinjiang region with the larger national and international markets provided fresh impetus for long-distance trade activities. Beginning with the 1870s, as statistical figures in the *Jiangxi Yearbook* for 1936 indicate, the volume of exports from this region climbed greatly.[7] Attracted by better profit margins and expanded demand, many post-Taiping small cultivators switched to the production of cash crops on a substantially bigger scale. As production became largely oriented to markets, they became, in increasingly

---

[4] Wright 1920: 7; see also Imperial Maritime Customs 1892–1901, 1911–1921.

[5] Wright 1920: 7.

[6] Chu 1936: 65.

[7] For historical statistical data on imports and exports from this province, see *JN* 1936: 993–1082.

greater degree, dependent upon those markets for the maintenance of subsistence. They thus became more vulnerable to obscure market forces.

This is evident in the growth pattern of the trade in tea—the most important export-oriented cash crop of the Xinjiang region. Almost all the districts
of this region were dotted with numerous small tea plantations, with major
areas of production concentrated in Fouliang, Pengze, Dexing, and Wuyuan
along the Anhui border; Shangrao, Yushan, and Guangfeng near the boundaries of Zhejiang and Fujian; and Boyang, Yiyang, Guixi, and Wannian in
the middle. Tea districts close to Anhui were especially famous for their
"Keemun" black tea, which was largely sold abroad. Other areas produced
both black and green teas for consumption within the province as well as for
export. With the boom in China's tea trade, the largely autonomous production and distribution base of the small rural cultivators began to erode.

The leap in China's tea trade began with the East India Company's purchase of tea for British markets in the mid–seventeenth century. By the early
nineteenth century, tea had become a major item of consumption in Europe
and America. Consequently, the volume of its export rapidly increased. By
1820, it constituted almost 75 percent of the total value of China's exports.[8]
The greatest development in China's tea trade took place between the 1860s
and 1880s, with total volume exceeding the two-million-picul mark in 1884.
Such an expansion was facilitated by the growing demand for Chinese tea in
the world market and a greater involvement of British, American, and Russian merchants in China's tea business.

The trade was initially carried out through the treaty port of Guangzhou.
Most of Jiangxi's tea reached Guangzhou through a land-river route, either
via Yushan-Changshan Pass of the Xinjiang region or via Meiling Pass in
southern Jiangxi. However, as the demand increased, both native and foreign exporters began to move to major tea-producing areas in central China
to break the monopoly of the Guangzhou merchants. Combined with this,
the opening of Shanghai as a foreign treaty port in 1842 resulted in the development of a faster and more convenient link through the Yangzi route
with major tea-producing central provinces of China. The export market
center therefore shifted from Guangzhou to Shanghai. By 1870, Shanghai
became the largest national tea market; Hankou, Jiujiang, and Fuzhou
emerged as the important intermediate collection and export centers.

The growing demand for tea encouraged a larger number of post-Taiping
small rural cultivators to maximize its production. Unlike other crops, tea

[8] Torgasheff 1926: 164; see also Wakeman 1973; Tan Chung 1973.

trees require maturity time of a minimum of two to three years after planting before the leaves can be plucked, and at least five years before they produce at maximum capacity. In spite of such a long development period, tea plantations spread to more and more districts of the Xinjiang region in response to tea's attractive market value. A British consular report from Jiujiang noted that tea planting began in Jingde district in 1861 and, by 1875, production had increased enormously, with some people earning huge profits.[9] The greater demand for black tea led wealthy persons like Hu Yuanlong of Guixi district to move to Qimen district in southern Anhui to start a large tea factory.[10] But, to a great extent, it was the small rural cultivators who switched to tea production. A survey of the tea plantations in Fouliang district found that most were less than seven mu in size.[11]

As demand for tea expanded in the late nineteenth century, specialized *chazhuang* (tea shops) and *chazhan* (tea warehouses) began to appear in the intermediate collection and export centers as well as in the major districts of production.[12] These were all linked with the larger chazhan of Shanghai. Gradually, a market network evolved that integrally connected the point of production with the point of distribution. The function of chazhuang was to procure the maximum amount of tea at the point of production. They carried out this task through their numerous commission agents who fanned out in villages and advanced cash or grain loans to small needy cultivators. They thus induced cultivators to continue producing tea and to plant larger areas. In return, they secured for themselves the guaranteed right to buy the tea at a pre-fixed minimum price.

During the tea-picking season, many chazhan also opened shops in small market towns and purchased production, often in cash. Money for such a business transaction was raised by numerous local chazhuang, partially through loans from Shanghai chazhan and partially through their own share capital. These chazhuang thus acted both as creditors and debtors. The Shanghai chazhan advanced loans to local chazhuang to procure a guaranteed supply of the maximum amount of tea at prices fixed beforehand to keep their monopoly in the competitive tea-trade market. Thus, a classic agricultural putting-out system operated at the point of production to meet national and international market demands.

Beginning with the 1870s, such chazhuang began to appear in larger num-

[9] *ZNYS* 1957, 1:449–50.
[10] Ibid., 1:450.
[11] Chu 1936: 33.
[12] Much of the ensuing discussion is based on Chu 1936: 6–66, and Abramson 1935.

bers in the Xinjiang region. By 1875 in Jiujiang, an intermediate market and export center, there were more than fifty large chazhuang and chazhan, each employing more than a thousand persons to look after the business. The work force included several thousand women who came from neighboring villages to process, grade, and pack tea.[13] Around the same time, these chazhuang also began to move to such important tea-producing districts of this region as Fouliang, Shangrao, Dexing, and Wuyuan. The first chazhuang in Fouliang was established in the 1870s and the number increased greatly during the latter part of the Qing era and the early Republican period. In the areas around Dexing and Wuyuan there were, at one time, more than three hundred small chazhuang.[14] In other districts, too, specialized tea businesses emerged.

Tea collected from each village through local middlemen or agents was brought to the chazhuang in the district town for processing and then sent to intermediate and national markets for export. These chazhuang, through their middlemen and agents, exercised tremendous control over the production of small cultivators. First, the agricultural putting-out system secured for them small cultivators' production at a cheaper rate. The advance of money or grain in exchange for tea naturally forced the cultivator to sell it at prices fixed beforehand. Control over the market by the middlemen at the point of production also limited cultivators' opportunities to take full advantage of prevailing prices.

Second, it was a common practice for the chazhuang to operate as a monopoly trade guild to avoid competition among themselves and keep the price of raw leaf suppressed. For example, in 1935, a notice issued by the Xiushui Tea Trade Guild in southern Jiangxi strictly warned its members that

> while buying the goods from the 12th inst. (29th day of the 3rd Moon) they should strictly comply with resolutions made by this Tea Trade Guild regarding the maintenance of the tea market. These are that for each catty of dry red tea the price is seven to eight hundred cash, and for the same amount of the dry green tea from eight to nine hundred cash, that any further reduction of the prices is to be [upon notification of] each member, and that the scale to be used should be, according to the tradition of the tea dealers, twenty ounces for one catty. Secret investigations are to be carried out by responsible officials of the Guild. Should any violators of the resolutions be found to pay an excess of

[13] *ZNYS* 1957, 1:450.
[14] Chu 1936: 37.

even one cash or to reduce even by one ounce the weighing or to substitute the price of dry red tea for that of the 'Ho' tea, they are liable to pay a fine.[15]

Such prior fixation of prices as well as the use of larger catty baskets, whose capacity was often fraudulently increased from the usual sixteen ounces to somewhere between twenty-four and forty ounces, inhibited the small cultivators from exploiting market potential for their own economic benefit. In fact, larger catty baskets were designed to take into account the weight of the leaf, which shrank when dried. But it was common for the middlemen to weigh tea in a basket that contained more than the amount required to yield the appropriate dried catty weight. They often made money for themselves by selling the extra leaves thus collected.

Finally, as indicated earlier, the production of tea required a growth period of at least two to three years before the first picking could be done. Hence, at a time of falling prices, it was difficult for the peasants to shift over to new areas of production by cutting the trees and planting different crops. The hope of getting better prices next year often prevented them from removing these long-maturing trees. Moreover, plucking of the leaf at the right time was necessary to get its full flavor. So, unlike other crops, the output could not be held back from sale even if prices fetched were low at that time. To deal with such eventualities, the only option for peasants was to plant intercrops between tea trees to provide for their subsistence.[16] However, this reduced the quality of the tea and further lowered its price.

It was not that the peasants did not profit from the expanding demand for tea. They did make money as long as the prices remained high. Moreover, they often countered middleman's tactics through such practices as mixing high-grade leaves with coarse ones and dust, or increasing the weight of leaves by wetting them. However, in spite of the trade boom, its pattern often restricted peasants from getting larger economic benefits. The price of raw tea leaf, which the small rural cultivators sold to the middlemen, varied according to national and international demand. According to the estimates of both Chu and Wright, the producer of tea, on average, received about 25 to 30 percent of its prevailing market price in Shanghai; the middlemen received from 50 to 55 percent; and expenditures for transportation, packing, and taxes consumed about 20 percent.[17] Such a structure of the tea trade naturally did not lead to capital formation at the point of production.

[15] Ibid., 50–51.
[16] Ibid., 32–33.
[17] Ibid., 30; see also the conclusion in Wright 1920.

The boom in the tea trade was, however, short-lived. From the 1880s onward, tea demand and price began to fluctuate greatly. The large production of tea in the colonial plantations of India and Sri Lanka greatly reduced British purchases of Chinese tea. Employing modern agricultural methods, these plantations produced larger amounts of better-quality tea at a cheaper price. Consequently, the export of tea from China declined. Its share of China's total export trade, which was about 75 percent in 1822, diminished to 16 percent in 1899 and to 4 percent in 1919.[18] The world tea market dealt mostly in black tea. Decline in demand for it was most harmful to the black-tea-producing belt of southern Anhui and northern Jiangxi where the famous "Keemun" tea was produced. Other black-tea-producing areas in China suffered too.

Just before the British withdrawal from the China tea market, however, the Russians entered. This temporarily revived the market, especially for the Chinese tablet and brick teas favored in Russia. Two czarist-Russian brick-tea factories were established in Jiujiang by Tokamakoff, Sheveleff & Company and Litivinoff & Company in 1875 and 1882 respectively. But internal developments in Russia began to diminish the demand for Chinese tea from 1916 onward. The total exported from Jiujiang thus began to decline, reaching a bare minimum in 1921. The world market for Chinese tea finally collapsed. This completely disorganized the once-thriving tea trade. Commenting on the contemporary crisis, Torgasheff remarked that "a great number of Chinese tea firms are entirely thrown out of their former situation. A great number of the planting lots have disappeared; others, even if still in existence, are not looked after at all, and plants are rapidly losing their productive capacity. It will take years to restore the plantations to their former condition." It was, as he further noted, "considered by the Chinese merchants and planters as some natural disaster, like a draught or pests" (see tables 3.1 and 3.2).[19]

Reverberations from the growing crisis in the fluctuating tea trade were felt all the way down from national, intermediate, and district markets to the point of production and the actual producer. By 1899, the number of chazhuang in Jiujiang had declined to four or five from an all-time high of between fifty and sixty.[20] In almost every district, the majority of chazhuang folded up as their profit margin was greatly reduced. The Jiujiang market

[18] Torgasheff 1926: 174–75. For various reasons for the decline of the tea trade see also *ZSGYS* 1957, 2:182–84.
[19] Torgasheff 1926: 222.
[20] *ZNYS* 1957, 1: 450; *ZSGYS* 1957, 2:186.

TABLE 3.1
Tea Exported from Jiangxi and Its Prices,
1863–1921

Period	Yearly Average Exports from Jiujiang (in dan)	Prices of Chinese Tea (in custom taels per dan)	
		Black Tea	Green Tea
1863–65	1,78,023.00	25.97	35.70
1866–70	1,75,342.00	25.00	34.78
1871–75	2,27,555.20	22.97	29.87
1876–80	2,55,080.60	18.48	22.40
1881–85	2,79,380.00	16.08	21.18
1886–90	2,76,991.20	16.27	18.56
1891–95	2,32,870.20	19.15	22.93
1896–1900	2,11,845.80	21.90	25.19
1901–5	2,39,951.00	19.14	30.04
1906–10	2,60,622.80	23.70	34.61
1911–15	2,71,035.00	29.21	41.13
1916–20	1,93,385.40	30.79	44.13
1921	84,372.00	26.85	31.98

Sources: Compiled from figures in *JN* 1936: 1006–77 and *ZNMT* 1983: 246.

TABLE 3.2
Tea Exported from Jiujiang, 1921–1935

Year	Total Amount (in dan)	Year	Total Amount (in dan)
1915	329,798	1925	175,242
1916	277,119	1926	161,092
1917	213,792	1928	167,677
1918	151,501	1929	160,144
1919	173,953	1930	109,818
1920	123,671	1931	100,820
1921	84,372	1932	80,421
1922	112,059	1933	65,472
1923	176,740	1934	87,646
1924	147,836	1935	30,421

Source: *JN* 1936: 1006–7.

was saved from final collapse until 1921 because Russian demand for tea and the establishment of the two brick-tea factories kept the export trade alive. But it never recovered from the crash of the tea market during 1917–1918, which led to the eventual transfer of the tea trade to Hankou. Jiujiang thus experienced the fate of Hekou. Chu notes that "the [Jiujiang] tea trade suffered a great setback when the great war broke out. Only three to four chazhuangs were able to stand the overwhelming current of depression and the quantities they produced were not to be compared with those of former days. Since 1927, they have suspended their business and changed to the status of chazhan undertaking only to transport and declare to the customs the tea for their client."[21]

The small rural cultivators bore the major brunt of the fluctuation in the tea trade. Describing the situation of the tea-producing region of northwest Fujian, adjoining the Xinjiang region, an investigative report of 1886 indicated that while, previously, it was quite common for tea cultivators to get at least twenty or more yuan for each hundred catties from the chazhuang, they were now getting only seven to eight yuan. Many of them, therefore, had either left off plucking the leaves and were letting the trees turn wild or had been picking only the small amount necessary for their own consumption. Both merchants and cultivators thus had no option but to leave the tea business. Those who had land shifted to subsistence crops, and those without it cut wood for subsistence.[22]

Other cash crops of the region, too, were influenced by the growing long-distance trade and the fluctuating trends in national and international markets. While tea was produced in almost all parts of the Xinjiang region, indigo, tobacco, and cotton were specialized cash crops of different districts. Closer integration of the local economy with larger commercial centers brought particular, specialized cash-crop production districts into the grip of wider extraneous forces.

Indigo was the predominant cash crop of Raozhou and Leping districts, where the phosphate-rich land promoted the bumper production of one of the finer varieties. The total output of these two districts was primarily exported to markets in China and abroad. The local need was met by importing coarser indigo produced in the Ganzhou and Jian districts of southern Jiangxi. Annually, between forty thousand and fifty thousand piculs of indigo were exported.[23] The volume of trade remained consistent until the end

---

[21] Chu 1936: 240.

[22] *ZSGYS*: 1957, 2:186–87.

[23] *JN* 1936: 1015–16. For details on indigo production in China, see *Chinese Economic History* 2:8 (1935): 11–17.

of the nineteenth century. However, the development of synthetic indigo in Germany and its production for commercial purposes soon decreased the demand for natural indigo in the world market. As textile mills in England and other countries switched to the German dye, their importation of natural indigo almost totally stopped. The consequences were felt in all major indigo-producing areas of the world. In India, for example, larger plantations, which were dependent upon English demand, were completely ruined. Many small cultivators, who had taken advances from middlemen to produce indigo, found no buyers for their product and no money to pay back their loans. They therefore revolted. The violent peasant uprisings that followed took place in the indigo-producing area of eastern India.[24]

In India, an effort was made to process indigo in the form of German dye, like paste. This was promoted in the China market but was not very successful. Meanwhile, however, synthetic indigo itself had captured the local market. The competition from these cheaper foreign products, primarily the synthetic dye, depressed the demand for and price of Chinese indigo. Even in those few smaller textile mills of Jiangxi which had surfaced in the early twentieth century, the use of foreign indigo for cotton printing had become widespread. In 1904, when the demand for local indigo was already declining, the provincial government imposed an additional levy on it to raise the money to start Western-type schools. This pushed its prices high, thus greatly diminishing its competitive value in the market. Moreover, indigo producers were further burdened by the levy.[25] The prospect of imminent and total socioeconomic collapse caused indignant peasants throughout the districts to rise in revolt.

Confronted with the depressed market and the weak state's indifference to their condition, some of the small cultivators shifted to tobacco, which promised better prices and could be cultivated on indigo land.[26] However, at the outset of the First World War, indigo prices began to soar once again. The war curtailed the amount of German synthetic indigo imported by Britain. This suddenly raised British demand for the local product, thus shooting its price up. In 1920, Stanley Wright noted that "at Jao chou [Raozhou] and Loping [Leping] where the best qualities [of indigo] are obtained, the price may run from ten to seventy dollars for a vat containing about a picul, the variation in price being due partly to difference in quality, but much more to extraneous causes such as European War, which by cutting off the

[24] See Natrajan 1953; Desai 1979.
[25] Zhang Zhenhe 1955: 188–97.
[26] ZNYS 1957, 1:427.

supply of foreign synthetic indigotin has created a boom in the old fashioned native grown dye."[27] Thus, the export of indigo from Jiujiang increased from 26,028 piculs in 1915 to 75,846 piculs in 1918.[28]

The export trade in tobacco also suffered from wide fluctuations. The districts of Guangfeng in the Xinjiang region and Yifeng in central Jiangxi were the two major tobacco-producing areas. The quality of their tobacco was among the best in China. Most of the exports from these areas were destined for the Japanese market. However, between 1875 and 1904, the volume of exports from Jiujiang port fluctuated wildly, reaching a high figure several times only to decline once again to less than half of that. Only between 1904 and 1918 was there a steady increase in exports.[29]

The districts of Boyang and Yugan in Shangrao prefecture were the main cotton-producing areas in the Xinjiang region. In the districts of Dehua, Hukou, and Pengze in northern Jiangxi, the output was only slightly less. Most of the local cotton was consumed in the province, feeding primarily the cotton-based rural handicraft industry. The demand of this industry was so large that the province imported raw cotton from Anhui and Hubei. Only a small portion was shipped to the Shanghai and Hankou markets for foreign sale. The production and price of cotton in China, as excellent studies by Chao and Kraus have demonstrated, went through both busts and booms arising out of cotton's growing linkages with the world market.[30]

The major impact on Jiangxi was that foreign yarn and foreign raw cotton began to enter the market from 1886 onward. By 1900, the dependence on foreign yarn had increased so much that imports of raw cotton steeply declined.[31] In addition, the price of imported yarn had become roughly equal to that of raw cotton exported from China.[32] In the wake of these new developments, the cotton producers were confronted with stiff foreign competition and lost their hold over local markets. This situation, as will be described later, also altered the traditional patterns in cotton-based rural industry. Between 1923 and 1933, cotton production rapidly declined. According to a 1935 report, "In 1923, the [cotton] output was as high as 170,000 piculs, but since then has been decreasing year by year, owing to the spread of bandit activities, frequent calamities . . . , and the increased

[27] Wright 1920: 62.
[28] Ibid.
[29] "Agriculture and Economic Conditions" 1935: 356.
[30] See Chao 1977; Kraus 1980; Huang 1985.
[31] *JJWT* 1934: 197–226; *JN* 1936: 1020–22.
[32] Chao 1977: 171.

import of foreign cotton piece-goods, causing a decline in cotton prices and forcing farmers to abandon cultivation."[33]

To be sure, the small cultivator profited as long as he earned surplus cash because of the steadily rising prices, but any short-term decline in market demand and price was enough to unbalance his socioeconomic condition for a long time. In an illuminating reassessment of Chinese agriculture and international economy on the basis of trends in the rice trade and prices in Yangzi markets, Loren Brandt correctly remarks: "By the turn of this century, despite the fact that Chinese rice imports were only a small fraction of domestic production and of total exports in the international market, rice markets throughout China had become highly integrated with their international counterparts. Attendant with this change, external factors came to play the major role in price formation."[34] Thus, given the nature of the market, which was largely dependent upon various extraneous national and international factors, even mild fluctuations often came as a shock to the small rural cultivator. The impact was similar to that of natural disasters in rural areas. Having little or no surplus to tide him over a financially bad year, the small cultivator naturally suffered more than landlords and merchants from such depression in market demands and prices. New pressures, especially since there was no protective umbrella of a strong state, constrained the natural development of the small-peasant economy.

PRESSURES ON THE RURAL HANDICRAFT INDUSTRY

For a large number of small rural cultivators, participation in the rural handicraft industry was traditionally a source of extra income. It provided them opportunities to improve their socioeconomic condition during agriculturally good years and to maintain their subsistence needs at times of crisis. In the Xinjiang region, these small home-based industries were primarily related to the production of tea, paper, and textiles. According to a 1873 report in the Pengze district gazetteer, the common traditional pattern in the countryside was that men produced millet, and women made cloth. Women, during their leisure time after spinning, reeled silk, and men, having surplus time after the harvest, either planted indigo or manufactured paper.[35] The small rural cultivator was thus both an agriculturist and a manufacturer. How-

[33] "Agriculture and Economic Conditions" 1935: 238–39.
[34] Brandt 1985: 189.
[35] ZNYS 1957, 1:518. ZNYS quotes similar descriptions from other districts of Jiangxi.

ever, in this region, pressures emanating from the expanding commodity economy and the deeper penetration of imperialism set in motion a process leading to the general depression of several flourishing rural handicraft industries.

In his study of the special characteristics of the post-Taiping rural economy, Liu Yao ascribes constraints on the further growth of the rural handicraft industry to three major developments in the lower Yangzi region.[36] Similar tendencies can also be discerned in the rural areas of the Xinjiang region.

First, the post-Taiping small cultivators depended considerably upon the rural handicraft industry. Due to the accelerated pace of commercialization of agriculture in the late nineteenth and early twentieth centuries, some of them gradually turned into "commodity producers." These producers kept primitive machines, employed wage laborers, procured raw materials at the point of production, and sold processed goods in the market. Some of them also got together and pooled their resources to establish joint firms. Because of their larger capital outlay, they were able to purchase better machines and increase their production.

Similar tendencies can be discerned in most of the chazhuang discussed earlier. In Fouliang and other tea-producing districts, they were organized on a share-capital basis with several landlords, rich peasants, and merchants providing cash, and tea-processing rural handicraftsmen contributing labor. They monopolized the purchase of raw leaf and its processing for sale in the market or shipment to Jiujiang or Shanghai chazhan. Noting their organization in Fouliang district, Chu wrote:

> The staff and workers of a chachuang [chazhuang] were in total number from fifty to over [one] hundred. Outwardly, this is more or less a village craft but taking its scope and organization into consideration it is actually a business of some magnitude. It is therefore obvious that when a district is in possession of several scores of such chachuang [chazhuang] having the nature of a factory, the people who rely on them for a living must be numerous. No wonder the proverb "the tea trade prosperity means the happiness of the entire population" is on the lips of all the inhabitants of the district.[37]

The emergence of these chazhuang naturally restricted the scope and business of the home-based tea-processing industry. Attracted by its financial potential, many independent cultivator-cum-handicraftsmen joined

[36] Liu 1981.
[37] Chu 1936: 41.

these firms on a full-time or part-time basis as joint owners or wage laborers. Many others found it simpler to depend upon these joint firms to sell their home-processed and -dyed tea. Thus, the eventual collapse of chazhuang as a result of the crash of the tea market resulted not only in the loss of capital for the landlords, rich peasants, and merchants but also in existential problems for a large number of rural handicraftsmen associated with the tea business.

The picture of the textile- and paper-based handicraft industries was essentially the same. It was not uncommon for a local landlord to keep three or four looms and employ wage laborers.[38] In Jiangxi, these small factories, as a report in the *Chinese Economic Journal* noted, "turn out coarse textiles only, and operate two or three looms each, and as such places are scattered all over the municipality and suburbs as a household industry, it is impossible to state accurately either the number of factories or workers."[39] Moreover, the newly emerging joint firms usually controlled the task of calendering and dyeing the textiles as well as coloring the paper. The lack of technical capability as well as the small scale of production in the family-based industry often precluded its performing these tasks itself. Thus, in order to make their products more competitive in the market, the rural handicraftsmen associated with the production of textiles and papers relied in an increasingly greater degree on these local firms for dyeing and coloring. Their production base was no longer independent.

Second, attracted by larger demands for some products in the national and international markets, a group of merchants moved to the rural areas and became direct purchasers of products manufactured by the local handicraftsmen. Acting either independently or in concert with joint firms, they were essentially middlemen-agents between the producers and consumers or bulk purchasing business concerns. By the early twentieth century, they controlled to a large extent the marketing of the rural products. This was a new development linked with the massive expansion of the commodity economy. In the case of cloth merchants, as Feuerwerker notes, "before the last quarter of the nineteenth century, [they] did not usually exercise . . . direct control over the weaving of the cloth which was commonly executed on their own account by peasant households."[40] But by the end of nineteenth and the beginning of the twentieth century, "the structure and functions of cloth

[38] See Abramson 1935.
[39] "Agriculture and Economic Conditions" 1935: 488.
[40] Feuerwerker 1969: 85–86.

merchants," as Chao demonstrates, "had undergone a long evolution."[41] From simple procurers of cotton cloth at village fairs, they turned into yarn sellers with the breakdown of the integrated, self-contained spinning-weaving process in rural households. Ultimately, their business included both the selling of yarn and the collection of cotton cloth manufactured to their specifications by the rural handicraftsmen.

The entrance of middlemen-merchant capital into the tea, paper, and textile handicraft industries promoted a characteristic agricultural putting-out system. This was marked by the mortgaging of rural household production to these merchants against either grain or cash loans, piecework wages, or the advance of yarn and other semifinished materials. Merchants thus secured guaranteed rights to semiprocessed tea, or such finished products as cotton textiles and papers. In many cases, the middlemen-merchants procured only semifinished products from the rural households and processed these in their own joint firms or in the larger manufacturing industries in towns, for sale in the market. Middlemen-merchant capital, with or without its own manufacturing facilities, thus controlled rural household products at both their point of production and of distribution.

In the absence of studies on these "agricultural put-outers," it is extremely difficult either to trace in specific detail or to measure the extent of their control over rural products. They should not, however, be ignored, for they played the crucial role of mediating between larger markets and the producers. They took away most of the economic benefits generally associated with a remarkable degree of monetization in the late nineteenth and early twentieth centuries. The profit thus earned was often invested in the purchase of land. Scattered comments of several merchant-landlords, such as Shao Xiangzhen of Yiyang district, indicate a general tendency of merchants, after they had entrenched themselves in rural areas, to shift gradually into landlordism.[42] Data on occupations of both city- and village-based landlords demonstrate that a large number of them were also businessmen.[43] The local handicraftsmen, thus separated from the market by these "agricultural put-outers," began to lose the leverage to get better deals for their products.

Finally, the predominant status of the rural handicraft industry in the region was greatly undermined by the growth of large-scale industries after the Sino-Japanese War in 1898. This was combined with the deeper impe-

[41] Chao 1977: 202–3.
[42] *FZM* 1982: 4–5.
[43] *YEWG* 1936: 77.

rialist penetrations, resulting in an enormous increase in imports without any tariff protection from the state for locally manufactured goods. The overall impact of such developments on the Chinese rural cotton industry, especially on spinning and weaving, has been illuminatingly discussed by several scholars.[44]

In rural Xinjiang, a thriving spinning industry had once consumed not only locally produced, but also imported, cotton. But the imported machine-made yarn, as well as those yarns produced in the burgeoning native industry, soon proved to be a cheaper and better substitute for the local products. In 1895, it was reported from Jiujiang that the imported yarn had become so cheap that the local people preferred to purchase it to save labor in producing handloom-made clothes rather than to use homespun yarn.[45] Consequently, after 1900, this region did not import any cotton for its spinning industry. Indian and Japanese machine-made yarn appeared in Jiangxi in 1874, and by 1898 constituted respectively 65 and 15 percent of total yarn imports. This trend continued until 1914. It was only during the First World War, which restricted the supply of foreign yarns, that the native machine-made yarn gained its supremacy. In 1920, Stanley Wright noted that "the outstanding feature of the Kiangsi [Jiangxi] cotton-cloth industry during the past fifty years has been the gradual decline and ultimate cessation of the import of raw cotton, and counterbalancing growth in the import of cotton yarn both foreign and native."[46] Spinning had been a more labor intensive industry than weaving, and its total collapse resulted in a massive loss of jobs in rural households.

Local weavers initially gained because of the availability of cheaper machine-made yarn. But they suffered in the long run. Massive imports of cheap cloth and the emergence of large textile and smaller knitting industries within the province and elsewhere in China offered stiff competition in the traditional market for handloom goods. The first textile factory in Nanchang appeared in 1912 with seven looms and, in 1924 and 1929, two more were established with, respectively, 22 and 151 looms. Similarly, the first knitting factory was set up in 1916, and the number rapidly rose to more than 120 by 1935 in Nanchang district alone.[47] These developments destroyed the monopoly of weavers in the market.

[44] See note 30 above.
[45] *ZSGYS* 2:227–31.
[46] Wright 1920: 50.
[47] "Agriculture and Economic Conditions" 1935: 488–90.

As in other areas of China, weavers did survive in the Xinjiang region.[48] But the qualitative decline in their living conditions has often been ignored. They survived partly because of their specialized production of the famous Jiangxi ramie cloth (xiabu) in Shangrao and neighboring areas and the consistent demand for it not only in China but also in Korea; and also partly because the quantity of both foreign and native machine-made cotton piece goods was still not sufficient to flood the market. The quantitative increase in their numbers, as Chao notes in his description of a general rise in the new weaving centers, was due to the availability of a great deal of surplus labor as well as their linkages with yarn-supplier merchants.[49] Such a situation would indicate a gradual displacement of handicraftsmen from their independent base of work and, finally, their total dependence on cloth merchants. They continued to work as weavers, as options for absorption elsewhere were limited, and they did so by cutting their own subsistence needs. A 1920 survey of Guangfeng district thus reports that the condition of rural handicraftsmen separated from their land was the worst in the district. They often worked at the lowest wages.[50]

Confronted with cheaper machine-made products, the rural paper industry of the Xinjiang region also suffered a major setback.[51] The most famous paper-producing and -exporting areas were Qianshan district and Hekou. The trade was carried out by paper-processing units, operating primarily as joint firms. Located in more than two hundred places in the district, they produced many varieties of fine papers as well as bamboo papers and coarser grass papers for printing, wrapping, window-glass substitution, and ceremonial purposes. The overall quality was inferior to that of Fujian paper. But its prices were lower. Wrapping paper had a ready market in Jiangsu and Zhejiang, where it was mainly purchased by silk shops. Between 1870 and 1900, the total value of annual exports was about forty to fifty thousand silver dollars. However, after 1900, the cheaper Japanese machine-made paper flooded the market in these two provinces. The demand for Qianshan and Hekou paper thus declined, reducing its total export value to about ten thousand silver dollars annually. Native paper also suffered from the import of Japanese printing paper, which could be used on both sides. Noting the causes of depression in the rural paper industry, the *Shibao* indicated that the production of paper meant for ceremonial purposes was greatly curtailed be-

[48] Chao 1977: 168–270; Feuerwerker 1969: 27–34.
[49] Chao 1977.
[50] Min Sheng 1920.
[51] *ZSGYS* 1957, 2:483.

cause either there was a decline in such superstitious practices as the burning of paper and its use as joss money or those who used it in these ways largely preferred to purchase cheaper and colorful foreign papers.[52] Finally, the establishment of large-scale paper manufacturing factories in southern Jiangxi and Hunan after the First World War completely dislocated paper production in rural areas. A large number of small cultivators-cum-handicraftsmen, who were actively involved in it with just a kettle used for the preparation of paper pulp, were doomed.

The pattern of these developments in rural Xinjiang negates conclusions indicating that expansion in the commodity economy and the long-distance trade, stimulated by the deeper imperialist penetration, did not disrupt the small-peasant economy in China. The emergence of steamships on Lake Poyang, not unlike the coming of railways to India,[53] brought about changes in the course of traditional trade routes; and new market centers changed the activities of old commercial towns. These new developments integrated rural market fairs and commerce with obscure national and international markets, on the rhythm of which the fate of a large number of small rural cultivators depended. The impact of a downward trend in demand and price on rural areas was no less severe than the effect of a natural disaster. The collapse of the tea and indigo markets and dislocations in the tea, paper, and cotton rural handicraft industries began the process of disintegration of the predominant small-peasant economy of the post-Taiping period.

In his well-researched study of the impact of long-distance trade on central and south China, Faure aptly concludes: "The Pearl River delta and Jiangnan were not sufficiently competitive for international trade in the long run, but it would be an erroneous reading of historical data [to infer] that there was not a great deal of economic benefit derived from long distance, including international, trade before their lack of competitiveness was brought to bear on the performance of their rural economies."[54] But it must also be added that the lack of competitiveness was inherently linked with the nature of integration of the rural economy with national and international markets. In fact, the development of long-distance trade brought about constraints on the growth of the small-peasant economy. The small rural cultivators, because of their lower scale of production and its control by the middlemen-merchants, were unable from the very beginning to participate in it competitively and earn a capitalist type of profit. In such a situation, the

[52] *ZNYS* 1957, 1:484.
[53] Chandra 1966.
[54] Faure 1985: 32.

possibility of their formation or accumulation of large-scale capital did not even arise. During the period of crisis, marked by either wide fluctuation in prices or decreasing demands for their products, the small rural cultivators were left with no financial cushion as the forces that mediated between them and markets simply disappeared or shifted to other profitable areas of business.

Moreover, greater dependence on the market also exposed the small rural cultivators to inflation. Faure justifiably notes the crucial role played by rising inflation in bringing about economic crisis in the Jiangsu countryside: "Throughout the 1870 to 1911 period, there was a silver deflation. Copper prices relative to commodities remained stable until 1895, but from 1896 to 1911, copper prices also declined relative to commodities. Hence silver prices relative to copper flattened out sometime in the 1900s. The silver deflation affected from the start all items originally pegged to copper but sold in silver. It was the copper deflation, however, which had the widespread effect of creating the runaway inflation which can be seen in every price listing for the 1900s."[55] The value of silver depreciated as the currencies of Western countries shifted from the silver to the gold standard. The copper deflation has been attributed to the circulation of newly minted coins that were pegged at a higher value and greatly reduced the worth of the large amount of old and already circulating copper cash.

In rural areas, in real terms, it meant more pressure on the small rural cultivator both as consumer and as tax and rent payer. The middleman-merchant operating in both silver- and copper-cash-linked markets attempted to cover his losses by raising prices and squeezing out as much as possible. The Jiangxi provincial government, confronted with the problem of remitting tax in full in its silver value in spite of its collection in full in copper cash, requested relief from the Qing court. In 1876, the one tael of silver due as a land and *ding* tax was commuted to 2,682 copper cash.[56] In 1910, at the request of the provincial governor, Fang Rugui, it was further readjusted to make it equivalent to 3,282 copper cash.[57] This led to an additional burden on rural areas. A larger economic study of the impact of inflation on local areas in Jiangxi is needed before one can begin to understand its total dimension. Without getting into the polemical debate over the impoverishment or enrichment of the rural cultivators from the beginning of the early twentieth

[55] Faure 1978: 432; see also Peng 1965.
[56] *Shenbao*, March 22, 1876; see also *ZNYS* 1957, 1:328.
[57] Kupper 1971: 30.

century, these trends do indicate that newer pressures brought about the regional decline.

THE STATE
AND THE SMALL-PEASANT ECONOMY

In exacerbating the destabilization of the small-peasant economy, the state, too, played a crucial role. During the late Qing–early Republican period, it was itself in crisis. The costly wars against the native peasant rebels and aggressive imperialist forces, especially from the mid–nineteenth century onward, had begun not only to deplete its treasury but also to weaken its control over the larger area under its authority. In the wake of persistent and increasing demands from imperialist forces and growing political chaos, it was never able to recuperate from the crisis. The political and financial exigencies of the state caused its greater efforts to raise larger revenues through various taxes and levies at the cost of stabilizing agricultural production through the repair of dams, dykes, and other waterworks.

Among the new taxes, the lijin was the most important. In Jiangxi, it was introduced in 1857 to raise money for the state's military activities against the Taipings. By the 1860s, lijin tax barriers and stations had spread over the whole of the province. In 1904, its collection apparatus was permanently reorganized under the administration of the Tongshuizhu. The head office was in Nanchang, and suboffices, stations, and barriers were located in prefectural towns and at various marketing points on trade routes. The commercially active northern and northeastern regions of the province soon contained the largest number of such stations and barriers in the province. In 1859, in Guangxin, Raozhou, and Jiujiang prefectures, respectively, ten, eight, and five substations were established, with numerous barriers in each district.[58] By 1920, the substations in these respective prefectures had decreased to five, four, and six, but the numbers were still not less than in other areas of the province.[59]

The lijin required payment of a levy on all export and import items passing through or coming into each district. The levy was roughly 10 percent ad valorem; rates, however, fluctuated. A 1903 report from the *Dongfang Zazhi* (Eastern miscellany) indicates that, in Jiangxi, exports of timber by river route from Jian, Ganxian, Wuning, Jianchang, and other areas; xiabu

[58] ZNYS 1957, 1:368.
[59] Wright 1920: 92–95.

clothes from Fuzhou, Jianchang, Yuanzhou, Guangxin, Ruizhou, and Ningdu districts; raw indigo from Leping, Yugan, and Pengze districts; porcelain from Jingde town; and radishes from Xinfeng district were specially taxed items.[60]

The imposition of lijin put further pressures on the small rural cultivator who customarily participated in a market either as a consumer or seller. More than the amount of the levy, it was the arbitrary nature of its collection as well as the corruption associated with it that denied movement of goods cheaply and more profitably. The duties were paid not at a single place either at the beginning or at the end of a trip but at all substations and barriers along the way. As Wright noted, a "consignment of rice from Fuchow [Fuzhou] to Kiukiang [Jiujiang] has to make eight district payments in five places, and all of them to offices under the control of the T'ung Shui Chu [Tongshuizhu]. Clearly, t'ung Shui [tongshui], in the sense of a consolidated tax paid once and for all, is a polite fiction." It proved to be "a rich source of income, not simply to the Government, but to all those—not a few—who had a finger in its working."[61]

Not only did this make goods purchased by the small rural cultivator expensive but also further discouraged his movement of goods beyond the local market fairs. Such a situation naturally promoted the firm control of middlemen-merchants who specialized in the movement of goods and were able to handle the corruption attached to the duty in a more expedient fashion through their larger connections.

In 1901, the state imposed another levy to raise indemnity payments resulting from the Boxer Protocol. It has been estimated that between 1901 and 1909, Jiangxi paid about 19.2 million taels into the Boxer fund. It thus contributed about 2.1 million taels per year, out of which 1.4 million taels were collected through new revenues and the remainder by directing the old levies to the fund. Besides that, it also had to raise 1.5 million taels to indemnify the local Roman Catholic mission for damages incurred during Boxer riots.[62] Prior to 1901, Jiangxi had a surplus of about 2.5 million taels, which, according to the British consul in Jiujiang, was "more than reasonably necessary to meet the bare requirements of the Provincial Government."[63] Larger demands naturally necessitated new levies on the small rural cultivators.

[60] *Dongfang Zazhi* 1:4 (1903); see also Fu 1929.
[61] Wright 1920: 95, 92.
[62] Kupper 1971: 32; see also Clennel 1903: 20.
[63] Clennel 1903: 20.

The province was, however, never able to recuperate from the fiscal crisis thus created. At the time of the 1911 Revolution, its budget showed a deficit of 2.5 million taels. Such a situation naturally increasingly prevented it from undertaking large waterworks repair projects or any other such programs for stabilizing agricultural production that involved large financial outlays. The neglect of waterworks led to frequent inundation. Consequently, except for two years between 1880 and 1910, there was hardly any year in which more than fifteen districts did not suffer from flood.[64] Bankrupt, the provincial government was forced to seek permission of the Qing court in 1900, 1901, and 1903 to utilize funds normally collected either as land tax or through the sale of official degrees for the repair of dykes and relief purposes in Hukou, Pengze, and other districts.[65]

Such tendencies continued even after the collapse of the Qing and the inauguration of the Republican period. While the increase in land tax was gradual, from .25 yuan in the 1880s to an average of about .70 yuan in the Xinjiang region in 1926[66] (though its real burden was much more in commuted value because of inflation), it was the imposition of various surtaxes and levies that considerably drained small peasant freeholders' surpluses. The number of these miscellaneous taxes greatly increased during the Republican period. In the whole of the province, there were ninety kinds of surtaxes. For example, in the 1930s, major surtaxes paid by the peasants in Boyang and Linchuan districts were for temporary state security, education, road construction, police, self-government establishments, public hygiene, public profits, and the like.[67]

Besides that, there were per-family population and salt taxes. In many districts, these surtaxes amounted to more than 100 percent of the land tax. For example, in Guixi district, the total value of these surtaxes had gone up to 300 percent of the land tax just before the peasant movement.[68] Members of the landed upper class, involved in tax-collection activities often added their own collection charges. It is therefore not surprising that most peasant riots in the late nineteenth and early twentieth centuries have been categorized by scholars as antitax riots.[69]

In the late nineteenth and early twentieth centuries, the small rural cul-

[64] See chap. 5, table 5.2.
[65] Kupper 1971: 28–29.
[66] See Wang 1935: 23–24; Abramson 1935; *JJWT* 1934: 64–70.
[67] *JJWT* 1934: 64–70.
[68] Wang 1935: 25.
[69] See chapter 5, 118–20.

tivator was thus confronted with several new pressures in addition to the problems traditionally linked with small-scale agricultural production. These pressures set off the disintegration of the small-peasant economy. Peasants found themselves in such a precarious position that, to use Tawney's oft-quoted phrase, even a ripple was sufficient to drown them. Floundering under both political and economic pressures, the state not only failed to provide any relief to them but also extorted extra cash from them in its effort to survive. Such a situation dictated the small rural cultivator's invocation of traditional defense mechanisms inherent in his socioeconomic structure and customarily actuated by the village leaders, that is, members of the landed upper class. An analysis of their performance is necessary to comprehend the nature of the growing crisis in rural areas.

Chapter Four

The Landed Upper Class
and the Crisis of Paternalism

Harassed and disarrayed by external socioeconomic forces, small rural cultivators naturally expected intervention from landed elites to support them in their attempt to maintain the security of subsistence. The landlords, after all, had customarily performed traditional paternalistic tasks as leaders of the clan, patrons of local socioreligious organizations, and representatives of the village in mediation with the state. But, in reading the local histories of the growth of the Xinjiang peasant movement, what strikes one most is not the numerous accounts of the landlords' closer linkages with the state and their easy and frequent employment of repression and violence but their bold disavowal of those roles which were traditionally expected of them by the peasants. Were they different landlords? Or, were they, in general, sometime before the beginning of the Marxist-led peasant movement, becoming increasingly indifferent to their peasants? One needs to ask: Why did the landlords not only fail to provide the traditional security of subsistence to the distraught peasants but also begin to impinge upon their customary subsistence rights? What made the peasants seek out not the landlords but radical intellectuals in the late 1920s for redress of their grievances?

Times were bad for landlords, too. Understanding how the landlords survived in a vigorous fashion in spite of the odds against them, especially after the Taiping Rebellion, requires comprehension of those historically available options which they chose and which, in turn, destroyed their previous relationship with the small rural cultivators. Why did a situation emerge in which paternalism and paternalistic values became increasingly relegated to the historic past? To be more precise, what led to the crisis of paternalism?

To begin with, what is paternalism?[1] It is generally agreed that when a

[1] My analysis of paternalism is based on studies by E. P. Thompson (see Thompson 1974, 1978a, 1978b).

social system is established, what perpetuates it is not so much the conflict but the norms of reciprocity between antagonistic classes. Gramsci remarked that supremacy of the dominant class in a society is expressed by a cultural hegemony that permeates the whole society and effectively mediates class consciousness and class struggle.[2] In any agricultural society based on social inequality, the imperative of the dominant class to control the labor value of peasants is expressed in the establishment of paternalistic relations. Paternalism thus historically defines the relations of superordination and subordination. It requires norms of reciprocity and generates reciprocal demands and expectations, for example, the deference of peasants in exchange for the landlord's recognition of the peasants' moral right to subsistence. Norms of reciprocity between the landlord and peasants represent, as Thompson notes, the "paternal-deference equilibrium in which both parties to the equation [are], in some degree, the prisoners of each other."[3]

The concept of paternalism has also been used in historical writing in a distorted "idealistic" sense. A society cannot be characterized as paternalistic. Any such characterization presents an unrealistic picture from above and mystifies the nature of the parasitic extraction of peasants' surpluses by emphasizing a balanced reciprocity. It is highly doubtful whether balanced reciprocity, as supposedly exemplified by the paternalistic relationship, ever existed in history. In fact, paternalism has no historical specificity.[4]

Without denying that paternalism is a loose descriptive term, it can be an important component not only of ideology but of the actual institutional mediation of social relations. To be precise, paternalism characterizes the nature of the relationship between two antagonistic classes. It is a useful analytic concept in discussing class relationships only if it is defined as mediating the cruel fact of exploitation inherent in the antagonistic class relations within a hegemonic order. In a rural society, paternalism suggests a delicate moral arrangement by which the hegemonic social forces grant peasants the moral right to subsistence, within the limits of what these forces think tolerable and possible in a particular historical situation, in exchange for control over the labor value of peasants. It thus, as Genovese explains, "implies class struggles and has no meaning apart from them . . . it has nothing in common with consensus history and represents its anti-thesis—a way

---

[2] For an illuminating discussion of Gramsci's concept of hegemony, see Williams 1960; Femia 1975; Joll 1978; see also Brenner 1976 and Lippit 1978 for discussions on social classes and agrarian structures respectively in Europe and China.

[3] Thompson 1978a: 163.

[4] Ibid., 137.

of defining historical content of class struggle during times of apparent social quiescence."[5]

Similarly, a crisis of paternalism does not necessarily mean a danger to the foundation of society or the hegemony of the dominant class. The crisis indicates the emergence of a sociohistorical situation when, for the perpetuation of established hegemonic order, it is no longer necessary for the dominant class to maintain its paternalistic responsibilities according to traditionally accepted forms. This results in the violation of the moral rights of the dominated class and the weakening of the link between antagonistic classes. It produces riots, uprisings, and rebellion, but not revolution, for the established cultural hegemony of the dominant class "induces such a state of mind in which the established structure of authority and even modes of exploitation appear to be in the very course of nature."[6] The prevalence of absentee landlordism, the shifting of primary emphasis from agriculture to commerce, and changes in the forms of dominant class force are some of the general factors that bring about the crisis of paternalism in a rural society.

In rural China, the gentry-peasant reciprocity of the paternal-deference equilibrium was expressed in terms of *ganqing*. Anthropologist Morton Fried, in his study of the Zhuxian village of Anhui province, wrote: "*Kan-ch'ing* [ganqing] expresses a relationship between two individuals who are not on precisely the same social plane . . . *Kan-ch'ing* [ganqing] is the primary institutionalized technique by which class differences are reduced between non-related persons or even . . . between distantly related kin. In this respect it differs from the state of friendship which, in many cases, makes a tacit assumption of equality."[7] Ganqing, however, does not express a one-sided relationship. The peasant imposes upon the gentry some of the duties and functions of paternalism and in turn obligations of deference are imposed upon him. For a peasant, deference means self-preservation and the security of subsistence, while, to the gentry, paternalism grants the maximum possible extraction of the peasant's surplus and control over peasant labor. Fried noted that "there are only protection of customary rights and *Kan-ch'ing* [ganqing] which ensure the tenant of his land year after year." And "even the wealthiest landlord had a certain interest in *Kan-ch'ing* [ganqing] because production may be spurred by it, cheating may be reduced by it, and it is within the grounds of propriety that all relationships can be

[5] Genovese 1976–77.
[6] Thompson 1974: 388.
[7] Fried 1953: 103.

carried out properly."[8] Expressed in the local vocabulary as "good," "not good," or, worst of all, "absent," the ganqing relationship keeps the balance between surplus appropriation (through tenantry, trade, or taxation) and subsistence demands.

The development of the ganqing relationship can be traced back to the crucial socioeconomic needs of lords to effectively control the labor value of peasants after the collapse of serfdom. Massive serf and serf-tenant uprisings in the late Ming and early Qing periods, combined with the antilandlord policies of the early Qing state, had progressively weakened the authority of the landlords over rural areas and loosened their control over the serfs. They were forced to relinquish their juridical rights to dues and serf labor. Rong Sheng, a historian of Ming-Qing peasant struggles, thus remarked, "By the Kangxi reign (1662–1723), the rich no longer dared to keep serfs."[9] In such a hostile situation, to ensure their socioeconomic survival, landlords were compelled to treat their tenants as human beings and to offer paternal protection.

Mark Elvin notes that in the sixteenth century a change gradually came over the attitudes of manor owners toward their serfs. If derived from "a greater sense of the precariousness of the master-serf relationship, and the need for the master to balance strictness with kindness."[10] Numerous documents on customs also reflect such a change in the old social relationship. A late Ming set of rules emphasized better treatment of tenants and stated, "When a family has long been rich, it declines and collapses. This is due to eating food produced by others without having any achievements to justify so doing . . . and is a course which brings retribution from heaven."[11] Similar views were expressed in another Ming work, "Compilation Concerning Everyday Affairs." It warned that "if one approaches them [inferiors] solely on the basis of authority, and follows after them with angry abuse, or harasses them with one's orders, then one's moral influence will decline day by day and the heart of one's inferiors will become increasingly estranged."[12] To be sure, such moral notions of paternalism had existed earlier in master-serf relationships, but their practice was essentially a prerogative of the master whose authority was secure. But as the master-serf relationship turned into a landlord-tenant relationship, and as the hostile situation in a village

---

[8] Ibid., 102–3
[9] Cited in Shi 1962: 25.
[10] Elvin 1973: 241.
[11] Ibid., 242.
[12] Ibid.

threatened a landlord's control over his peasants, paternalism took on a measure of reality. In return for providing means of production and the security of subsistence, landlords sought deference from the peasants.

The necessity for paternal practices is well reflected in three policies formulated by a Jiangsu landlord. He prescribed, first, "when a tenant without capital tills your land, lend him two *dou* [peck] of seeds per *mu*. At the autumn harvest, collect the rent but do not add interest. In times of drought or flood, energetically help the tenant, and in normal times you will be repaid." Second, "when you have something to be done and call upon the tenant, pay him for his labor. If a tenant family raises pigs, sheep, chickens, or geese; and plants vegetables or fruits, buy these things at fair prices if your family needs them." And third, "if a tenant family conscientiously carries out good deeds [being filial, loyal, trustworthy, upright, etc.] you should give them wine and food on special occasions for their labor. If they fight [with the lord?] try to settle it by exhortation. Only as a last resort take away their land."[13]

Numerous such descriptions in books about local customs, laws, and everyday affairs indicate a consensus on the role played by the ganqing relationship in providing a moral basis for social harmony and maintaining the traditional order based on inequalities. These projected images, in turn, reinforced the peasants' conceptions of "fair" practices and their "just" rights and obligations.

As indicated earlier, it is difficult to suggest specifically when or whether the ganqing relationship historically existed in its "ideal" sense. However, since the ganqing and its images played an important historical role in maintaining the traditional order, it is possible to trace developments over the time during which there occurred not only the gradual weakening, but also, ultimately, the elimination, of sociopolitical and economic imperatives for these "moral" bonds. The beginning of these historical tendencies can be associated with the growth of modern landlordism in the eighteenth century. The emergence of a new class of commoner landlords, from the ranks of Qing officials, merchants, and rich commoners, followed by the expansion of the commodity economy and commercialization, promoted absentee landlordism and new sources of wealth outside agriculture. This diminished the imperative of attaining socioeconomic mobility solely through agriculture and active participation in rural areas and thus began to weaken the basis of traditional and customary moral linkages.

[13] Wei 1972: 149.

Equating these "new landlords" with an "agrarian bourgeoisie," Marianne Bastid argues that significant changes began to take place in Chinese rural society at the end of the eighteenth century that transformed it from a feudal, or traditional, agrarian society to a bourgeois, or modern, agrarian society. She thus observes:

> One crucial difference between the agrarian bourgeoisie and the old rural elite is that the status of the agrarian bourgeoisie did not depend primarily on the central government's bestowal of titles and degrees. Its loyalty and indebtedness to the central government were therefore far more tenuous. Another difference is that the power of the agrarian bourgeoisie within the local community did not rest primarily on the upholding of customary bonds and the fulfillment of customary duties (such as repair of public works and mediation with government authorities). Rather, it was a matter of wealth and strength.[14]

This is an apt description of the nature of the class that had begun to establish itself after the end of the eighteenth century. But not until 1926, when the Guomindang began to establish its authority, can one speak of the full domination of this class over the rural areas. The old ruling elite, as Kuhn's study has demonstrated, was able to survive the abolition of the examination system in 1905 and the collapse of the dynasty in 1911.[15] Instead of assuming that the old ruling elite was totally replaced, it would be more correct to say that, by the late eighteenth century, a symbiotic relationship between the ruling elite and the "agrarian bourgeoisie" had begun to emerge, as the interest of both of them coincided in the expropriation of the peasants' surpluses. As the formal status of an aristocrat was also a means to wealth (certainly more profitable than investment in land), the emerging class of commoner landlords strove to either attain the status of, or to maintain a close link with, traditional rural elites to protect their landed wealth. However, the growing symbiotic relationship between officeholding and the ownership of surplus land and liquid wealth began to destroy the balance between the customary and private interests of the landlord gentry and the public interests of the officials, a balance that had been effectively maintained by the early Qing emperors through restricting the power of the Ming aristocratic-official landlords.

In fact, beginning with the end of the Qianlong reign, the state itself increasingly lost the power to maintain the balance between the landlords

[14] Bastid 1976: 125–26.
[15] See Kuhn 1970, 1975.

and the officials. After a relatively long period of peace, it was confronted with a series of large-scale peasant uprisings starting with the White Lotus and culminating with the largest of all, the Taiping Rebellion, in the mid–nineteenth century. Increasing penetration of foreign imperialists not only led to several costly wars but also threatened the empire. All this rapidly depleted the financial resources of the state. Politically weakened and financially bankrupt, the state needed more cooperation from the landlords to police the rural areas and to collect taxes and other revenue. The Tongzhi restoration thus respected the socioeconomic privileges of the landed upper class, for, as Mary Wright explains, the reliance on them for local control was universally held to be not only inevitable but right and proper.[16]

But, already threatened by the similar destabilizing impact of the peasant uprisings and the long-term economic decline, landlords were themselves taking over the tasks of local control. They developed their own apparatus of sociopolitical and economic power. This increasingly lessened their dependence upon either the deference of peasants or the authority of the state to maintain the traditional order. As Chuzo Ichiko notes: "The gentry realized that whenever the officials could not protect local lives and property, they themselves must form self defense corps consisting of farmers directly under their influence. Since under such circumstances, there was no need for the gentry to obey governmental authorities, the balance between the gentry and government officials collapsed."[17]

The landed upper class could not have done otherwise. The common crisis thus brought both the weak state and the distressed landed upper class together to maintain the status quo. The state promoted members of the landed upper class in its organization of the local militia forces. It also provided them opportunities to attain formal official status through the purchase of degrees and granted full rights to landownership as well as to collect rent and taxes. In return, the landed upper class looked after the political and economic needs of the state. This cemented the link between them and consequently reshaped the nature of landed-upper-class influence in the countryside.

During the initial stages of the Taiping Rebellion, as Kuhn's excellent study of local militarization in late imperial China demonstrates, the weakness of the state necessitated massive organization of militia groups (*tuan lian*) by many powerful and large landholding lineages. They raised such forces

---

[16] See Wright 1957: 7, see also Wright 1968.
[17] Chuzo Ichiko 1971: 298–99.

under the leadership of the landed upper class to defend themselves.[18] A local chronicler of the Se lineage of Qianzhang (the present Yongxiu) in Jiangxi wrote that it was the need for survival that led to the formation of militia groups. "Since the beginning of the rebellion, there were many communities that dared not organize *t'uan lian* [tuan lian] (thinking they could remain uninvolved), but were destroyed nonetheless; our lineage reckoned that it was better to militarize and thus stand a chance of survival."[19] Other lineages of Jiangxi, such as Liu of Zixi and the Wan of Hexi, "which boasted extensive landholdings, and intricate connections with the bureaucracy,"[20] rose to fame and commanded considerable power by organizing large militia groups and supporting the state in its attempt to quell the rebellion in 1852. Liu Yunzhan, a *zhuren* who belonged to the Liu lineage of Nanchang, was so successful in organizing a local militia that he was asked by the state to form the Jiangxi Army. He became the key link between the rural gentry and the provincial bureaucracy during the Taiping period and was consequently granted many higher ranks.[21]

Local militarization was, however, not limited only to a few powerful lineages in a province. Kuhn indicates that besides simplex organization, comprising single-lineage local militia groups, there were also a large number of multilineage simplex and multilineage multiplex organizations, consisting of members from more than one lineage. Both the Se and Liu lineages of Jiangxi were multiplex organizations; many people having different surnames joined their powerful militia groups.[22]

If local militarization activities strengthened the control of the landed upper class over the rural areas, of no less significance was the state's promotion of the purchase of degrees and the institutionalization of their holders' customary power to manage efficiently the task of tax collection. The policy of increasing the number of degree holders provided the state with much-needed revenue during the time of greatly increased military expenditures and also created a large number of local followers who were as anxious as the state to maintain the established order. According to a Qing edict of 1853, the contribution of 100,000 taels to the military fund by the gentry, merchants, and commoners of a province entitled it to enlarge its civil and military *zhuren* quota. A donation of 2,000 taels by a ding, *zhen*, or *xian* in-

---

[18] Kuhn 1970: 76–105.
[19] Ibid., 81.
[20] Ibid., 80.
[21] For a study of the Liu lineage and its role in the Jiangxi Army, see Kuhn 1970: 152–65.
[22] See Kuhn 1970: 64–92.

creased its civil and military *sheng yuan* quota. Excess collections similarly allowed a region to increase its degree quota. The contributors were rewarded with the grant of a degree.[23]

Under this policy, the sheng yuan (the lowest rank of gentry) quota of Jiangxi, which was one of the richest provinces of China and which contributed heavily to the military fund to combat the Taiping Rebellion, was raised by 56 percent. Thus, between 1855 and 1862, the number of sheng yuan degree holders in Jiangxi increased from 39,830 to 62,197; it was highest number in all the provinces.[24] Moreover, the number of *qiansheng* (a rank of gentry acquired through purchase), which was highest in Jiangxi before the Taiping Rebellion, totaling 38,552, was enlarged by 50 percent. During the reign of Xianfeng, a total of 191,336 taels was paid to purchase 2,175 qiansheng degrees.[25] The number of *qianshen* degree holders remained lower, suggesting that more people preferred sheng yuan status after the Taiping Rebellion. Chang Chung-li writes that "Kiangsi [Jiangxi] was the province which most fully exploited the permission to expand the sheng yuan quota by making contribution to the military fund."[26]

The trend toward attaining gentry status through direct or indirect purchase firmly established the link between wealth and rank. A wealthy landlord or merchant could now easily acquire a degree and maintain both informal and formal status in the sociopolitical structure. Chang Chung-li's compilation of data about the economic status of the gentry confirms that a growing number of new gentry in the late nineteenth century belonged to the wealthy families.

Moreover, during the post-Taiping period, official endorsement by the weak Qing state not only of the landed upper class's customary tax collection rights but also its participation in private rent collection further strengthened the alliance between the two. Suzuki writes that the growing involvement of the state in collection of private debts was one of the most important innovations in the post-Taiping Jiangnan land system.[27] Immediately after the rebellion, the first priority for the financially bankrupt state was to strengthen and expand its tax base. Following the dictum that "government tax comes from private rent," it paid special attention to the protection of rent collection activities of the landed upper class in order that the latter

---

[23] Translated in Chang 1962: 83–84; see also Chang 1955.
[24] Chang 1962: 110.
[25] Ibid., 110–11.
[26] Ibid., 111.
[27] Cited in Grove and Esherick 1980: 415.

would be financially secure enough to pay its taxes. To aid collection it created special "collection agencies," which acted as official tax and rent collecting organizations.

The state also promoted the establishment of rent bursaries by the landlords. Originating in 1863, these bursaries were organized privately by the big landlords to facilitate collection of rents for their land, and taxes and levies from peasants on behalf of the district government. Yuzi Muramatsu's study of the bursary system indicates that a single bursary often managed several thousand mu of land, extending to more than one district. It acted as an agent for many small- and medium-scale landlords in collecting rents and depositing taxes. It also kept blank forms signed and issued by the district government authorities for ready use in legally prosecuting delinquent tenants and small freeholders.[28] The grant of official and legal rights to both rent bursaries and "collection agencies" to realize private debts and government taxes demonstrate the fusion of state and the landed-upper-class interests. Thus, "the fusing of state and gentry power not only meant that private obligations were made public, it also meant that public functions were privately assumed."[29]

Such tendencies had become so embedded in the rural structure that it became increasingly difficult to separate the landlord from the local instruments of power and control. The last attempt of the collapsing Qing state to save itself was the move to local self-government in the first decades of the twentieth century, which, in principle, represented no departure from the traditional concept of the "select orthodox" gentry as maintainers of a proper relationship between the bureaucracy and local interests. Chuzo Ichiko has convincingly suggested that this policy, instead of restricting the local members of the landed upper class, provided further opportunities for its conservative members to expand their influence to the point that they occupied all the important posts in local government.[30] The abolition of the examination system, the collapse of the dynasty, and the consequent formation of the Republican state did not have any demoralizing effect on them.

The crisis of paternalism within the post-Taiping hegemonic order is perhaps most aptly described in a sarcastic commentary by Tao Xu (1821–1891). In reaction to the publication of a posthumous anthology of the writings of Jiangsu's great fiscal reformer and Confucian theoretician, Feng Guifen, he wrote:

[28] Muramatsu 1966: 566–99.
[29] Grove and Esherick 1980: 415–16.
[30] Chuzo 1971: 302.

Reading over the essays on tax equalization [*zhun-fu*] . . . I could not but be moved. How truly glorious is the philanthropic spirit which seeks to abolish the system of privilege enjoyed by the grandee households [da hu] and to render the assessment rates equal for all. Why is it, then, that the age speaks not at all of the benefits of equalization, but murmurs instead only of Master [Feng Guifen's] accomplishments in negotiating the reduction of our taxes?

There can be no disputing the credit earned by Mr. Feng in drafting [for Li Hongzhang] the memorial which moved the court to lessen our taxes by one third. . . . But in the very same memorial, Mr. Feng speaks incessantly of the plight of the tenant farmers who comprise 90 percent of the local population. Why is it, then, that the benefits of this one third discount have not been conveyed to the tenant farmer?

In the "Memoir on the Tax Reduction," Mr. Feng . . . speaks of rent reduction in tandem with tax reform. Is it permissible to speak of both projects together, yet not implement them simultaneously?

In the same piece, Mr. Feng rebukes a certain official for his ignorance of Ku Yen-wu's [Gu Yanwu] discussion, in the Jih-chih lu [*Rizhilu*] (Diary of daily learning), of the procedure for "apportioning [deficits produced by resurveying] among the [rate payers] of the entire county in question." Yet in this very work, Mr. Feng speaks cheerfully of rents as high as twelve bushels of rice per mou [mu]. It does not seem, to judge from this, that Mr. Feng himself adhered to the prescriptions of Mr. Ku [Gu], who proposed a rent ceiling of eight bushels.

I raise these points for the consideration of those who peruse Mr. Feng's anthology believing its author worthy only of praise, and innocent of misdeed, or who seek to excuse Mr. Feng on the grounds that he had at least intended that rents too should be trimmed.[31]

This long passage reveals the glaring contradiction between the theory and practice of the landed upper classes in the late nineteenth century. It indicates that the post-Taiping hegemonic order was characterized by the rhetoric of paternalism, not by its application. The result was steady erosion of paternalistic obligations and the corresponding socioeconomic bonds of the customary ganqing relationship.

This can be better understood from the fact that in spite of Mr. Feng's rhetoric about the sufferings of tenants, the landholding of his bursary (as Yuzi Muramatsu's study indicates) continued to increase manyfold during the late 1860s and early 1870s. During the same period, the condition of the tenants of his bursary rapidly deteriorated, and many of them were unable

[31] Translated in Polachek 1975: 216.

to pay rent.[32] It is, thus, the ability of the landed upper classes to effectively control the labor value of peasants, without maintaining reciprocal paternalistic obligations, that constitutes the major characteristic of the post-Taiping hegemonic order.

Remarking on Tao's sarcastic criticisms of the contemporary elite, James Polachek aptly observes that "in 1876 (as opposed to 1911), the sins of these worthy gentlemen were still mainly those of omission, not of commission."[33] The emphasis on "omission" should be taken seriously, for it meant that the elite abdicated those crucial paternal services which provided subsistence to peasants during difficult years, while continuing to demand economic and extraeconomic services from peasants traditionally guaranteed under the ganqing relationship. Under a "philanthropic facade" and the illusion of paternalism, peasants were thus subjected to the worst kind of oppression. In sins of commission, there are at least no illusions for the peasants since the exploitation is direct.

Noting the changing nature of the landlord-peasant relationship, Tao writes:

> The gentry of Soochow [Suzhou] have shown themselves to be obsessively concerned with imposing their will upon the local rural population. In former times, it was often at the pleasure of landlords to make special concessions to indigent sharecroppers who were stricken by sickness, death in the family or natural calamity. But the landed proprietors of postbellum Soochow [Suzhou] were of a new and remorselessly tightfisted variety. The unfortunate lessee who could not meet his rent obligations in full, or whose holdings failed to produce the required ten percent profit for their owner, would be shunted off to the yamen to be caged like an animal until a more fortunate kinsman might pay his fine or until his desperate wife could auction her children to raise the requisite sum.[34]

Finding that contemporary landlords worried only about making the countryside safe for rentier interests and ignored the spirit of charity, Tao finally accuses them of hypocritical greed and deliberate apathy. Polachek, agreeing with Tao's observation, writes that "from what we know of the behavior of Soochow's [Suzhou] landlord class during the late Ch'ing [Qing], and from what glimpses contemporary Chinese and foreign sources afford into the economic condition of the Shanghai hinterland during the same pe-

---

[32] See Muramatsu 1966: 566–99.
[33] Polachek 1975: 217.
[34] Ibid., 216.

riod, it seems likely that at least his [Tao's] final two indictments, greed and apathy, are justified."[35] While "greed" was hardly new, it was basically the increasing "apathy" of the dominant class toward peasants that exposed the greed latent in paternal relations. I warned earlier that it is hazardous to view the landlord's paternalism as a desire to have balanced reciprocity of exchange; instead, it should be seen as justification of a system of exploitation. Hence, paternalism does not preclude "greed," but rather confines greed to a tolerable limit so that the peasants' moral right to subsistence is not violated. "Apathy," as Tao pointed out, was indeed a new development and one with serious consequences. Apathy, whether of commoners or rulers, applies to those situations in society in which people look increasingly to private solutions for public problems. It thus precludes paternalism. In post-Taiping China, the greed and apathy of the landed upper class created the crisis of paternalism.

Thus, after the Taiping Rebellion, the state's institutionalization of the landed upper class's customary authority over the rural areas was perhaps the most distressing development for the peasants. It fused the landed upper class's informal status with formal power. The consequences of this change in its form of power have not adequately been studied in the existing scholarly literature. Kuhn does not view this change as radical. "It appears," he writes, "that growing out of the turmoil of civil war was enhanced power for the local elite, often exercised within the formal apparatus of the sub-district government. The importance of the development cannot be overemphasized, for the power of the elite in the old system had been exercised primarily through informal channels."[36] He further notes that the "informal power had indeed been the elite's own preference. . . . But now the gentry often found it necessary to oversee local administration in its own interests, a role to which they had become habituated by the growing importance of local defense associations during the years of crisis. At least one of the roots of the old order—the power of traditional elites in rural China—seems thus to have survived the Taiping holocaust in a surprisingly vigorous fashion."[37]

Although Kuhn rather cautiously notes the strengthening of the elite's power as merely a vigorous survival, in a more realistic sense and in the context of the landed upper class's pre-Taiping status, it signifies its acquisition of a monopoly of force and of the means of violence in the rural areas. It also evinces the coincidence of the interest of both the landed upper class

[35] Ibid., 217.
[36] Kuhn 1970: 215; see also Kuhn 1975.
[37] Kuhn 1970: 215–16.

and the state in the expropriation of peasant's surpluses for maintenance of their own sociopolitical and economic power. This consequently turned the members of the landed upper class into virtual rulers in their areas, prepared the ground for localism and provincialism of the later period, and dispelled any socioeconomic or political need to maintain a paternalistic relationship with the peasants. As Wakeman observes:

> As control fell almost entirely into the hands of the local elite, taxes and rents, public and private fused together. The rural gentry had ostensibly become master of its own estates.
> One possible consequence of this fusion was the intensification of class conflicts. During the high Ch'ing [Qing], gentrymen, however venal, at least pretended to stand for local paternalism. But now urban rentiers were represented by rent bureau bailiffs, often moon lighting policemen, who destroyed the particularistic *kan-ch'ing* [ganqing] (rapport) which once united rural landlords and their tenants.[38]

The period after the collapse of the Qing state and before the beginning of 1927 can best be seen as an era of the landed upper class's rule in the Chinese countryside. It marked the rapid institutionalization of those tendencies which had developed in the wake of a crisis—the mid-nineteenth-century peasant uprisings and the accelerated expansion of the imperialist-stimulated commodity economy—and which had ultimately fused together the state and the landed upper class's power in local areas. The change from the Imperial to the Republican state did not greatly alter the configuration of force in local areas. After the Revolution of 1911 in Jiangxi, as Samuel Kupper remarks, "the traditional establishment at the local level, including landlords and former degree-holders, were able to solidify their control over collection of taxes. Wu Chieh-chang's [Wu Jiezhang] initial telegram to the various hsien [xian] left the responsibility for collecting taxes with the former officials and instructed them to work in conjunction with the local self-government associations, dominated by the same traditional establishment that had always controlled the rural regions."[39] The achievement of succeeding governors such as Li Zhun, he notes, "is to be found in the unaltered socioeconomic structure and in his being able to satisfy the traditional elite's desire for peace and order."[40]

[38] Wakeman and Grant 1975: 23.

[39] Kupper 1971: 262.

[40] Ibid., 352. For a general description of the late Qing see Fairbank and Liu 1980; Cohen and Schrecker 1976.

During the early Republican period, moves to curb the power of the landed upper class thus failed. The Republican state envisioned a subdistrict administrative system (*zu zhih jiu*) where administrative matters as well as the traditional tasks assigned to the landed upper class were to be handled by a headman, the *chuzhang*, or *chudong*. The headman was nominated through the ballot system with voting rights limited to those having property and education or those formally appointed by the district magistrate. But this scheme fell short of serving the purpose for which it was intended. Kuhn writes that "if we look beneath the normative provisions of the administrative codes there is convincing evidence that the 'ch'u' [*chu*] in actual practice was very little influenced by the quasi-modernism of tsu-chih [*zu zhi*], but was mainly a gentry organization that evolved from the multiplex and extended multiplex associations formed during the mid and late nineteenth century."[41]

Local and provincial assemblies, elected on a limited franchise, thus were completely in the control of the landed upper class. The case of a big landlord of the ninth district of Yiyang (Jiangxi), Zhang Niancheng, who used his gentry connections to stand for election, illustrates how easy it was for a big landlord to manipulate such elections in spite of the opposition of radical intellectuals. In her biography of Fang Zhimin, his wife Miao Min writes: "Since the establishment of the Republic in 1912, the staging of 'elections' had become common over the whole country, providing fat incomes for local gentry who manipulated the elections. They framed the list of voters and used these lists to bargain with those of the gentry seeking election. Then after buying the votes, the candidate would hire people to write their names on the ballot and thus get elected."[42] Anybody who opposed them or attempted to expose their corruption and illegal extraction of "election funds," as did Fang's youthful friends in the case of the landlord-gentry member Zhang Niancheng, was simply put into prison.

In fact, the power and influence of the landed upper class had become so embedded in the rural structure that during the early Republican period it was impossible either to dismiss or discipline members of this class through traditional reformist means. In many places, they enjoyed an almost autonomous status. They controlled and taxed local areas at will and ignored the state's rule and regulations. Their private militia forces dominated the countryside. During periods of political chaos and vacuum, such as immediately

[41] Kuhn 1970: 219; see also Young 1970.
[42] Miao 1962: 6.

after the Revolution of 1911 and after the collapse of the warlord state in 1926, these forces had assumed total administrative control of this region. Describing the rural political situation before the arrival of the Northern Expedition troops in Yiyang and Guixi districts, Shao Shiping notes that these private militia forces, in alliance with local bandits, had not only initially usurped power in the area but also claimed a right to it before the military commander of the newly arriving revolutionary army.[43] Fang Zhimin and members of the peasant associations had to wage their fiercest and most numerous struggles against these forces in order to establish and expand their hegemony in the countryside.

The militia forces of such landlords as Zhang Niancheng and Shao Xiangzhen frequently moved to villages from their base in the market town of Qigongzhen, to collect rent, debts, and levies. They even collected a "footwear levy" for their own pockets.[44] Moreover, the connivance between these and other landlords of this market town with the local police official, the pock-marked Yu, for the extraction of peasants' surpluses indicates the total interdependence between the state and the landed upper class. In the twin Luoti-Lanjia villages, the attempt by the local tax official to collect a newly imposed coal levy with the support of a local landlord, Luo Kuangshan, turned out to be an occasion for the members of the peasant association to launch their struggle.[45] Local histories of the Xinjiang peasant movement are replete with scattered references reflecting the power exercised by the landed elite in close alliance with state apparatus of local control.[46] These references and incidents should not be ignored, as they demonstrate the dominant trend of rural reality just before the beginning of the peasant movement in the Xinjiang region.

Confronted with the weakness of the state and the new larger economic pressures, the landed upper class had thus developed its own means for maintaining sociopolitical and economic hegemony over the rural areas. Instead of being a leader of the peasant community, it had become that community's supervisor. It no longer needed to represent the interests of peasantry by bargaining with the state for the reduction of taxes or petitioning for funds for dykes and granaries until its own socioeconomic status was threatened. Now as a representative of the state, its hegemony depended less upon the maintenance of norms of reciprocity with peasants and sanctions

[43] Shao 1958: 242–43.
[44] Fang and Miao 1977: 3–4.
[45] *FZM* 1982: 119–20.
[46] For example, see *HQPP* 1957–60; *HSFB* 1958–61; Fang and Miao 1977; and others.

of its legitimacy from "below" and more upon its control over the means of repression and violence. Such changes afforded the landed upper class opportunities to redefine paternal-deference equations on its own terms and project its paternalism in its own images. This, as I will examine in detail in chapter 5, evinced its indifference and apathy toward peasants and its greed in maximizing profits at the cost of peasants through the introduction of new forms of tenancy and rent collection as well as commoditization of various customary "use rights" or "entitlements."

Yet these developments did not mean that the Xinjiang rural society had turned into an arena of explicit class struggle; or that the landed upper class and the peasants had stood against each other to perpetuate or establish their respective "class rules." Antagonistic class relationships were still verbal, couched in terms that manifested the growing imbalance within the paternal-deference equation. Peasants had begun to complain frequently that the landed upper class had turned into "local bullies," "evil gentry," and "cannibals," and was increasingly indulging in "unfair" and "unjust" practices. But landlordism itself was not denounced. Only the landlords' redefinition of their paternalistic functions was rejected. Moreover, there were "good" landlords too, who at least pretended to respect the subsistence needs of the peasants. The solution still favored was that "bad" ones be humiliated, punished, and, in extreme cases, executed. The "goods," however, were to be spared—a tendency that was evident in numerous peasant riots and uprisings and that remained strong during the early period of the peasant movement throughout China.

In fact, the paradox of paternalism is that it depends much upon such visible hegemonic functions of the dominant class as the arbitration of justice and the administration of the law, as well as pretensions of generosity through charity and participation in ancestral worship and local socioreligious ceremonies. It depends less upon its invisible function—the extraction of peasant surpluses. Such visible functions of the landed upper class did not change over the long course of time. They remained consistent from the earlier period until the time of the peasant movement in the late 1920s. A local gazetteer from Jiangxi notes numerous examples of the performance of such paternalistic functions by the landed upper class.[47]

Li Chengan of Taihe, for example, was an assistant *zhou* magistrate during the Daoguang period. He established a "charity granary" and managed the clan temple, school, and sacrificial ceremonies in his village. In the same

[47] See Chang 1962; Hu 1948.

area, Xiao Wei, another assistant zhou magistrate, contributed funds for the establishment of a foundling home during the Jiajing period. In the Xingguo district of southern Jiangxi, as Masao Mori notes, community granaries and charitable granaries existed in almost all the villages from the eighteenth until the early twentieth century.[48] After the suppression of the Taiping Rebellion alone, more than four hundred granaries were set up by landlord families to provide for the peasants' subsistence needs during the period of poor harvests. The notorious landlord Zhang Niancheng, of Yiyang district, besides acting as the arbitrator of justice and administrator of law, provided funds for the repair of local bridges, maintenance of roads, operation and management of a local school, and subsistence of calamity-stricken peasants. His performance of such tasks, as an author notes, led a majority of people "to not recognize his ugly face."[49] Fang Zhimin, during his childhood, had attended landlord Zhang's school. The clan registers of landlord families from districts of northwestern Fujian and on the boundary of Jiangxi indicate that from the early nineteenth century until the 1930s, landlords systematically set aside in their wills at least 30 percent of their total land as "food land," "ancestral land," or "educational land." This was meant to provide for the needs of the local community and was a symbolic manifestation of their performance of paternalistic services.

Such descriptions, if not viewed in terms of the historically changing force of the paternal-deference equation, obscure the rural reality. In his investigations of Xingguo district in 1930, Mao found, instead of community and charity granaries, a large number of "food-lending" organizations. They advanced food at a high interest rate to peasants during the preharvest period.[50] Mori's study indicates the gradual modification of these granaries over time into the food-lending organizations that turned their landed-upper-class managers into grain lenders.[51] The ostensibly paternalistic purpose of these organizations was thus lost. Landlord Zhang, in collusion with local police officials, instigated lawsuits against peasants and extorted money from them.[52] Local militia of Yiyang district raised by the landlords to ward off bandits terrorized the peasants and collected its own "footwear" levy. Such new public functions as the establishment of schools, or the organization of elections, became occasions for the landlords to impose fresh levies. Lands

[48] Mori 1975: 621–38.
[49] *FZM* 1982.
[50] Mao, in Mori 1975: 607–11.
[51] See Mori 1975: 638–40.
[52] Miao 1962: 6.

previously kept aside by clan landlords to serve various paternalistic purposes in the community became a means to increase their own wealth.[53]

The frequent scattered references to such practices, beginning in the early twentieth century, are themselves examples of how easy it had become for the landed upper class to redefine its paternalistic functions in such a way that these became instruments for the extortion of peasants' surpluses and for maximization of profits. The shift in the form of landed-upper-class power altered the nature of its traditional moral role in the countryside and its relationship with the peasants. It is in this rapid decline of the force of the old paternalist-deference equation leading to the crisis of paternalism that the source of the twentieth-century agrarian crisis can be traced. The consequences of the crisis of paternalism, in material terms, can be seen not only in the landed upper class's vigorous survival but also in its increasing accumulation of land at the cost of harassed and disarrayed small rural cultivators.

As noted earlier, in his survey of rural Xinjiang during 1884–1885, Jamieson found that only in rare cases did the land of a big landowner exceed fifty mu. But by 1920, it was not uncommon to find landlords whose holdings amounted to several hundred mu. Agricultural surveys of the early Republican period indicate the presence of big landlords in various districts of north and northeastern Jiangxi. In Hengfeng district of the Xinjiang region, for example, the landlord Jin Lian owned two thousand mu of land. There were several other landlords whose landholdings were anywhere from five hundred to one thousand mu.[54] A 1920 survey of Guangfeng district reported that "the majority of peasants are either landless or extremely poor. They have houses with kitchen garden land or ancestral land. The land of extremely big landlords does not exceed one thousand to two thousand mu. In the district, there are not more than four or five such families. Those who own between ten to one hundred mu of land are mostly people who live in the city. In the village, most of the peasants own less than ten mu of land."[55]

In the same region, in Guixi district, the income of several landlords from rent was said to be six to seven thousand dan. Landlords Guan, Wan, and He of Guangze county possessed several hundred to thousands of mu. Landlords Lu and Chen of Lichuan, a district on the border of Xinjiang, had more than a thousand mu of land each. Their lands were located along the

---

[53] See Zheng 1984, 1985.
[54] See Abramson 1935: 96–113.
[55] Min 1920: 54.

road between Lichuan and Guangze.[56] It should be noted that owning land at various locations was not an uncommon practice in China. Those studies which rely on the statistical data of a particular area often fail to reveal the total mu of land a landlord residing there actually possessed. One of the famous examples is that of the Taoist Arch-Magician and Heavenly Teacher who lived on Longhu Mountain in northern Jiangxi. His landholdings were said to have extended over eight districts in the valley of the Guangxin River.[57] Another prominent landlord, Zhou Ruihuai of Xingguo district in southern Jiangxi, had land in three hundred different locations in Jiangxi and in neighboring provinces. His total holdings amounted to more than 100,000 mu. Ruan Mo's article on the agrarian situation in Jiangxi also mentions two prominent landlords in the province who owned respectively 300,000 and 400,000 mu of land at different locations.[58]

The situation in southern Jiangxi was much worse, for it was comparatively less affected by the Taiping Rebellion. According to a survey, Xitan village in Wanzai district consisted of about five hundred households, of which eight were those of large- and medium-scale landlords. The major landlord owned about four thousand mu of land, and each of the others controlled between two hundred and five hundred mu.[59] Xingguo district, where one of the largest landowners of Jiangxi resided, had several landlords possessing hundreds of mu each. Landlords Tao, Tian, and Chang of this district received more than three thousand dan of grain as rent. Ruijin (later the capital of the Chinese Soviet Republic) was the home of landlords Tong and Yang who received two thousand dan of grain in rent. In addition, there were ten families who received rents of more than a thousand dan each. In 1926, 3 percent of the entire population in Ruijin consisted of landed gentry with an average landholding of a hundred to three hundred mu.[60]

A 1934 survey of the districts of Fouliang, Guixi, and Leping in Xinjiang indicates that the average landholding of big village landlords was less than 200 mu in the first two districts and 281 mu in the last. On the other hand, the landholdings of the big absentee landlords consisted of more than three hundred mu. While absentee landlords possessed larger landholdings, there were a greater number of village landlords.[61] All of them, however, were

[56] Wang 1935: 5–6.
[57] Miao 1962: 48.
[58] See Abramson 1935: 96–113.
[59] Ibid., Wang 1935.
[60] Wang 1935: 5–6.
[61] *YEWG* 1936: 77.

engaged in various other occupations in addition to landowning. Business, official, and leisure activities combined kept them busy most of the time. Some of the village landlords indulged in farming also, but none of them wholly depended on it for a living and maintenance of their status.[62] This reflects the increasingly blurred distinction between different status groups and indicates the difficulty in examining twentieth-century rural society in China purely in terms of landlord-tenant relationships. The fusion of several roles and interests enabled the landed upper class to completely dominate and control the rural areas.

It should also be noted that opportunities for either the downward mobility of the landed upper class or the upward mobility of peasants were becoming more and more restricted, especially in the early twentieth century. The 1934 statistics from three districts of Xinjiang region indicate that in Guixi, Leping, and Fouliang, respectively, 90, 67, and 87 percent of landlords' land was inherited from their ancestors.[63] This suggests that, in spite of the division of land under the peculiar inheritance system, most of the landlords, especially in the early twentieth century, were able not only to keep their ancestors' land intact but also to increase their landholdings. Hilary Beattie, in a study of the land and lineage in Tongcheng district of southern Anhui, finds no rapid impoverishment of successive generations of landlord families due to the division of property by inheritance. He explains: "When lineages made cash income through usury it was invariably reinvested in more land, unless used for some specific short term purpose like the building of an ancestral hall; this holds true right down to the twentieth century. Though other sources of income were undoubtedly available to the members of the elite families, the combination of landowning and usury seems likely always to have provided the most secure basis for livelihood."[64]

Recent studies on the nature of village clan landlords and their continued strength in local areas in northwest Fujian, adjoining the Xinjiang region, indicate also that the division of property under the family inheritance system did not adversely affect the socioeconomic position of landlords.[65] This was primarily because the traditional custom of a landlord was not to divide all his land but to keep a portion of it, roughly one-third of the total, for purposes of clan-related tasks. The portions were called by various names such as "ancestral land," "Taoist sacrificial ceremony land," "prosperity

---

[62] Ibid., 172.
[63] Ibid., 80.
[64] Beattie 1979: 138–39.
[65] See Zheng 1984: 33–35; Zheng 1985: 45–51.

(zhengchang) land," "educational or book lamp land," "corvee land," "yearly administrative supervision land," "food land." These became part of common clan properties to provide benefits for the poor members of the same descent group. However, as studies by Zheng as well as Chen Han-seng indicate, these common properties began to turn into a modified form of private property.[66]

Entrusted with the management of the common clan land, the powerful village landlords regarded it as their own property and rented it out to maximize their private gains. Hu thus wrote that this "danger was inherent at all times in a social structure as extensive as the *tsu* [*zu*]. It is only increased by the modern age with its emphasis in money economy centered in big cities as well as *its disregard for old cultural values*, which have very much weakened the social controls that made the common property an institution of benefit for the group" [emphasis mine].[67] He further wrote that "the feeling of responsibility to the common descent group is becoming lost under the impact of modern commercialism, with its attitudes of maximizing personal gain."[68] Consequently, in the land reform investigations conducted in postliberation northwestern Fujian, it was found that "village clan" landlords possessed more than 50 percent of the total land in the rural areas as compared with the 20 percent owned by the nonclan landlords.[69] In some cases, like the multiplex militia organizations discussed by Kuhn, the clan properties were also managed by landlords with two or three different surnames. These clan lands were rented out on short-term leases and had tenancy conditions similar to those of nonclan land.[70] Such control over common clan properties enabled the landlords to earn benefits from them and further expand their landholdings. It therefore seems improbable that the division of property necessarily led to the downward mobility of the landlords.

On the contrary, it was peasants who suffered most from the division of property under the Chinese inheritance system. A survey of northern Jiangxi in 1933 reflects the rapid decline of the landholding of peasants. It found that 79 percent of the population owned 27 percent of the land, and the rest of the population owned 73 percent of the land. This suggests increasing fragmentation of land among peasants, shrinking their landholdings to tiny parcels. In his study of Hunan peasants, Mao correctly mentions that

---

[66] Zheng 1984: 34–36; Zheng 1985: 51–55; Chen Han-seng 1936: 37–39.

[67] Hu 1948: 90.

[68] Ibid., 99.

[69] See Zheng 1984: 35.

[70] Ibid., 36.

"a large portion of China's big landlords are descendants of the Ch'ing officials and nobles; some are present day officials and militarists. There is also a group of rich urban merchants who have bought land. There are very few who have raised themselves to the status of big landlords by their industrious cultivation of the land."[71] The upward mobility of peasants during the early twentieth century thus seems to have been a very rare occurrence.

It was, in fact, downward mobility of peasants that characterized rural China in the early twentieth century. Edwin Moise's discussion of downward social mobility convincingly demonstrates that the resources of a poor family in prerevolutionary China declined very rapidly as compared with those of the higher status groups. "The simple fact is that the families at the bottom end of the economic scale tended to die out. The poorest men were often unable to have children at all; any children they did have were rather likely to die young. This means that the poorest fifteen percent of the men in one generation could not be the children of the poorest fifteen percent of the preceding generation."[72]

In this context, it becomes clear that there were good reasons why Mao Zedong would be so impressed later by the peasants' attack on the landed upper classes, for neither the late Qing nor the early Republican state was able to restrain them.[73] Mao realized that any attempt to ameliorate peasants' conditions and to effectively relate the rural areas to the center called for destruction of the domination of the landed upper class over rural areas. The Guomindang, in a different context, reached the same conclusion. It found it necessary to attack the rural gentry in favor of urban classes, whose interests were ill-served by the former.

The crisis of paternalism, resulting from greed and apathy of the landed upper class, is also a theme that appears frequently in the literary works on peasants and peasant society in the early decades of the twentieth century. In the novels of Wu Zexiang,[74] which are praised by critics for their realistic and honest portrayal of society in central China, villagers are always working hard to fulfill the demands of the landlord. In *Fan Village*, one of the peasants confides: "Our six and four fifth *mu* have yielded twenty-five piculs of rice. Several days ago he asked the miller, who would only give him a dollar sixty for a picul. Today he asked a rice dealer, who would not even pay a dollar sixty. Just paying back what miller had advanced us in food

[71] Mao, in Schram 1969: 241.
[72] Moise 1977: 4.
[73] Mao, in Schram 1969: 252.
[74] *Chinese Literature* 11 (1959): 61–101.

stuffs will take thirty dollars. We might as well pay the landlord with our lives. He is hard as iron and won't let go half a penny that's his due. If we harvest one grain, he wants that one grain. Three stewards kept a watch on threshing. All our rice is being held at the mill."[75]

In a story by Jiangxi native Chen Nong the tenant Tai Sheng, not unlike Wu Zexiang's villagers, cries "murderer," "robber," "cannibal" at the landlord who systematically takes his crop away, does not even allow him to keep his customary bonuses, and still complains that the customary feast is inadequate. The landlord finally leaves when it is evident to him that Tai Sheng can surrender no more because he has nothing left to give.[76]

Peasant complaints about landlords' abdication of paternalistic responsibilities are also evident in their songs. These songs testify to the peasants' concern with meeting the minimum subsistence requirements of their families and their antagonism toward the unpaternal landlords. A hill song from northern Jiangxi provides an example of their sentiments.

The sunset is red, so red;
I advise my employer to stop work now.
Other houses are having dinner
But we are still in the middle of the field.

The sun sets on the western hill with a spot of red,
On my hoe hangs a lantern.
If you, our employer, have candles enough,
We are not afraid to work until the sun rises in
the East again.[77]

These songs express the peasants' antagonism toward overlords who forced them to work long hours without providing decent working conditions. The agricultural laborers' songs from Nanchang (Jiangxi) and the cowherds' songs from Zhangding (Fujian) depict in even harsher terms the life of peasants.[78] In the last line of one song, the peasant is left to "go home empty handed for the New Year" due to the expropriation of wages by the master. In another song "he owes the master 300 coins" even after working the full season.

[75] Ibid., 99.
[76] Chen Nong, translated in Isaacs 1974: 392–93.
[77] See Chiang 1963 for the hill songs he collected during his childhood days spent in a village of Jiujiang district, northern Jiangxi.
[78] Ho 1954: 126–42.

Beginning in the late nineteenth century, there is an abundance of evidence from novels and folk songs for the crisis of paternalism and qualitative changes in the nature of landlord-peasant relationships. The sudden burgeoning of such novels and folk songs during this period is strongly reflective of the increased domination of members of the landed upper class over the peasantry and their evolution from "paternalistic" figures to "local bullies and evil gentry." The impact of these changes was most strongly experienced by the small rural cultivators of the Xinjiang region in such material terms as changing tenancy conditions and the circumscribing of traditional use-rights and entitlements. The effect was also discerned in new pressures on their surpluses by the landlords, which arose out of the latter's attempt to maximize gains during the uncertain sociopolitical and economic climate.

Chapter Five

Exploitation, Protests, and Uprisings

The crisis of paternalism signified decay of the past order, traditional relationships, and old values in the rural society in China. The failure of the
landed upper classes to maintain their paternalistic obligation to peasants
turned them into landlord-merchant-moneylenders. In the eyes of peasants,
the landed upper class lost their raison d'être. The peasants began to char-
acterize their landlords as "cannibals," "murderers," "robbers," "hard-
fisted," or "iron-hearted"; and one must not ignore the sudden burgeoning
of such phrases in the literary sources and folk songs of the late nineteenth
and early twentieth centuries in an analysis of the agrarian crisis. It would
be naive and simplistic to look for evidence of the rage and injustice felt by
peasants only in such sources. But simple points must be made. When one
examines the evidence and analyzes the changes in the nature of tenancy
relations, including the increasing rents and the introduction of various new
levies by the landlord, the existential dilemma of peasants, which prompted
rage and indignation, becomes manifest. To understand the impact of these
changes in intensifying the grievances of peasants requires an explanation of
the moral economy of peasants, that is, their notion of economic justice and
their view of exploitation—which defined to *them* the legitimacy or illegitimacy of claims on their product.

Peasant land tenure, scholars agree, is characterized by a network of human relations rather than impersonal access to real estate on "Western lines."
T. Shanin thus writes that the peasant economy is embedded within the
rural society and "all the essential units of social action—the family farm,
the village, and the still broader networks of interaction and domination—
appear in the peasantry as the basic units of economic life."[1] The moral economy of peasants closely links the network of social relations and the subsis-

[1] Shanin 1973: 27; see also Saul and Wood 1971; Shanin 1971.

tence economy on the basis of the peasants' conception of moral order. Combined, they form a crucial determinant of the peasants' ultimate security.

In a revealing analysis of the peasants' moral economy, James C. Scott argues that the peasants' conception of moral order can be understood through the subsistence ethic, which arises, in turn, from the existential dilemma of their lives; that is, the fear of dearth, or food shortages.[2] Noting the noncapitalist economic nature of peasants' production, he maintains that the precapitalist village social organization serves above all to secure the subsistence of the community, which is continually threatened by vagaries of natural disasters and external social demands. The compelling need for the security of subsistence forces peasants to minimize the risk element in production and to follow the "safety first" principle in their social and economic behavior.[3]

The "safety first" maxim prevents peasants from following those practices which might endanger their subsistence, and entails various social arrangements within the community to assure, through reciprocal exchange relationships, a minimum subsistence for all inhabitants. In his anthropological study of Chinese villages, Fei Xiaotong notes the significance of a distinct moral standard in the socioeconomic life of peasants that defines to them a range of socioeconomic wants as either proper and necessary or extravagant and luxurious. He writes that "a standard is thus set up to control the amount and type of consumption. This standard is a measurement of plenty and deficiency by people themselves."[4] There is, thus, a precise consensus among the peasantry as to what constitutes subsistence and the reasonable limits of external demands. Peasants evaluate various claims by landlords and the state within this context of the right to subsistence and the norm of reciprocity. Barrington Moore writes: "The contribution of those who fight, rule, and pray must be obvious to the peasant, and the peasant's return payment must not be grossly out of proportion to the services received. Folk conceptions of justice, to put the argument in still another way, do have a rational and realistic basis, and arrangements that depart from this basis are likely to need deception and force the more they do depart."[5]

Peasants feel exploited when external demands violate their minimum subsistence needs and threaten the customary reciprocity in services rendered by the landlord or the state. The major criteria to judge exploitation

[2] Scott 1976: 2–12.
[3] Ibid., 14.
[4] Fei 1939: 119.
[5] Moore 1966: 471.

or social and economic injustice within rural society becomes not only how much the landlord and the state extract from the peasants but what effects their claims have on the minimal subsistence needs of peasants. This view of exploitation is radically different from those notions which attempt to measure the living conditions of peasants solely through the construction of statistical indexes of rent, grain price, grain production, and the like. The denial of the crucial significance of social exchange and redistributive mechanisms in the life of peasants most often results in contradictory conclusions. As Scott aptly indicates, the reduction of rent at the time of a near famine results in an improvement in terms of exchange between tenants and landlords, in spite of the decline in the standard of living, while a deteriorating exchange relationship during the time of a buoyant market might not bring any benefit to tenants.[6] Thus, it is possible that objective exploitation and human experience of exploitation may run in opposite directions. One must examine to what extent new demands affect the reciprocal exchange relationship and the peasants' right to subsistence.

Changes in Rural Xinjiang during the Late Nineteenth and Early Twentieth Centuries

Major consequences of the Taiping Rebellion on the Xinjiang region were the rise of small peasant freeholders and the prevalence of permanent tenancy. The Qing state granted the right of ownership to those peasants who immigrated to Taiping-devastated areas and began tilling unclaimed land. Landlords, on the other hand, provided the incentive of "permanent tenancy" to attract tenants to reclaim their wasteland. These changes were not a result of any transformation of the rural socioeconomic structure but of the necessity to repopulate and reclaim wasteland in order to recover revenue, either through taxes or rents. As both the landlord and the state survived the rebellion and as the political superstructure was still based on the extraction of peasant surpluses, there was, at best, only an illusion of change. The socioeconomic condition of peasants registered no actual improvement in the long run.

Moreover, the suppression of the Taiping Rebellion not only strengthened the ties between the landed upper class and the state, but also estab-

[6] Scott 1976: 161.

lished the former's firm control over rural areas. The weakened Qing state recognized landed-upper-class power to indulge in local militarization and tax collection. The combination of both political and socioeconomic power allowed the members of this class to expropriate peasants' surpluses through tenancy, trade, or taxation to maintain their hegemonic authority. The primary victims of change in the form of landed-upper-class power were small peasant freeholders and permanent tenants; that is, the small rural cultivators.

THE TENANT—THE PREDOMINANT
FIGURE OF THE RURAL WORLD

From the late nineteenth century onward, a remarkable increase in the surplus landholdings of landlords radically altered the somewhat "balanced" pattern of landholding resulting from the Taiping Rebellion. Naturally, this was at the cost of small peasant freeholders, many of whom lost their land and became tenants. Various statistical data, compiled during the early Republican period, confirm the rising number of tenants and the diminishing landholdings of the small peasant freeholders.

In 1911, tenants comprised 71 percent of the total rural population in Jiangxi.[7] According to the land statistics of the Shangye Bu (Department of Commerce), the number of tenants in Jiangxi amounted to 76 percent of the population in 1931. In his survey of different regions of the province, Wang Hao found that during the same period in the Xinjiang region, 40 percent of the population were tenants and 44 percent were part-owners and part-tenants.[8] The counties of Guixi, Leping, and Fouliang contained, respectively, 80, 72, and 85 percent of peasants who depended upon rented land for their subsistence, either fully or partially. The number of tenants who rented all their land was particularly high in southern Jiangxi, where they constituted 78 percent of the population, while the number of part-owners–part-tenants was only about 13 percent.[9] This suggests that between 70 and 80 percent of the peasants in Jiangxi had to rent land in order to maintain their marginal subsistence in the early twentieth century.

Among economic historians, however, there has been a great deal of po-

[7] Li Shiyue 1972: 244.

[8] Wang 1935: 6–8; see also Buck 1937b: 55–56; Yan 1955: 261–78; *JJWT* 1934: 51–106; *JN* 1936: 629–38; *YEWG* 1936: 11–12; Abramson 1935: 89–113.

[9] Wang 1935: 6–8.

lemical discussion over the question of the exact percentage of the different economic categories of peasants in Jiangxi. Mark Elvin, in an article on the early Communist land reform and the Jiangxi rural economy, rejects the assumption that the majority of peasants were tenants. "It is certainly hard to conceive what the 'rural feudal power' spoken of by Mao Tse-tung can have meant in a world such as that described by Buck, where one half of the farmers were owners, less than one third part owners and 17 percent tenants."[10]

The most striking fact in Buck's data, based on surveys of the rice-tea region (this included Jiangxi) by different agencies between 1929 and 1931, is the agreement over the percentage of owners in rural areas.[11] Most of the controversy thus lies in the percentage of part-owners–part-tenants. Given the complexity of the landholding pattern, different economic criteria for the classification of peasants result in startlingly different conclusions. For example, it is not known whether a small landowner who leased out all his unfertile land to tenants and rented fertile land from a landlord for himself would be considered a landlord, part-owner, or tenant. Moreover, the category of part-owner, as will be demonstrated in the discussion below of the landholdings of small peasant freeholders, includes those peasants who had either unproductive or very small patches of land insufficient for the subsistence of their families. Forced to rent land for their survival, they were, therefore, also part-tenants and subject to the same kind of exploitation experienced by the tenants.

The absolute economic categorization of peasants thus does not help in comprehending the rural situation. Instead of presenting a mass of inconclusive statistical data (which are surprisingly abundant for the early Republican period), it is more important to indicate that the critical survival of the majority of peasants depended upon rented land and tenurial conditions. This assumption is based on the result of different surveys and the belief of economic historians in the apparent existence of large numbers of part-owners–part-tenants in rural Jiangxi.[12] If Mark Elvin, relying on one set of data, does not find a large number of economically classifiable tenants, this conclusion does not invalidate the assumption here that between 70 and 80 percent of the peasants in Jiangxi had to rent land for their subsistence.

[10] Elvin 1970: 165; see also Myers 1967: 210–22.

[11] Buck 1937b: 55–56.

[12] In a recent study Esherick (1981) estimates, after taking into account various statistical figures, that in Jiangxi tenants and owner-tenants respectively constituted 39 and 34 percent of the total population, and they together rented roughly 59 percent of the total land.

Before proceeding to an examination of tenurial conditions and the mode
of exploitation, it is necessary also to point out the diminishing landholdings
of small peasant landowners and the nonexistence of a strong class of agricultural laborers in rural Jiangxi. The average landholding of a small peasant
landowner was eight to fifteen mu after the Taiping Rebellion, when Jamieson surveyed the rural area during 1884–1885. However, by 1927, the average landholding of a small peasant landowner had gone below five mu.
According to rural surveys, in the districts of Yiyang, Hengfeng, and Guixi
of the Xinjiang region, the largest number of peasants owned less than five
mu of land.[13] The surveys indicate that the majority of small peasant landowners had land barely sufficient for subsistence. Kang Chao's recent studies based on fish-scale registers and landholding records of the landlord families also confirm the existence of a numerically large number of tenants and
small freeholders with barely sufficient land.[14] Possessing only a tiny
amount, many small peasant freeholders were forced to either rent land as
tenants or find work as laborers.

Scholars have pointed out a very thin distinction between the rich and the
middle peasant in terms of landholding. A 1933 Communist document even
stipulates that those middle peasants who did not own enough land should
be allotted land in the same fashion as poor peasants and workers.[15] Both the
rich and the middle peasants are distinguished on the basis of their differing
exploitation of poor peasants and workers. For example, both may have
owned land, but a rich peasant employed agricultural laborers for a longer
period than a middle peasant. Where neither hired agricultural laborers, a
rich peasant is defined as one who received a comparatively larger share of
the grain from the land and commanded higher interest on loans. Such differentiation between them suggests that neither were large landowners but
were either self-sufficient or the comparatively-better-off peasants in the villages. They did not comprise more than one-third of the total rural population in the Xinjiang region.[16]

Agricultural laborers were always a small minority in rural Jiangxi. The
growth of their numbers was inhibited by the increasing diversion of capital
away from agricultural enterprise and the predominance of landlordism. In

[13] Wang 1935: 2.
[14] See Chao 1981, 1982.
[15] For example, see Hsiao 1969: 103–22, 254–57.
[16] Difficulties of the Communists in correctly identifying each category of peasants in
Jiangxi are noted by Zhang 1984; Xia 1983; *Zhongyang geming genju di shiliao xianbian* 1982,
3:398–414; see also Buck 1937b: 55–56.

1929, only 10 percent of the farms employed agricultural laborers in northern Jiangxi.[17] Full-time laborers were not much in demand, for a big landowner often found it easier and more profitable to leave his land to tenants in exchange for rent. In Jiangxi, most of the full-time laborers worked on monastic and ancestral land. They generally owned their own means of production, such as a hoe, a plow, cattle, and the like. Those laborers who did not possess their own means of production were mostly employed on the farms of the large landowners, and their wages were comparatively lower. Many of them were not paid any wages at all if they were the offspring of poor peasants who were given to large landowners to pay off a debt or were bought during a period of crisis for the poor peasants. The personal lives of such laborers were completely controlled by their masters. For example, they had to have their master's consent in order to marry. Besides working on the master's land, agricultural laborers also performed such domestic chores as cutting firewood, bringing water, cleaning house, and transporting gifts and messages. They were thus servile laborers.

Among agricultural laborers, seasonal laborers, connected with agriculture and agricultural industries, were much in demand. In rural Xinjiang, there were more seasonal laborers than full-time agricultural laborers. Many of them were hired to work on tea plantations and in textile and porcelain factories. Their wages were determined either by the hours they worked or according to their total output. For example, the spinners in the village textile industries received wages commensurate with each *zhang* of cloth they produced. Seasonal laborers, involved in the agricultural process during harvesting or tilling seasons, were generally poor peasants or migratory laborers. Having small plots of land of their own, they often worked on others' land in the village during the peak agricultural periods to earn extra money. Their lives are thus described: "One day they do field work on their land or the land they have leased; the next day they work as hired laborers in someone else's field; and the day after they work as coolies transporting goods from the shops in the city."[18] Migratory laborers were either poor peasants from other regions or workers from the city who found harvest work more remunerative in labor-short areas. Unlike full-time agricultural laborers, seasonal laborers were free from precapitalist bonded relationships.

The need for both full-time and seasonal laborers varied from area to area. They were less in demand in those villages where a precapitalist labor ex-

[17] Wu 1935: 11–12; for the discussion below see also Abramson 1935; Min 1920; *Agrarian China* [1938] 1976: 69–79, Tawney [1932] 1966.

[18] *Agrarian China* [1938] 1976: 71.

change or a self-help system predominated. This system was more prevalent in the less commercialized and tenant-dominated areas, simply because there was not enough surplus cash or grain to pay wages, and smaller landholdings did not require many laborers. Tenants usually borrowed a hoe or cattle for a day or two in exchange for a certain customary period of field work.

The lack of a large class of agricultural laborers and the decline in the landholdings of freeholders thus polarized the rural social structure between the landed upper class on the one hand, and rent-paying peasants, or the class of exploited small rural cultivators, on the other. In the absence of any better phrase, I have used "the class of small rural cultivators" to denote declining post-Taiping small peasant freeholders and tenants. It was this class that grew out of the post-Taiping changes in land tenure and was typical of rural Xinjiang in the early twentieth century. Its existential condition, to a great extent, depended upon the nature of its relationship with the landed upper class.

Tenurial Conditions
and the Mode of Exploitation

As the forms of landed-upper-class power changed, the traditional paternal relationship between members of this class and peasants began to break down. The impact of the subsequent crisis was most strongly felt by peasants in the changing conditions of their tenure. Landlords imposed many new demands and renounced their traditional obligations to provide tenants' subsistence. The prevalent permanent tenancy system, in which tenants enjoyed almost as much right to land as did the freeholders, began to be replaced by those tenancy arrangements which ignored tenants' need for the security of, and their right to, subsistence. New demands and coercion by landlords altered the basic nature of this tenancy system to the extent that it became difficult or impossible for tenants to maintain their permanent rights. Various tactics, used by landlords to curtail tenants' rights, are described in documents from different regions of Jiangxi.

A 1924 document from Hengfeng district establishes that the landowner who asked peasants to till his land was known as a *bu tian* (tributary), and the tenant was called the *tao* (lessee).[19] There were two copies of the tenancy contract. The *bu zi* (tributary document) copy was kept by the tenant and the *tao zi* (lessee document) copy was held by the landlord. The tenant had

[19] *ZNYS* 1957, 2:88.

to pay a security deposit (*ding jia*), the amount of which depended upon the size of the land and mutual agreement. Both bu zi and tao zi copies of the contract recorded the amount of rent to be paid and the discount to be granted during any disaster period. The tenant who kept the bu zi copy had the right to permanent tenancy. Only when he delayed his payment of rent could a landlord legally take back land, either for himself or to rent it to other tenants. The tenant could also mortgage or sell his right to tenancy simply by signing an agreement stating his desire to withdraw (*tui qian*).

In both cases a landlord returned deposits to tenants after deducting the amount of rent owed. On the other hand, when a landowner transferred his right to land to another landowner, the new owner was supposed to be responsible for collecting the deposits made by the tenants from the old owner. If he did not do so, it was his responsibility to return a deposit anytime a tenant chose to withdraw. However, in actual practice, landowners never returned deposits to the tenants. New landowners frequently complained that they were instructed neither about the deposits nor their amounts by the old owner. When such cases went to court, they were usually resolved in favor of the owners, who had begun to exercise a great deal of influence over the local administration.

Another practice frequently encountered in the southern part of this district was that the bu zi copy of the contract (kept by the tenant as legal proof of his surface rights to land) was not signed by the landlord, while the tenant was forced to sign the tao zi copy of the contract that was kept by the landlord.[20] While in such cases the landlord usually demanded a lower security deposit, the tenant's mobility was restricted. The tenant could not sell, transfer, or mortgage his rights to others as his private property. Moreover, since a tenant had no legal evidence of his rights, a landowner could claim back the land at any time. Such a breach of contract seems to have occurred often when a tenant refused to pay increased rent or new surcharges, or when the landlord viewed his tenant as lazy and unproductive.

An example from Yichun district of Jiangxi is instructive in this regard.[21] It demonstrates the tendency of the landlord to extract the maximum possible surplus from permanent tenants by arbitrarily changing the silver standard. In 1929, in Yichun district, the educational land of Chang Li College was originally the property of the ancestors of the current permanent tenants. For some unknown reason, ancestors of these tenants were forced to

[20] *ZNYS* 1957, 2:88.
[21] *ZNYS* 1957, 3:254.

sell the bottom-soil rights to their land in exchange for surface rights. This land was later seized by an overbearing member of the gentry, one Li Tianrui. To increase profits, Li called a meeting of the managers of educational land from the four districts of Yi (chun), Fen (yi), Ping (xiang), and Wan (zai) and decided to increase rent by changing the silver standard. The traditional standard was six qian and five fen of silver, equal to one diao and 950 wen of copper cash. This was changed into a grain system whereby one dan of grain was equal to ten dong, which in monetary value was the equivalent of three silver dollars. According to this new system, the traditional measurement of 1 dan = 10 dong = 100 sheng was altered to 1 dan = 10 dong = 150 sheng. This made tenants pay more as rent.

Confronted with such demands, the tenants of Li Tianrui delayed their payment of rent. The landlord then dispatched the court police and tax collectors to the village with the cooperation of the district magistrate Ou Yangxiang. The tenants were beaten and their dwellings were destroyed. Finally, tenants Su Dongcheng, Yuan Manrui, Qian Licheng, Li Yongxing, and Wang Zhengxiang were arrested and held for a ransom of eighty-four foreign silver dollars. They were also forced to sign documents restricting their permanent tenancy rights. Such demands and coercion by landlords, as the narrator of this incident remarks, "completely changed the meaning of permanent tenancy."

Such oppressive tactics by landlords had become prevalent by the early twentieth century. These indicate landlords' unwillingness to maintain traditional reciprocal exchange relationships with the tenants and their desire to make tenancy arrangements flexible enough to squeeze cultivators at will. It is difficult to point out exactly when permanent tenancy was replaced, for the change took place over a long period in the late nineteenth and early twentieth centuries. But by the latter part of the period, new forms of tenancy predominated in the rural structure of Jiangxi.

New systems of tenancy, which became prevalent in Jiangxi in the early twentieth century, were known as *ding qi* (limited-period tenancy) and *bu ding qi* (tenancy with no fixed period). In the Xinjiang area, the average length of the fixed-period tenancy did not even cover the major portion of a tenant's productive years. In most cases, it was for a maximum of ten years and a minimum of one year.[22] However, before the beginning of the peasant movement in 1927, the bu ding qi tenants dominated rural areas. These tenants had no guarantee of the right to use land after a harvest. In such tenancy

[22] Wu 1935: 12–13.

agreements no fixed period was mentioned. According to the 1924 data, tenants having rights to use land for less than a year constituted 65 percent of all tenants in Xinjiang, while the number of fixed-period tenants was 25 percent and that of permanent tenants had shrunk to only 10 percent. By 1934, approximately 70 percent of tenants belonged to the bu ding qi category.[23]

The enormous increase in ding qi and bu ding qi types of tenancy radically reduced the security of subsistence enjoyed by a tenant under permanent tenancy. The tenant was now completely dependent upon the landlord for the grant of usufructuary rights to land year after year. He had no other option but to comply with any demands by the landlord if he wanted to maintain the security of his tenure. He could neither sell, mortgage, nor transfer his rights, nor could he leave his land until the harvest season was over. The landlord, on the other hand, had far more flexibility in evicting the tenant. Any delay in the payment of rent was a common excuse to force the tenant out. The landlord could also demand the eviction of the tenant simply by accusing him of being lazy, a bad cultivator, or an inefficient night soil gatherer, or by merely indicating his desire to till the land himself. It might seem, as Chen Han-seng writes, "that no landlord can afford to be arbitrary in shortening or lengthening a lease to suit his own purpose, for the tenant would soon find it less safe to lease his land than that of other owners, and accordingly he would find that the bids for renting his land are lower than those received by other landlords. But, actually, this seemingly obvious cycle of economic cause and effect, like so many others, does not take place in China. The land hunger is so great that a landlord can easily find a new tenant at any time that a lease falls in."[24] Thus only the tenant bore the burden caused by the insecurity of tenure.

The significance of these new systems of tenancy lies not in the creation of a capitalist wage-labor type of agriculture but in the withdrawal of earlier guarantees of the tenant's right to subsistence. New systems neither ensured the earlier feudal type of subsistence protection inherent in the lord-tenant relationship nor established the capitalist type of pure economic relations in which wages guaranteed minimal subsistence to ensure efficient production. The tenant was still at the mercy of the landlord, and land was still the major source of his family's survival. He therefore paid excessive rent and levies in order to keep the usufructuary rights to land even though the nature of the rent and levies ignored his subsistence requirement.

---

[23] Yan 1955: 324.
[24] Chen Han-seng 1936: 50.

In rural Xinjiang, changes in the length of tenancy were accompanied by a shift from sharecropping to the system of fixed-rent payment either in grain or cash. In the traditional sharecropping system, as exemplified by the "substitute cultivator," the landlord assumed all the risks of agriculture and met the tenant's minimum subsistence needs. Under this system, the tenant tilled the land for the landlord not in exchange for rent but for labor. He was essentially a full-time agricultural laborer, except for the one major difference that he did not receive a fixed wage. All means of production—agricultural tools, seeds, fertilizers, farming cattle—as well as a house were supplied by the landlord. The tenant, in addition to tilling the land, served his landlord's household in many ways. During his time away from the fields, he cut wood, fetched water, worked as a courier, and performed other services. In exchange, he received 20 to 30 percent of the harvest, leaving the remaining 70 to 80 percent for the landlord. The tenant was required to feast the landlord with warmth and courtesy when he came to collect the harvest. In a disaster year or in a financially difficult period, the landlord generally provided either grain or cash to the tenant to ensure his family's subsistence needs. This earliest form of tenancy still existed in Xinjiang, especially in the districts of Yugan and Guixi, at the beginning of the twentieth century, but by then less than 10 percent of the tenants were involved in it.[25]

The two most prevalent forms of sharecropping in Xinjiang were the "three-cornered" and the "four-cornered" systems, whereby both landlord and tenant shared the risks of a bad harvest and profited during a good agricultural season. In the "three-cornered" system, the yield was divided into three portions by ropes or sticks on the field, out of which the landlord took two portions, leaving one for the tenant. Similarly, in the "four-cornered" system, the harvest was divided into four equal portions of which the share of the landlord was three portions.[26] While these systems did not fully ensure the tenants against a bad harvest, equal sharing of the risks by both landlord and tenant protected the latter during extreme situations. Moreover, as the landlord's income depended upon the yield, he was as much interested in the progress of the harvest as the tenant. He was still not completely withdrawn from the agricultural enterprise.

During the early twentieth century, however, fixed-rent payment in grain or cash, and not sharecropping, had become the predominant part of ten-

[25] Wang 1935: 9–10.
[26] Ibid., 11.

ancy. This was a result of the increasing withdrawal of the landlord from agricultural enterprise and the village. The renunciation of paternalistic obligations was part of this withdrawal as well. In this new fixed-rent system, the landlord completely abdicated his responsibility in the agricultural process, and all the risks of production were now transferred to the tenant. Comparing fixed rents with sharecropping, Scott writes, "Fixed rents—in cash or in kind—would in safety-first terms be the most onerous. The amplitude of crop yield fluctuations are reflected in full in the tenant's income, and while the sharecropping system claims no rent if there is no harvest, the fixed rent system demands its inexorable due even if not a single stalk matures."[27] Thus, with more and more tenants belonging to the fixed-rent system, as table 5.1 indicates, the landlord assured himself a steady source of income, while the conditions of tenants fluctuated according to the yield in any particular year.

It has generally been argued that the fixed-rent system provided tenants incentive to increase productivity, for any production over the fixed amount

TABLE 5.1
*Percentage of Tenants in Each Type
of Rent System in the 1930s*

| District | Sharecropping | Fixed-Rent System | | Substitute-Cultivator System |
		In Grain	In Cash	
Zixi	10	30	60	
Hukou	7	90	10(?)	3
Fouliang	12	60	20	8
Leping	2	60	38	
Boyang	5	80	10	5
Duchang	15	80		5
Xingzi	25	70	5	
Dean		100		
Yugan	10	70	10	10
Wannian	25	74	1	
Yiyang	25	75		
Guixi	20	60	10	10
Jinxi	20	50	10	20
Jinshu	10	60	30	

Source: Wu 1935: 11–12.

[27] Scott 1976: 46.

of rent belonged to tenants.[28] A tenant could use fertilizers and plant new, improved varieties of grains to raise the output from his field and consequently his income. But, in fact, there is no evidence that the tenant's situation in Jiangxi improved in the early twentieth century, for the fixed-rent system was accompanied by a simultaneous shortening of the period of tenancy. The short length of tenancy, which in most cases neither exceeded one year nor guaranteed renewal of the contract, inhibited any effort by the tenant to improve the land in order to increase production. He was concerned only with producing enough for his family's subsistence. In this situation, the material basis for any capitalist rationalization simply did not exist.

The most frequent complaint of the landlords in Jiangxi, as Wu Shunyu notes, was that tenants did not put as much energy into the landlord's land as they would have into their own land and willfully wasted the leased land. If a tenant was not going to till the land, he did not fertilize it. The subsequent poor harvest then became a pretext to demand a reduction in rent. In fact, at the time of leaving the land, tenants often dug up earth to make bricks and earned cash by selling them.[29] Besides this, the landlord's imposition of higher rent on poorer-quality land and the fragmentation of his surplus land into tiny parcels to rent to tenants were essentially countermeasures against the tenants' destruction of his property. These severely restricted any profits to tenants from the fixed-rent system.

Rent for land was fixed on a seemingly contrary scale: the better the quality of land, the less the amount of rent. For example, in Pengze district of Xinjiang, the fixed rent in comparison with the per-mu grain yield was 42 percent on the best land, 45 percent on the medium-grade land, and 72 percent on the worst land,[30] a fact puzzling to most classical economic rationalists. But it becomes understandable in light of the economic rationale of the landlord masterminding the arrangement. Chen Han-seng explains, "The

---

[28] For example, Rawski (1972: 150) writes that "of three kinds of rent systems, we have seen that cash rents were most, and share-cropping least advantageous to the tenant, with fixed rent falling in between." Similarly, quoting from Japanese sources, Myers (1970: 229) argues that "in the land tenure system where rent is a fixed amount payable in kind, tenants are inclined to use more fertilizer. As a result, income rises and any extra goes entirely to the tenant. Under the share rent system, even though the tenant introduced more fertilizer, only a part of the increased gain in productivity went to him while the remainder went to the landlord. The tenant had little incentive to add more fertilizer, and the good management of the land developed more slowly."

[29] Wu 1935: 35–36.

[30] Ibid., 19.

tenant of good land often supplies more means of production per mou [mu] than other tenants because such investment is certain to pay. Improving the soil, he is actually in a better position to bargain with the landlord who cannot afford to lease his good land to a tenant who cannot or will not keep the fertility of soil. It is for this reason that the landlord gets less rent from the tenant of the best land, paradoxical as it may seem, than he gets from the tenant of the medium grade land."[31] Thus, the poor paid more. On the worst-quality land, the landlord fixed higher rent so that the tenant was forced to improve overall productivity of the land in order to meet the demand for higher rent.

The same logic was at work in the fragmentation of land into tiny pieces for rent. The landlord, who possessed a large amount of surplus land, usually leased his land only in tiny pieces. A study of a similar situation in India explains the underlying reasons for such practices. It found that landlords favored offering tenants land in small parcels so that the latter would work harder and use land in the best manner. The logic was as follows: "It would seem that a tenant family, with limited alternative resources of income, is bound to work intensively to meet its needs, and the larger the family the greater the compulsion to do so. Additionally, an insecure tenant may want to prove himself 'efficient' by putting in hard labour as he is afraid of losing the lease otherwise."[32]

Kang Chao's studies of the areas adjoining the Xinjiang region indicate that on average a landlord leased somewhere from thirty to forty plots to tenants. As Kang has also demonstrated, in only very rare cases did a landlord own more than several hundred mu of land, so the average size leased to tenants must have been very small.[33] A similar situation has been noted by Muramatsu in his study of Fei clan landlords' records. In spite of their large domain, the average size of the individually leased plot was 2.65 mu. He thus remarks that in "pre-war Central China the average generally accepted as necessary for subsistence was 3 *mu per capita* (not per family). So it is clear that the scale of cultivation undertaken by the tenants who farmed the lands managed by the landlord bursaries was really very small, and not very far above bare subsistence level."[34]

Moreover, the highly unpredictable agricultural cycle prevented tenants from enjoying the fruits of the fixed-rent system. As mentioned earlier, in

[31] Chen Han-seng 1936: 56.
[32] Bharadwaj and Das 1975: 237.
[33] Chao 1981, 1982.
[34] Muramatsu 1966: 577.

the fixed-rent system, the tenant's subsistence needs were completely ignored and he was forced to pay a fixed amount of rent even when none of
his stalks matured. The burden on the fixed-rent-paying tenants is evident
when one finds that between 1898 and 1911, there were eleven years in
which the state had to grant temporary relief to various districts in Jiangxi
because of natural disasters (see table 5.2). An average of eighteen districts
were granted tax relief in each year of a great disaster. In 1903, thirty districts of the province suffered from damage by flood and drought. In 1907
and in 1908, natural disasters created food shortages in twenty-seven and
twenty-eight districts respectively.[35] In such an abnormal agricultural cycle,
the tenant had no opportunity to produce enough even for his own subsistence. In a bad year he lost more than he received in a good year. Thus, the
fixed-rent system did not improve socioeconomic conditions of tenants but
helped landlords to stabilize their income at the expense of tenants.

When one examines the changing nature of tenancy arrangements in conjunction with the deterioration of the paternal relationship between the landlord and the tenant, the subsistence dilemma of tenants becomes more dis-
cernible. New practices and demands by the landlord reflect not only his
abdication of the moral obligation to guarantee the tenant's subsistence needs
but also his general withdrawal from agricultural enterprise. In Jiangxi, a
survey of landlords' behavior during the early twentieth century notes that
out of forty-five districts of the province, in twenty-four the landlords were
not even interested in going to their villages to see the harvest and collect the
rent. The rent was either collected by the agents of a landlord or was taken
by the tenant to the landlord's house. In fifteen districts, the landlord came
down to the village to collect rent; and in the remaining six districts, there
was no fixed practice.[36] Thus, the landlord-tenant relationship was becoming increasingly limited to the extraction of rent.

As the landlord began to withdraw from the agricultural enterprise, the
customary practice of reducing or canceling rent also declined. The fixed-
rent system, which was popularly known as the "iron-rent" system, stipulated no reduction in rent even when the harvest was destroyed.[37] Where
there was a provision for the lowering of rent in a disaster year, the amount
of discount was to be decided by the landlord. The standard practice in
Xinjiang was to invite the landlord to inspect the land and the yield. He
then decided whether or not the demand for a discount was justifiable. If he

[35] Kupper 1971: 28–29.
[36] Wu 1935: 22–24.
[37] Wang 1935: 10.

TABLE 5.2
Frequency of Disasters in Jiangxi Province,
1847–1910

Year	Number of Districts Affected	Nature of Disasters	Year	Number of Districts Affected	Nature of Disasters
1847	43	Flood, drought	1891	21	Flood, drought, hailstorm
1848	21	Flood			
1849	18	Flood	1892	20	Flood, drought
1850	21	Flood, drought	1893	1	Flood, drought
1851	12	Flood	1894	—	—
1852	13	Flood, drought, soldiers	1895	21	Flood, drought, insects
1853	—	—	1896	17	Flood, drought,
1854	20	Flood, drought, soldiers	1897	27	Flood, drought, insects
1855	36	Soldiers	1898	28	Flood, drought,
1856	7	Soldiers			insects
1857–62	—	Soldiers	1899	35	Flood, drought, storm, insects
1863	20	Flood, drought, soldiers	1900	31	Flood, drought, storm, insects
1864–78	—	—	1901	29	Flood, drought, storm
1879	29	Flood			
1880	30	Flood, drought	1902	22	Flood, drought, storm, insects
1881	—	—			
1882	35	Flood, drought	1903	17	Flood
1883	35	Flood, drought	1904	—	—
1884	19	Flood, drought	1905	27	Flood, drought
1885	25	Flood, drought	1906	25	Flood, drought
1886	14	Flood, drought	1907	24	Flood, drought
1887	34	Flood, drought	1908	32	Flood, drought
1888	33	Flood, drought	1909	21	Flood, drought
1889	14	Flood, drought	1910	14	Flood, drought
1890	18	Flood, drought			

Source: Statistical data compiled by the Economic Research Group of the Chinese Academy of Social Science, in *ZNYS* 1957, 1: 721–22.

found it was, either a discount was granted to the tenant or the existing crop was divided equally. In the districts of Shangrao, Yugan, Yujiang, and Jiujiang, the custom was generally to divide the crop equally after a bad harvest, but in Yiyang and Guixi districts, the reduction of the rent depended upon the subjective estimate made by the landlord.[38] In the latter case, the reduction varied according to the good or bad nature of the landlord. Since the landlord most often did not come down to the village to collect rent, he was not able to estimate objectively any partial loss to a tenant's harvest, especially since his agents generally did not accurately report the nature of the harvest. And even when there was a disastrous harvest, if the landlord visited the village at the request of his tenant, he expected to be served the customary feast.[39]

Other essential services traditionally provided by the landlord also were reduced significantly. The landlord was no longer willing to supply all the means of production and customary rewards to the tenants. In the districts of Hukou, Shangrao, and Yugan, the only reward a tenant received was a one-time gift of food or a 260-wen tip when he went to the landlord's house to pay the rent. In Yiyang, a landlord provided a grain loan and a room, but no agricultural tools were supplied. If the tenant did not own tools, he had to rent them. In Guixi, while agricultural tools and a waterwheel or a windwheel were supplied to the tenant, no rooms or plowing animals were given. In some places, only seeds were delivered during a bad harvest year.[40] These practices suggest the breakdown of the earlier "substitute-cultivator" system, to which the origin of the tenancy system can be traced and under which the landlord provided all the essential tools of agriculture to the tenants.

The growing imbalance in the reciprocal exchange relationship between the landlord and the tenant is reflected in the fact that while the landlord repudiated his obligations to tenants, the tenant was still required to demonstrate his deference by advancing cash gifts to or arranging feasts for the landlord and his agents. Traditionally, these gifts and feasts were means by which a tenant expressed his gratitude to the landlord for various favors. In any given year, there were several occasions when the landlord, tax collector, and the middleman were feasted by the tenant to express the harmonious nature of the relationship. While most of the tenant's services to the landlord were customary, by the early twentieth century these had become fixed to the extent that an equivalent amount was demanded in cash or in

[38] See Wang 1935: 10; Wu 1935: 30–32.
[39] Wu 1935: 35.
[40] Ibid., 35.

grain as levies without even considering the situation of the tenant. More-over, many once-only occasions, such as the beginning or the end of the tenancy contract, turned into annual events with the shortening of the pe-riod of tenancy. This, too, provided more occasions for imposing and col-lecting levies.

Among the most common levies in Jiangxi was the fee for the welfare of the landlord's family, known as *xiao zu qian* (small rent money). *Luo nian qian* (money for passing a year) was a levy demanded after the completion of an agricultural year to defray the landlord's inspection expenses. Even when the landlord preferred not to inspect the land, the levy had to be paid. The system of *yu zu* (advance rent), by which a tenant was required to pay one dan of rice to secure tenancy rights for the next year, was also common in Jiangxi. A horse expense (*fu ma fei*) was paid by the tenant at the time of the renewal of the contract to compensate the landlord for the expense of his visit. Presentations of firewood, chickens, ducks, and fish were required at several occasions as were feasts, including meat and wine, for the landlord and tax collectors. The custom of *zu tian qing jiu* (feast with wines at the time of the beginning of the harvest), *zu fan* (feast on the occasion of the rent payment), *xiang zhu huan dao liang dong jiu* (feast for the renewal of the ten-ancy contract), *jiu fei* (wine fee for the tax collector), among others, are ex-amples of a large number of such levies.[41]

Without the landlord's reciprocal performance of his paternal duties, these feasts lost their traditional symbolic meaning for the tenants. Forced to arrange a lavish feast according to the traditional customs, the tenant found these occasions burdensome. Chiang Yee, son of a landlord in the Xinjiang region who was sent to represent his family at such a customary feast, was appalled by the number of dishes served by the tenant. But his family had warned him beforehand that he was not to grant any favor re-quested by the tenant after the dinner. His experience is worth quoting.

During harvest time, when the rice grain was all gathered, our tenant farmers called on us again and invited some elders to go to the country to see the year's crop and settle payment. This was only a formality, since the payment was usually arranged beforehand, but it was a pleasant social occasion. . . . Before I set out my uncle told me that I had no special duty to perform and was merely to enjoy the good dinner provided; I was to be polite and observe care-

---

[41] Tanaka 1930: 115–16; Wang 1935: 16–17; Wu 1935: 26–28. For the development of se-curity deposits and the advance-rent system, which secured tenants the right to till the next season, see Jiang 1980.

fully the customary procedure, and if the tenant should mention prices or ask a favor, I was to give no definite answer. . . .

It made me feel odd that they [tenants] did not address me on this occasion by name but called me shao-hsien-sheng [xiao xiansheng] (Young Sir). . . . I wondered why the farmers spent so much money on this dinner, for I had never seen them eat and drink like this during my year among them when their meals had invariably been simple, meat and chicken being included only very occasionally. Here there were two huge chickens besides other meats (chiefly pork). . . . At the end of dinner I asked that my extra bowls should be given to some of my old playfellows. . . . One of the farmers seemed pleased that I should remember my old friends, but another teased me and said he would have put more into his own belly if he had known that I was going to give my share away. After the dinner, the farmers began to talk business, and I had to avoid the issue by saying that it would be better to leave that to my uncle.[42]

This reflects how much such feasts cost to peasants who ordinarily subsisted on frugal diets. Further, it indicates the prevalent pattern that was marked by landlords' increasing unwillingness to reciprocate the ganqing demonstrated by the peasants. These feasts had thus lost their traditional significance of creating a morally cohesive pattern in rural relationships and had turned into a meaningless and burdensome exercise for the peasants.

In Jiangxi, as mentioned earlier, the tenants often complained about the custom of arranging a feast when, during a bad year, the landlord visited them to inspect the harvest and to estimate any reduction in the rent demanded. These occasions forced the tenants to take out loans or pawn their tools or clothes. It was therefore not just a case of an occasional small expense that did not affect their basic economic condition; feasts meant the accumulation of more debts at higher interest rates. The problem was serious enough to warrant the attention later of the peasant movement in Jiangxi. Not surprisingly, one of the major demands was the abolition of such customs.

With the growth of short-length tenancy, the landlord also demanded a security deposit. Paid by the tenant at the time the tenancy contract was signed, it secured the landlord against any threat to his rent or any attempt by the tenant to escape after the harvest without paying rent. In most cases, the deposit was either close to or more than the amount of rent. In a study of northern Jiangxi during 1927, Tanaka illustrates that the amount of the

---

[42] Chiang 1963: 240–42.

security deposit demanded by the landlord ranged from three to five yuan per mu.[43]

In many districts, payment of the full deposit was generally beyond the means of the poor peasant signing a tenancy contract. He usually borrowed the sum and paid the interest on it periodically. In Wuhu, Guichi, and Tongcheng districts of southern Anhui, it was a customary practice for the tenant to deposit only about one-third of the total security deposit and then to pay an annual interest of six to seven catties of rice on each yuan owed. This was called "interest rice," and the land on which the deposit was owed was known as "interest land." Moreover, theoretically, the deposit was to be returned to the tenant after the expiration of the contract. But, if a tenant delayed his payment of rent or was short of rent, the landlord most often confiscated the deposit.[44]

The short length of tenancy also provided the landlord with an opportunity to increase the amount of the deposit each time a new tenancy contract was signed or an old one was renewed. In many cases, the increase in the security deposit was the result of the landlord's practice of shifting the burden of taxes onto the tenants. Chi Min-chiu writes: "Taxation certainly had much to do with such a rapid increase, for it was difficult to oppose a tax increase or to advance the rate of rent, and thus the landlord was forced to raise rent deposits by various means."[45] In the worst cases, as in Baoshan near Shanghai, the security deposit increased 300 percent within a short span of ten years (1923–1933), and in regions where the income of the tenant was slightly higher, the deposit went up about 500 percent.[46]

Besides such levies, the landlord often employed dubious means to extract more from peasants. One of the most common practices was the introduction of a bigger basket to measure the amount of grain rent. In some districts of the Xinjiang region, the rent-measuring basket was five sheng bigger than the standard *shi*. The agents of landlords made sure that a tenant did not fill the basket with wet or adulterated grain. In the majority of districts, the landlord often did not sign the tenancy contract, but the tenant was required to hand over his signed contract. Oral tenancy contracts provided an opportunity for landlords to either increase the rent or evict the tenant without any legal constraint. Expenses for dyke building or repairing, originally borne by the landlord, were also charged to the tenants. In some areas, a fee

[43] Tanaka 1930: 115–16.
[44] *Agrarian China* [1938] 1976: 98–99.
[45] Ibid., 101.
[46] Ibid.

for bandit protection was included in the rent. Tenants in Jiangxi also often complained of the practice of *zuo shikang* (to sit on the stone wall), which customarily required tenants to pay frequent courtesy calls on the landlord with gifts and inquire if the latter needed any service. They were not supposed to enter the inner hall of the landlord's mansion but to wait by the stone foundation of the outside door until the landlord found time to meet with them.[47] These practices and demands of landlords suggest the extent to which relations became strained between them and their tenants. The traditional redistributive mechanism of the village community was disrupted. The tenant was left with no subsistence options and, most important, no patron to fall back on. Thus even a slight fluctuation in rent became a threat to his survival.

In a tenant's budget, rent was the most onerous item of expenditure, often taking more than half of his income in a harvest year. But the introduction of the fixed-rent system and the growing reluctance of the landlord to meet the subsistence needs of peasants during periods of harvest failure not only transferred all the risks of agricultural enterprise to the tenant but also significantly reduced his income. As the landlord stabilized his income at the expense of tenants, any decline in the yield, under the fixed-rent system, raised the percentage of the tenant's total income or harvest to be paid as rent. This consequently unbalanced his budget, even if the amount of rent did not change over the period. In the Xinjiang region between 1864 and 1927, although in some districts rent remained constant, in many it had enormously increased by the early twentieth century. The pressure of rent had become so acute that a tenant often found it hard to pay even in an agriculturally good year, and a bad year generally forced him either to take out a loan at a high interest rate, to resist payment of rent, or to starve to death.

In any study of the amount of rent in rural China, the wide variety of rents makes accurate estimation extremely difficult. In Jiangxi, there were different types of rent related to different tenancy systems, and the amount fluctuated according to the quality of land. Tanaka Tadao notes fifteen major types of rent prevalent in the province during the early twentieth century: (1) *gan zu* (dryland or upland rent); (2) *shui zu*, or *wen jie* (wetland rent); (3) *zao zu* (interest-land rent, which meant, for example, that if a tenant borrowed ten dollars from the landlord, he worked to pay one dan of rice as interest in the second year); (4) *ban zu* (early rent, which involved early payment of half of the rent to pay land taxes); (5) *wan zu* (late rent, which meant

[47] Wang 1935: 16; Wu 1935: 35–36.

that half of the rent was to be paid in the second half of the year to pay land taxes); (6) *zhe zu* (this rent was paid with a quantity of grain equivalent in cash value to the amount of the rent, and since the price of grain usually fell at the time of yield, this provided an opportunity for the landlord to collect a large amount of grain at low prices); (7) *zhun zu* (rent on the traditional banner land, which was relatively higher than other rents); (8) *tian zu* (bottom-soil rent); (9) *pi zu* (surface-soil rent); (10) *shan zu* (rent on the mountainous land); (11) *yuan zu* (rent for the vegetable gardens); (12) *yu zu* (rent for the tilling rights during the next year); (13) *qian zu* (rent in cash); (14) *mao zu* (rent at the time of returning the sickle to the landlord after harvest); and (15) *gong zu* (labor rent).[48] Such a wide variety of rents resulted in great disparity, not only in each district but also within villages in a district.

Sufficient information about the amount of rent as compared with the total yield is not available in the historical records of the late nineteenth century. There are, however, some scattered references. In his study of the land tenure of Jiangxi in 1883–1884, Jamieson mentions that the yield per mu in a good year on the best land was about four dan of unhulled rice, out of which the landlord took two dan as rent. The winter wheat crop, which yielded one to two dan per mu, belonged to the tenants.[49] After the Taiping Rebellion, the average rent in Jiangxi was thus about 40 to 50 percent of the harvest.

Local gazetteers of Jiangxi give the amount of rent fixed for educational and temple land. If these amounts are examined, estimating an average yield of three dan per mu, a rent figure close to 45 percent of the harvest becomes evident. For example, the local gazetteer of Yiyang district provides the following information on the amount of rent on its 12.3 mu of educational land: According to its statistics, the village of Taotanpan had four patches of educational land consisting of 2, 3.3, 2, and 2.3 mu, on which a rent of, respectively, 2 dan, 5 dou; 4 dan; 2 dan, 8 dou; and 3 dan, 2 dou was paid. In Dadangpan village, a rent of 3 dan, 5 dou was collected on educational land of 2.3 mu. In the village of Hujiawenqian, on .4 mu of land the yearly rent was 5 dou.[50] Perkins's estimate of the average rice yield per mu for Guangxin fu, to which the district of Yiyang belonged, is 2.5 dan.[51] This indicates a rent of about 50 percent of the harvest. However, before the peasant move-

[48] Tanaka 1930: 113.

[49] Jamieson 1888: 97–98.

[50] *ZNYS* 1957, 1:269–70. This monumental work also cites rent data from the district gazetteers of Guangfeng and Hukou of the Xinjiang region. Their figures are not very different from those for Yiyang district.

[51] Perkins 1969: 320.

ment of 1927, as Tanaka's study indicates, in many parts of northern Jiangxi the amount of rent demanded reached more than 70 percent of the yield.[52]

As the amount of rent was fixed according to the total yield in a good year, any fall in production significantly raised the total percentage of rent in comparison with the total harvest. As noted above, between 1898 and 1911 Jiangxi suffered from natural disasters for a total of eleven years. Given this frequency of natural disasters, one can assume that more often than not tenants ended up paying a larger percentage of their total harvest than what was fixed. Moreover, it has been established that a tenant, besides paying rent, was also required to contribute cash or grain for surtaxes and levies demanded by the landlord. If that amount is added on, the amount of rent actually paid increases considerably.[53] For example, D. K. Lieu notes that in the Zhangshu district of southern Jiangsu, the rent was fixed at 50 to 60 percent of the harvest, but in 1926 when an investigation was made, it was found that the actual payment averaged 70 percent of the harvest.[54]

As mentioned earlier, the amount of rent was usually higher on the worst-quality land, and such land was given to those tenants who did not own their means of production. This indicates that the pressure of rent was higher on poor tenants than on those who cultivated the best land of the landlords and owned their means of production. For example, in the districts of Leping and Pengze, tenants paid 40 to 45 percent of the total harvest on the best-quality land and 55 to 70 percent on the worst-quality land.[55]

The growing subsistence problem of tenants can, perhaps, be best com-

[52] Tanaka 1930: 113–14.

[53] Rawski (1972: 144–46) writes that "historians who have cited rent figures to argue that tenants were oppressed must remember that frequently the rents were not paid." In support of this argument, she mentions the incidences of default in rent payments with impunity noted in Hunan gazetteers and in the Jiangsu bursary records studied by Yuzi Muramatsu (1966). More-over, in the absence of any evidence that the rising rent forced tenants into nonfarm activities, it has been implicitly assumed that the landlord in early-twentieth-century China was not exploitative and peasants did not experience any hardships. These points seem unconvincing. Muramatsu (1966: 599) himself points out that only in rare cases did the rent remain unpaid for more than a year, for a tenant who delayed paying rent was often publicly beaten, arrested, or locked up in a cangue. The rural world was, therefore, not characterized by stronger tenants but by "powerful domination which landlord and bursary were able to exercise over their land and tenants" in the early twentieth century. I have already indicated in chapter 1 that without putting cases of defaulter tenants in a historical context, any conclusions derived from these incidences would be meaningless. Following Scott (1976), I feel that the amount of rent was not as crucial for tenants as the new forms of tenancy systems that ignored their minimum subsistence needs.

[54] Liew 1928: 466.

[55] Wu 1935: 19; see also *YEWG* 1934: 51.

prehended by an examination of rural indebtedness. In 1933, a survey indicated that 98 percent of the peasants in Jiangxi were in debt.[56] This figure was the highest in central China. While such a high percentage of indebted peasants can be attributed to the destruction caused by the civil war between the Communists and the Nationalists, their number before the Communist movement could not have been less than 60 percent of the total population. The same study indicates that out of 98 percent of the indebted peasants, 57 percent were in perpetual debt.[57] Buck's survey for the period 1929–1931 also points out that in two districts of northern Jiangxi, Pengze and Fouliang, 61 and 56 percent of the peasants, respectively, were in debt.[58]

Credits obtained by the peasants were mostly "distress loans" meant primarily to meet subsistence requirements. Studies by both Buck and Nan confirm that these were generally taken out not for agricultural enterprise or the improvement of land but to meet subsistence needs and social demands. Food shortages, lack of clothes, and the daily needs of peasant households accounted for the highest number of loans. Next in frequency were loans to meet expenses connected with marriages, births, funerals, and religious ceremonies.[59] This suggests the increasing inability of peasants to perform those tasks which were necessary for their existence as a part of the village community.

Further, loans were always accompanied by a higher interest rate. These rates varied from moneylender to moneylender and region to region. They also differed according to the purpose for which they were taken. Commonly, interest rates ranged from 40 to 80 percent annually, but during bad harvests, they increased enormously—approaching 150 to 300 percent.[60] Between 1796 and 1820, the interest rates were below 3 percent per month in Jiangxi. By 1884, in some places in Jiujiang an interest rate of 4 percent was charged.[61] Before the peasant movement, the interest rate had reached 5 percent per month during normal periods and 20 percent monthly during a bad year.[62] If a tenant borrowed one dan of rice, the custom of *fang zhe* demanded the return of two dan after the next harvest. As peasants took loans to meet subsistence needs and not to increase production through the improvement of land or the application of fertilizer, their income remained con-

---

[56] Nan 1937: 30. For the development of pawnshops in modern China, see Luo 1979.
[57] Nan 1937: 92.
[58] See Buck 1937b: 55–56.
[59] Nan 1937: 92; Buck 1937b.
[60] For example, see Abramson 1935.
[61] *Shenbao* February 9, 1884; see also ZNYS 1957, 1:575.
[62] See Abramson 1935.

stant and, consequently, they often found themselves in perpetual debt. Not surprisingly, an enormous number of peasants were in perpetual debt during the early twentieth century.

Such a situation favored the moneylender, who was generally also a landlord. By providing loans sufficient only for subsistence needs and taking agricultural products as partial payment, he gained control over the entire process of production. The landlord-moneylender profited more by simply lending money at a higher interest rate than by improving efficiency and increasing output. Scholars have noted that in many places, usury replaced rent as the major source of income for the landlord. For peasants, this meant perpetual indebtedness and subsequent bonded status. Tawney thus remarks that in China "as far as poor peasants are concerned, permanent indebtedness is the rule rather than the exception. They pawn their crops in summer, their farm implements in winter, and their household belongings throughout the year."[63]

By the early twentieth century, new tenancy arrangements and the increasing demands of the landlords had significantly reduced the security of the peasants' subsistence. The landlord shunned his paternal responsibilities, for, backed by the state, he no longer needed local sanctions and support to maintain his position. He provided fewer services to peasants and demanded more in return. This unbalanced the paternal-deference equation and narrowed peasants' subsistence resources. The peasants now assumed all the risks of agricultural enterprise. Consequently, they often found it impossible to meet their subsistence needs not only during crop failures but even in normal seasons.

PEASANTS' PROTESTS AND RIOTS

If, during the twentieth century, landlords repudiated their paternal obligations, peasants also withdrew their deference. The imbalance in the paternal-deference equation meant a break in the customary ties between the landlord and the peasant. It altered the peasants' traditional work and leisure patterns, disrupted their use rights, and destroyed the redistributive mechanism of the village community. The rural world turned into a hostile battleground where both landlords and peasants bitterly resented each other's corrupt practices.

[63] Tawney 1932, 1966: 62.

The peasants were not unconscious victims of the strength and power displayed by the landlord. By the early twentieth century, their struggle to retain as much as possible of the products of their labor had intensified. They vigorously protested the violation of their customary rights and accepted the cultural hegemony of the landed upper class only on their own terms.

The larger outlines of political power and the established structure of authority were, however, still strongly entrenched in the daily experiences and lived values of the peasants. Thus, as long as the cultural hegemony of the landed upper class did not snap, and as long as images of its power and authority remained strong in the popular mentality of subordination, this hegemony defined for peasants what forms of social and political actions were possible, and limited the scope of peasants' political actions. As a result, more often than not the protests of the peasants included a conservative proclivity to restore equilibrium. The peasant ideology legitimized the punishment of those landlords who violated their moral right to subsistence and unbalanced the paternal-deference equation. The ideology did not envision the overthrow of the social order itself. Traditional expectations bred rebellion, not revolution. Scott writes:

> The central goals envisioned by the peasants are often limited—even if the means employed may be unlimited. They take up arms less often to destroy elites than to compel them to meet their moral obligations. Where a shred of the paternal normative structure remains, peasants often invoke it; where such a restoration is inconceivable, peasants often attempt to drive out the collectors of taxes and rents (or to move beyond their reach) and to reestablish an autonomous community.[64]

During the early twentieth century, peasant riots and rebellions increased in Jiangxi. C. K. Yang, in his study of the statistical pattern of mass actions in China, finds that the number of documented peasant rebellions in Jiangxi suddenly grew between 1896 and 1911.[65] The major peasant rebellions in the reign of the last two Qing emperors, Guangxu and Xuantong, are listed in table 5.3.

Insofar as these rebellions were conscious political actions of peasants to compel landlords to fulfill their traditional paternalistic duties, they followed

[64] Scott 1976: 192.

[65] Yang 1975: 182. For general discussions on Chinese peasant uprisings see also Wakeman 1975, 1977; Billingsley 1981.

TABLE 5.3
*Major Peasant Rebellions
in Districts of Jiangxi, 1900–1911*

Location	Year	Causes
Xingguo	1904	Local opposition to German-Chinese mining
Leping	1905	Bandit activity, opposition to school taxes
Southern Jiangxi	1905	Secret society, bandit activities
Dean	1906	Tax collection
Duchang	1906	Secret society, bandit activity, increase in the price of rice
Linchuan	1906	Bandit activity
Pingxiang	1906	Revolutionary uprisings, famine
Ruichang	1906	Destruction of likin barriers
Yuanzhou	1906	School tax levy
Fengcheng	1907	Registration of population
Nankang	1907	Bandit activity
Pingxiang	1907	Student protest
Yudu	1907	Registration of population
Ganxian	1908	Boxers
Leping	1908	Bandit activity
Boyang	1909	Bandit activity, floods
Dayu	1909	Bandit activity
Jian	1909	Confiscation of the opium crop, rice riots
Fuzhou	1909	Rice riots
Linjiang Prefecture	1909	Rice riots
Xinyu	1909	Rice riots
Yichun	1909	Bandit activity, school taxes
Dean	1910	Bandit activity, famine
Jianchang	1910	Bandit activity, famine
Nanan Prefecture	1910	Bandit activity
Hunan, Guangdong, and Jiangxi border area	1910	Bandit activity
Wanzai	1910	Bandit activity
Wuning	1910	Bandit activity, famine
Xinchang	1910	Bandit activity
Yiningzhou	1910	Bandit activity
Yongxin	1910	Confiscation of opium crop

Source: Based on Kupper 1971: 36–37.

culturally set patterns. Rebel peasants knew their targets and the scope of their action so well that even the landed upper class predicted the forms of protests. The *Guide to Famine Preparedness* compiled in the late eighteenth century thus warned landlords against abdicating their paternal obligations in such an extraordinary period: "When there is a famine the people easily cause disturbances, such as forcing the sale of grain. If those who have grain refuse to sell it, every one becomes a 'guest at their table.' "[66] Discussing the range of peasants' political action, the *Guide* observed: "The poor and the rich live in different worlds. The rich exploit the poor and the poor hate the rich. The poor are always waiting for something to happen to give them an excuse to act. As soon as there is a famine, they will riot. First they will steal rice. Next they will steal from the rich. Finally, they will gather in great masses to plunder. If this happens, the rich will be harmed by the poor. After a day or so, the poor will be punished by the government. . . . This certainly is not in the interest of the poor or the rich."[67] To prevent such a situation, the *Guide* emphasized the opening of granaries, prohibition of grain exports, reduction in rice prices, rents, and taxes, and the establishment of pawnshops.

Peasants' riots and rebellions thus resulted from the apparent violation of local practices. The normative justification for resistance appeared whenever landlords or the state failed to observe what Scott argues was "the priority of local subsistence over outside law and the priority of local subsistence needs over outside claims on the local products."[68] Peasants legitimized their action in riots and uprisings by the same ideology that demanded protection from the traditional paternalists against illegal extraction of the surplus and respect for local, customarily defined subsistence needs. In an extreme situation of dearth, this also dictated the revival of the traditional redistributive mechanism to reduce rents and share grains. One account observes that "due to the generosity of some families, contributions were first made (voluntarily) to buy food for the destitute. But as time went on, the catch phrase 'share the famine' was invented; now whenever rice is expensive, it has become customary for poor people to assemble themselves in groups and beg for rice door to door. If their wish is not satisfied they promptly seize the rice by force."[69] Rebel peasants undertook these actions when the customary redistributive mechanism failed. Thus, when the post-Taiping landlords be-

66 Cited in Marks 1984: 80.
67 Hsiao 1972: 445.
68 Scott 1976: 45.
69 Hsiao 1972: 445.

came increasingly unwilling to perform their essential traditional paternalistic tasks as long as their power to expropriate peasants' surpluses through other means remained secure, peasants periodically resorted to violent political struggles to resist landlords' total control over their socioeconomic lives and punish those who frequently violated the traditional norms. Peasant riots and uprisings were, therefore, strong political expressions of indignation; they were not undirected fury but predictable responses to certain actions.

Among peasants' political actions in the post-Taiping period, the most numerous category is classified as tax riots. Wiens notes that "anti-tax revolts in the nineteenth century became as frequent as the anti-rent incidents in the seventeenth and eighteenth centuries, since once the government pressed tenants to pay rents for the sake of tax income, tenants-farmers joined the rank of landowners to fight for a common cause against a common exploiter."[70] Similarly, K. C. Hsiao, in his illuminating study of rural China, remarks that "by far the most fertile and important source of riots was official extortion in connection with tax collection . . . they appeared more often after the opium war."[71] I earlier noted that, especially after the Taiping Rebellion, both the state and the landed upper class increasingly relied upon each other's support in tax and rent collection activities. The consequent fusion of landlords' political and economic power provided them opportunities to extort money from the rural cultivators either through imposition of various levies disguised as collection charges or by passing the burden of taxes directly on to them. Thus, as paternal landlords turned into oppressive tax and rent collectors, rural cultivators reciprocated by punishing them.

Lucien Bianco notes that "what would appear to have been the most acute area of social tension, namely the tension between the landlord who lived off the land and his tenants who had to remit almost half the volume of the crop, produced in fact less frequent and usually less violent conflicts than the conflicts which were generated by the collection of land taxes."[72] He writes that it was probably the attitudinal difference that made revolts against an impersonal government more possible than actions against "very personal and local figures of landlords" to whom tenants were tied by various social and economic relationships. It is true that tenants' struggles against landlords largely depended on the nature of the socioeconomic relationship between them. Tenants resisted their oppressive landlords only when this relation-

[70] Wiens 1980: 33–34.
[71] Hsiao 1972: 441.
[72] Bianco 1976: 315.

ship turned exploitative and violated their minimum subsistence needs. But accounts of such resistance were often less well documented because, as compared with more fully recorded peasant riots and uprisings, they remained quite trivial in scale. Both tenants and landlords dealt with each other on the basis of individually suited actions. This made resistance more a personal than a collective struggle. Confronting landlords' wider control over instruments of repression and violence, tenants often resorted to such means as suicide, murder, escape to other areas without paying dues, and use of corrupt practices to reduce the amount of cash or grain to be paid.

The relative absence of detailed documentation of such resistance, however, does not suggest that tenants generally remained docile and apart from the larger peasant riots and uprisings. In fact, the fusion of rent and tax collection activities at the top brought both small peasant freeholders and tenants together as a class of small rural cultivators to wage struggles against the exploitative practices of the state and the landed upper class. They, as a class, resisted excessive economic and extraeconomic demands placed on them, which not only violated the traditional norms but also retarded their natural socioeconomic growth.[73] The nature of larger socioeconomic changes produced uniformity in experiences of exploitation and reactions to it. It blurred the distinction between groups of small rural cultivators. One does not find any of the riots or uprisings linked only with a particular socioeconomic category of peasants. Tax riots thus symbolized the collective struggle of the exploited rural cultivators who attacked such manifestations of the state and landed-upper-class power in the countryside as the local tax collection offices, tax agents, and corrupt officials and landlords, and finally threatened the very basis of the latter's traditional local political and economic authority. This is reflected in the nature of tax riots in the Xinjiang region.

In this region, a large number of tax riots were sparked by the levy for educational funds and the establishment of schools. Education was one of the major themes of the reform movement of 1901. A great emphasis was placed on the restructuring of the educational system along Western lines. Soon after the announcement of reforms, a large-scale campaign was started

---

[73] It was this class of peasants that most vigorously participated in the Xinjiang revolutionary movement. The peasants' declining socioeconomic status and loss of customary rights made them indignant enough to make revolution under the guidance of Marxist intellectuals. It is difficult to say whether this class can be considered middle or poor peasants. Broadly, it may be called the middle-peasant-in-decline, a category similar to Wolf's revolutionary middle peasant (Wolf 1969). See also Alavi (1965), who advances the hypothesis that the middle peasants are initially most militant, but a revolution takes root when the poor peasants join it.

to raise funds for this purpose. Mary Wright has noted the enthusiastic support of officials, merchants, and local elites for this campaign. But the major reason for their enthusiastic support was, perhaps, the favorable opportunity the campaign afforded them to extract the peasants' surpluses. This fact does not receive adequate expression in Mary Wright's bland statement that "there was certainly some local misappropriation of educational funds, and in some cases sharp resistance by the peasantry to an innovation for which they paid extra taxes but which seemed for gentry benefit."[74] Moreover, for traditional peasants, such modern schools in the cities were meaningless and provoked traditional resistance to this new wind of change.

In 1904, for example, the imposition of levies on indigo to expand new educational programs brought about a large-scale antitax uprising in Leping district—a famous indigo-producing area in the Xinjiang region.[75] Grown in abundance in this hilly and phosphate-rich land, indigo was the most viable commercial crop for many local peasants. It provided sufficient returns for the maintenance of subsistence needs. According to the Leping district gazetteer, at the end of each autumn harvest season local peasants sold coal, limestone, indigo, sugar cane, *shaojiu* (liquor), and other products to the Jiangsu, Hunan, and Hubei markets, and, in return, purchased salt and salted goods for their daily use in the winter. However, beginning with the last decade of the nineteenth century, massive imports of cheap indigo paste as well as synthetic dye from outside suppressed the price of indigo in local markets. Profits of indigo-producing peasants thus greatly shrank. Moreover, in 1902, peasants in Leping district were suddenly informed that they could not carry indigo out of their villages for sale in the market without paying a lijin tax on each basket. On a "Tianjin basket," which held 105 *jin* of indigo, a tax of 262 copper cash was to be paid. On the "road basket," which had a capacity of 100 jin, 250 copper cash was demanded. The tax on a "village basket" of 90 jin was 225 copper cash. This further lowered the peasants' income from the local trade in indigo.

But what sparked the riot was the imposition of still another levy on indigo. In 1904, Leping's district magistrate, Tu Linguan, and the city-based members of the landed upper class decided to raise funds for the establishment and maintenance of new "Western-style" schools by collecting a surcharge on the sale of indigo. This surcharge was over and above the recently introduced lijin tax. While its amount was not high, being only one copper

[74] Wright 1968: 25.
[75] The following discussion of the indigo riots is based upon Zhang Zhenhe 1954: 188–97; *North China Herald*, October 17, 1904, 5, and November 4, 1904, 5; ZNYS 1957, 1:963–64.

cash per dan, its imposition infuriated the indigo-producing peasants whose economic status was already declining. They finally rebelled.

The leader of this uprising was Xia Yanyi. Xia was an active member of a local branch of what was probably the Hongbang, or Honglian, Secret Society. After the suppression of the Boxer Rebellion of 1900, many of its participants had escaped to remote villages in various districts of the Xinjiang region. There, they continued to act as a nucleus in organizing local branches of their secret society on the plank of antiforeignism. Thus, when Xia Yanyi took up the cause of the exploited indigo-producing peasants, he naturally related the source of the latter's plight to increasing activities of the Christian missionaries and the establishment of new Western-style schools. The fusion of the Boxers' antiforeignism with the indigo tax resistance extended the scope of the uprising. It soon received support from not only the class of exploited rural cultivators but also other branches of the local antiforeign secret societies. This strengthened the rebel forces.

On July 21, 1904, Xia Yanyi, leading a force of several hundred peasants, entered the district city. Rebels stayed in the town for several days. They destroyed the properties of Christian missionaries and the local yamen, as well as the lijin, salt-tax, and the district antismuggling barriers. Two gunboats, employed to check bands of smugglers operating on waterways, were burned. The rebels searched for and attacked corrupt and oppressive members of the local elite as well as personnel of the antismuggling checkpost. It appears that members of the local branches of an antiforeign secret society that traditionally thrived in this region were also involved in salt smuggling because of their location near the boundaries of three provinces. As the state's antismuggling forces frequently harassed them, rebels directed their struggle against those forces too. Thus, indignant peasants' systematic destruction of all those offices which exercised tremendous control over their socioeconomic life, and their selective attacks on those members of the local elites and their agents whom they considered corrupt and oppressive, indicate their purposeful participation in the uprising. To defend their traditional rights, they set upon state and landed-upper-class symbols of oppressive power.

Rebels kept the district city surrounded for several days and disconnected its communication link with the outside world. Their success swelled the number of active supporters to about three thousand. As rebels' power strengthened, village landlords' control and authority in their native areas began to be threatened. This resulted in their disagreement with and opposition to the city-based absentee landlords, who had advised the district mag-

istrate to impose an additional levy on indigo. Further, it also seems probable that the dispatch of persons by the district magistrate to collect the levy
directly in the local areas was considered by the village landlords to be a
deliberate attempt to downplay their influence and to deny them any profit
from the levy collection activities. Confronted by the powerful rebel force,
the local landlord, along with the head of the local baojia office, Cai Mou,
supported the indignant peasants in order to protect his property. Other
rural landlords, like Wang Detai, Zou Kewang, Wang Dingwo, and Wang
Xixian from Dongxiang and Xixiang villages, as well as Ding, Wang, and
Ye of Nanxiang village, followed suit. The ease with which these landlords
were able to penetrate rebel organizations demonstrates that their symbolic
expression of paternalistic concern over unjustified levy collection was sufficient to gain peasants' deference. It also indicates that the competition
among landlords to expropriate peasants' surpluses sometimes created divisions within their ranks. But these divisions were transient. When superior
state forces began to suppress the rebels, village landlords were the first to
betray the uprising and to ally themselves once again with their counterparts in the city.

When the strength of rebel forces increased enormously, the district magistrate, Tu, bribed a rebel peasant and sent secret messages to the prefectural
officials in Raozhou asking for immediate military help. The reserve military
troops of Zhu Zechun, garrisoned in the prefectural city, were sent at the
end of September to Leping to quell the rebellion. Zhu arrested Xia Yanyi's
wife as well as one of Xia's close friends. Infuriated by this, Xia demanded
their immediate release. Failing that, he threatened to attack the city and kill
the local elite. A frightened Tu set them free. Xia, nonetheless, carried out
his threat to resist the advances of Zhu Zechun's troops. Using cannon, rebels opened the gate of the city, burned the houses of district officials, including the home of the indigo tax collector Wang, and released all the peasants
detained in the district prison. Zhu's troops were defeated and he himself
had to escape in disguise. Rebels and militia forces of the village landlords
together guarded all the strategic points leading to the city. Their success
extended their influence up to southern Anhui.

Eventually, the state intervened with a larger force. The Daotai of Jiujiang, Rui Cheng, was sent to Leping via Boyang with a force of about one
thousand soldiers and a few gunboats. As soon as this force reached the
northern outskirts of the city, local officials, merchants, and landlords once
again united to welcome it. The village landlords betrayed Xia Yanyi and
aided and escorted Rui Cheng's forces to the city. Weakened by the betrayal,

rebel forces moved out of the city, dispersed, and escaped. On October 19, the city was reoccupied by the imperial forces after more than three months of turmoil. A fine of twenty-eight thousand silver dollars was imposed on the peasants to cover the cost of restoration of destroyed official and missionary properties. The fine was, however, not collected because of the fear that it would spark another uprising. This massive anti-indigo tax uprising thus petered out.

Similarly, in 1906, the local landlord-gentry of the district of Yugan imposed a white-soil levy on peasants to raise educational funds.[76] This restricted peasants' traditional rights to use lime, available in abundance in nearby mountainous areas, to improve the quality of the soil. Moreover, the collection of the levy itself was mishandled by the manager of the local rice mill and the school committee members entrusted with the task. Peasants sent petitions to the district office for the redress of their grievances. Local officials were dispatched to investigate the case, but they failed to reach a settlement. Consequently, the peasants became impatient and a riot started at Miaofang village in the Honghuadun area. More than a thousand peasants gathered. They attacked and destroyed the properties of the officials and landlords who were members of the corrupt school committee.

Such antitax riots took place in almost all the areas of Jiangxi. In May 1906, in Ruichang district, peasants rebelled to protest the collection of a levy for education.[77] They attacked the tax collection office and destroyed all the account books and tax warrants. Tax collectors and their guards were severely beaten. At another place, peasants became indignant over the forced collection of taxes during rice shortages. They looted the tax collection office. The tax collector and his guards were injured, and his wife and concubine were raped.

In 1909, in Yichun district, the task of establishing modern schools was entrusted to a member of the landed upper class, Lu Yuanbi. He arbitrarily converted the cash value of the tax into a higher grain value and extorted a huge amount of rice from peasants, embezzling all of the extra amount thus collected. Originally, the school tax was ten cash, but he forced peasants to pay in rice worth more than fifty cash. When peasants learned about this in mid-July they stopped the transport of tax rice to the city and secretly sent messages to other villages to do the same. On August 3, peasants from all the neighboring villages gathered and marched to the city. They killed several members of the local militia but were forced to retreat because of heavy

[76] *Shibao*, June 14,1906; see also *ZNYS* 1957, 1:964.
[77] *Shibao*, May 2, 16, 1906; see also *ZNYS* 1957, 1:964.

casualties. On August 6, they again attacked the city with locally made long guns, destroyed four gates of the city wall, injured the police chief, and killed many policemen. The local militia retreated to the inner section of the city and continued to struggle. The riot was suppressed only after the army was summoned on August 12.[78]

In 1909, the countryside in southern Jiangxi was similarly disaffected due to the collection of a levy for taking a census. A report by E. S. Little in the *North China Herald* noted on October 2, 1909:

> Considerable irritation has been caused in South Kiangsi [Jiangxi] by the taking of the census. The matter was put into the hands of the native gentry, who immediately realized that it afforded a fine opportunity for feathering their own nests, and they have imposed so called taxes varying from 100 cash to a family to 30, 20, and 10 cash for each man, woman, and child respectively. Unfortunately, the natives imagine that foreigners are mixed up with the census in some way. They give credence to the report that their names are being sent abroad to foreign countries where a malign spell will be cast over them, and all sickness and misfortune are put down to this cause. In some districts, the gentry are reported to have collected large sums by these illegal methods.[79]

As a result, violence erupted in several districts and many landlords were killed. Little writes that "the populace has lost confidence in the officials to such a degree that when proclamations are pasted up they are mutilated or destroyed."[80] Thus, once again, the landed upper class attempted to extort peasants' surpluses in close alliance with the state on every possible pretext, resulting in the interplay of antiforeign sentiments of local people and secret societies to create in combination an explosive situation in rural areas. Such occasions provided an opportunity for rural cultivators to band together to resist not only illegal taxes and levies but also all other exploitative practices.

To be sure, as noted earlier, members of the landed upper class knew what actions of theirs would invoke protests from peasants. Their frequent violations of traditional and customary local practices were, therefore, not unconscious or bizarre acts but resulted from the strengthening of their power in the post-Taiping period, which made them feel secure enough to expropriate peasants' surpluses with impunity. Time and again, when they believed that their exploitative actions would bring about large-scale protest

[78] *Dongfang zazhi* 6:1 (1909): 365–66; *North China Herald*, October 2, 1909, 21.
[79] *North China Herald*, October 2, 1909, 5; see also "Ji Jiangxi diaocha hukou zhi fengchao" 1909.
[80] Ibid.

and threaten the basis of their authority and control in rural areas, they attempted to pacify the peasants by either reducing rents and taxes or petitioning to remove a particularly oppressive tax collector or district magistrate from the explosive area.

In 1920, for example, a widespread natural disaster (apparently locusts) struck Boyang district in the Xinjiang region.[81] This severely destroyed crops and financially ruined a large number of peasants. The whole region experienced a massive dearth of food-grains. Finally, the district magistrate of Boyang, Jiang Bozhang, called a meeting of the local landlords to discuss the situation. It was agreed that if rents were not reduced immediately, peasants would be forced to sell their children for food and would turn into bandits. They finally decided on a 30-percent reduction in rents. This defused the explosive situation.

Similarly, in 1923, an antitax riot in Majia village of Leping district was averted because of timely action by the district magistrate.[82] A provincial official, Cai Zhengdong, had issued an order for the advance collection of local taxes. As the harvest season was not over, peasants found it difficult to pay their taxes in advance. All the villagers, therefore, gathered together and requested the district magistrate, Liu Mengjiu, to postpone the tax collection. Infuriated by their demand but at the same time fearing the eruption of large-scale violence in this traditionally rebellion-prone area, Li sent some troops to the village to take action before the peasants got organized. About fifty peasants were arrested and more than three hundred houses were burned. Moreover, a strong force was stationed at a local checkpoint to restrict the movement of peasants in and out of the village. Fearing further reprisals, about three thousand displaced peasants refused to come back to the village to reconstruct their houses. They sent a petition to the provincial investigation bureau in Nanchang for redress of their grievances. Their petition was promptly rejected. They also approached their clan leader and the landlord Ma, who was also a member of the first provincial assembly, to plead their case in Beijing. Probably due to his alliance with the ruling class, Ma did not actively work to help the peasants. Finally, in desperation, homeless and wandering peasants attacked with homemade weapons the district magistrate Liu and his small band of police when they were on their way to the village for inspection. Liu survived. Many more peasants were arrested.

[81] "Qianze yundong" 1920.
[82] Zhang 1923: 312.

The peasants finally organized themselves with the support of local bandit forces and prepared to launch an attack to kill all the officials and landlords of the region. Threatened by this development, Liu finally resigned and advised the provincial official Cai to postpone the advance tax collection to calm down the peasants. This finally averted what could have become a large-scale antitax riot. Once again, peasants vigorously resisted the violation of their traditional norms, used all customary means to redress their grievances, including forcing the local elite to undertake its paternalistic duties, and, failing that, took up arms to punish a corrupt official. However, as soon as the district magistrate resigned and a promise for the postponement of tax collection was made, peasants returned to their village in satisfaction.[83]

Discussing peasant riots and uprisings of the pre-Guomindang era, Bianco notes that "the forms of peasant protests (their submission of petitions and their attempts at using gentry members or locally born officials as emissaries who could intercede in the capital on their behalf) were, if anything, more traditional."[84] However, the "traditionalism" of these riots and uprisings did not turn them into futile exercises. They should be seen as conscious and meaningful attempts by indignant peasants to defend their rights. The moral outrage of the peasants against the imposition of levies without any concern for their subsistence needs formed the basis for struggle in all these riots. Many of the levies were obtained by the local elites through circumscribing peasants' entitlements and taxing their traditional use-rights. In addition, tax collectors often ignored local crop failures and insisted that peasants pay the full fixed revenue. This violated peasants' prior claim to the harvest. As many of the local landlords were also directly or indirectly involved in tax collection activities and profited from additional exactions, the peasants were deprived of customary protection from their landlords. Traditionally, landlords often petitioned to have taxes reduced. They bribed the tax collectors to collect a lesser amount, or delayed their arrival on some pretext, or simply altered village records. When the interest of both tax collectors and landlords coincided in extraction of peasants' surpluses, grossly ignoring local subsistence needs, peasants attacked them.

---

[83] Similarly, in 1910 peasants rebelled near the Lu Mountains in northern Jiangxi because the tax collector Yue Yiding ordered them to pay unpaid taxes and levies in a busy farming season after a crop disaster caused by a severe flood. When the local members of the landed upper class ignored rebelling peasants' demands for the postponement of tax collection until the new harvest season was over, the peasants entered the city. Proclaiming them bandits, the district police official Xu Wenkan called the army, which suppressed the uprising. See ZNYS 1957, 1:953.

[84] Bianco 1976: 322.

Rice riots, too, were frequent in the Xinjiang region. Unlike the antitax riots, in which peasants attacked tax collection offices and punished those landlords and officials who participated in the illegal extraction, in rice riots they revived the traditional redistributive mechanism. R. Bin Wong, in his illuminating study of food riots during the Qing period, demonstrates that these eventuated because either commercial, state, or customary spheres of grain circulation failed "to make grain available on terms and in quantities demanded by people expecting their needs to be met"[85] during periods of poor harvests or natural or artificial local scarcities. The most common targets in such riots were wealthy households that belonged to the customary sphere of circulation—those "whose large stores of grain could be sold or lent directly to the poor, marketed locally, and/or purchased by merchants for sale elsewhere."[86] Granaries belonging to both the state and the customary sphere of circulation were another target. Within the sphere of commercial circulation, the hoarding of grain or its movement elsewhere by traveling merchants, brokers, and rice shops at the time of dearth made them the third most common targets of food rioters.

In 1901, for example, consequent upon the extensive flood damage, many rice riots occurred in both the northern and southern regions of Jiangxi. In Nanchang, two weeks before the new harvest, rice from both the village and city markets disappeared. In spite of the fact that rice was only two thousand copper cash per dan and the local granary, managed by the gentry official Liu Xinyuan, was full, the landed upper class failed to provide rice at this crucial moment of subsistence needs. It also ignored peasants' petitions to transfer rice from other regions to this area. Consequently, peasants assembled and looted rice at several places.[87]

In 1910, peasants in Fuzhou district protested the transfer of rice by local merchants to other regions at a time of dearth in the local area. When rice merchants and local elites ignored the demands of the peasants, about a thousand of them gathered together and attacked the rice shops. The news soon spread to other villages. By the next day, the number of indignant peasants had increased to about ten thousand. They marched to the town of Hedongwan and destroyed most of the rice shops. When the police arrested several of them on the charge of robbery, peasants followed the policemen up to the district city and pressured the district magistrate to release those in custody. In order to pacify the peasants, the district magistrate finally

---

[85] Wong 1982: 785.
[86] Ibid., 770–71.
[87] *ZNYS* 1:980.

released the arrested persons and the riot thus ended. Similar rice riots took place at several other places in Jiangxi at this time of dearth. Rebel peasants attacked granaries and looted rice shops, and then swiftly dispersed.[88]

It should be noted that the destruction and looting of the rice shops was not a mindless act. Peasants attacked only the forestallers and those merchants who hoarded rice, increased its price, and exported it to other places in Jiangxi during the period of dearth. The moral right to subsistence dictated that rice should be consumed locally and should be distributed at a fair price in the affected local area. Those members of the elite who violated this ethic and failed to perform their paternalistic tasks were severely punished by the peasants. Thus, in many instances, either during food shortages or when rumors of peasants stealing rice spread, the landed upper class forced district magistrates and merchants to send rice to distribute or sell at fair prices to peasants.

In 1910, in Hukou district of the Xinjiang region, the landed upper class prevented a serious rice riot by petitioning the district magistrate to send five thousand dan of rice for distribution in the area.[89] In Jian district of southern Jiangxi, when some landlords and merchants hoarded rice and attempted to transfer it to other regions during a period of dearth, infuriated peasants felt that customarily they had the first claim over the rice extracted from them. They guarded all the river ports and confiscated all the rice meant for export. The local elite, taking this as a warning, requested the district magistrate to supply rice to the area and to forbid price increases.[90]

It was a frequent practice of indignant peasants to stop boats carrying rice on the river route and to prevent their movement until peasants were given their share of rice during times of food shortages. They plundered the houses of the rich, often apologizing to them by saying that they resorted to such actions because their families were starving. In many cases, landlords and merchants were made to sell their surplus rice at fair prices. Through various similar acts, peasants exercised social control and set up restrictions on the consumption and hoarding of grain. Informed by an egalitarian and collectivist ethic, they attempted to revive the traditional redistributive mechanism of the village community. Rice forcefully acquired was often cooked communally and distributed among those who were starving.

In Mao Dun's novel, *Autumn Harvest*, the starving peasants of Yang-jiaqiao, after stealing rice from a middle peasant, old Tong Bao, who man-

[88] *Dongfang Zazhi* 7:10 (1910): 28–29; see also *ZNYS* 1957, 1:979.
[89] *Dongfang Zazhi* 7:5 (1910): 29.
[90] Ibid.

aged to borrow it from a rice merchant, say: "We share what food we have, don't you understand! Live or die together! Who told you to beg for that bit of rice? You can borrow but others cannot. Are you going to live alone and let everybody else starve? . . . You cry bitterly as if your father-in-law had died. We eat up your rice, but we will get back rice for you. You have nothing to cry about." The band of starving peasants force the local gentry, after robbing their houses, to plead with pawnshop operators and rice merchants to open a "door of convenience" by giving up a bit of rice. When peasants surround the town, local gentry and merchants agree to distribute rice and to charge no interest on pawned items. The forced opening of the "door of convenience," the threat of the advancing "peace preservation corps," and the approaching harvest season finally end the rebellion.[91]

Mao Dun's deep knowledge of central China's village life leads him to portray very correctly the general character of all rice riots in this famous short novel. Not only does this description indicate the peasants' strong belief that all in the village community should share during the famine but also demonstrates their extraordinary sense of discipline in managing traditional redistributive mechanisms during the period of food shortages. Although there are numerous short and sketchy riot reports, prepared either by the state or outside observers, there is no detailed narration of the nature of indignant peasants' actions. But the reports, nonetheless, indicate peasants' strict enforcement of traditional redistributive mechanisms on both the landed upper class and their own members during difficult periods.

Both antitax and rice riots thus demonstrate the moral outrage of peasants at the violation of their subsistence needs. Their attempt to restore the paternal-deference equation by attacking carefully selected targets, their symbolic warning to landlords and officials to respect customary practices and norms, and finally their swift dispersal after direct action, suggest the limited objectives of these riots and uprisings. Additionally, peasants' political actions, as exemplified by such riots and uprisings in which they attempted to restore their world by force, were extraordinary and rare moments in their lives. "Aside from these 'moments of madness' (and even during them!)," as Scott writes, "much day to day reality of peasant life is the effort of the family to assure itself an adequate food supply."[92]

In their day-to-day activities, peasants responded to heavy exactions and the reluctance of the landlord to perform paternal services with acts of false

[91] For a more complete translation see Isaacs 1974: 302–36.
[92] Scott 1976: 230.

deference or nondeference. For example, peasants in Jiangxi responded to the growing coercion by landlords by demonstrating their lack of deference through employment of clandestine devices that enabled them to retain more of the products of their labor. Wu Shunyu notes that it was a frequent practice of the tenants to fill the landlords' rent baskets with adulterated or wet grains. Often, when the old landlord sold his land to other persons at the close of the harvest season, peasants did not pay their grain rent. Moreover, landlords in Jiangxi frequently complained that if a tenant decided not to till the land after a year, he did not put enough fertilizer on it and wasted the land by not working on it as hard as on his own land. When the land produced less, the tenant demanded a reduction in rent. If a landlord's land became flooded, the tenant let the land lose its productivity and demanded a rent reduction.[93] Increasing reports of such common complaints evince peasants' growing unsentimental and unfilial attitude toward the landlords.

Finally, peasants jealously guarded their own culture. The dominant landed upper class continuously strove to expand its hegemony by imposing its own cultural values and ideology of "order" on peasants. Such institutions of ideological control as the Xiangyue lecture system, Xiang yin jiu ceremonies to honor old persons, local sacrificial activities of the state, and *shexue*, or the village schools, which were employed by the state and the landed upper class to instill the established Confucian ideology into peasant culture, had increasingly become futile.[94] For example, the most important apparatus of ideological control in China was the Xiangyue lecture system. The state appointed Xiangyue lecturers who at periodic intervals delivered discourses in their localities on imperial Confucianism and on the official interpretations of unlawful and antisocial activities. But the wide gap between the theory and the actual practice of these lecturers, who generally belonged to the landed upper class and who ignored material and spiritual comforts for peasants, turned this system into an ineffective means of control.

This system, as John Watt writes, "in the seventeenth and eighteenth century . . . was still of concern to Kiangsi [Jiangxi] local officials. By the early nineteenth century it was no longer mentioned in Kiangsi [Jiangxi] district gazetteers. . . . The subject was quietly dropped."[95] By the early twentieth century, the Xiangyue lecturers were assigned to tasks different from

[93] Wu 1935: 35–36.
[94] Hsiao 1972: 184–205.
[95] Watt 1972: 196.

indoctrination. For example, Martin Yang, in his study of Daidou village in Shandong, found that

> the Hsiang-yueh [Xiangyue] was the tax collector. Originally, his chief duty was to convey to the villagers the emperor's instruction as to how to be a filial son and to see that social customs and the people's daily life were in conformity with the Confucian ethics. Gradually, the Hsiang-yueh [Xiangyue] became merely a political orderly for transmitting orders from the county government to the village and dispatching reports on the village affairs to the local officials. Finally even these circumscribed duties stopped and he became merely a tax collector, a position which did not command much respect.[96]

In fact, peasants avoided as much as possible any participation in the state- or the landed-upper-class-controlled ceremonies, as these activities in the hands of corrupt officials had become a tool to extort money from them and harass them. Huang Liuhang, a celebrated bureaucrat, noting the futility of the Xiang yin jiu ceremony, wrote: "When a villager hears that his name is included (in the list of guests), he feels as if he is falling bodily into fire and hot water. Some of them make open confessions of their sin, or take off their clothing and show the scars left on their bodies as a result of the punishment by blows (thus to disqualify themselves for this doubtful honor)."[97]

Thus, any positive and significant impact of these different means of ideological control on peasants seems doubtful. They at best create an illusion of peasant society at a standstill under the heavy weight of the culture of the upper class.[98] But the vigorous resistance by a robust popular culture, either through violent and nonviolent struggles or through its own socioreligious

[96] Yang 1945: 173.

[97] Cited in Hsiao 1972: 214. Hsiao also notes that one of the "sordid usages" of this ceremony was to demand "gifts" in return for the invitation (Hsiao 1972: 627).

[98] This illusion has, perhaps, led Maurice Freedman (1974: 39) to assert the close unity between elite and peasant cultures. He writes: "How could China fail to constitute a community of ideas when the political center made itself responsible for disseminating its belief by the spoken and written word, when literacy, however thinly spread . . . was an institutionalized part of rural life, when the elites were based as much in the countryside as in the towns and when social mobility ensured a steady interchange of styles between the common run of men and the highly literate?" This is a picture of a rural society set deep within a hegemonic elite culture, but within it independent paths were followed. Wolf (1974: 9) points out that "the evidence we have seen of close correlation between the beliefs of laymen and their perspective on society argues that there has always been a vast gulf between the religion of the elite and that of the peasantry." This gulf widened more as the crisis of paternalism led peasants to protect their own culture vigorously.

ceremonies and ideological expressions of dissent, impeded such efforts at indoctrination. The existence of this popular culture reflected the powerful and dominant system's weakest area of control over peasants. Its vocabulary reserved the most scornful and choicest words to describe the landlords—so much so that in numerous local descriptions of the growth of the Xinjiang peasant movement, compiled by the peasant participants, the actual names of landlords many times hardly appear.

To conclude, one must ask: What did all these acts of peasant protest achieve? Did not the inevitable cruel suppression turn them into historically meaningless and futile exercises that failed to bring about desired social changes? There is no doubt that peasant protests, expressed both in riots and other acts of nondeference, were inherently conservative insofar as there was no real effort to seek any structural changes in rural society. Moreover, peasant participants in riots eventually submitted to the superior forces of the landed upper class. Their goals remained parochial and the scope of their sociopolitical actions was limited. They thus present a picture of a confused lot desperately searching for a means to ameliorate living conditions that had deteriorated due to unfair pressures.

The peasants' goals were indeed limited. But this limitation was a result of the survival techniques historically available to them within their cul-ture—which existed independently but within the overarching structure of a larger society. Thus, as long as the cultural hegemony of the landed upper class remained strong, peasants viewed their problems in terms of the crisis of paternalism and attempted to invoke the paternalistic order. The paradox-ical nature of the peasants' sociopolitical actions becomes meaningful when these actions are analyzed in the context of a wider social order.[99] In his excellent study of slave uprisings, Genovese remarks: "Should we say of the slave revolts, as Marc Bloch did of peasant revolts of mediaeval France, that they qualified as disorganized outbursts which counted for little or nothing when weighed against the achievements of the peasants in building their vil-lage communities? The question, however compelling, must be turned around: What could the slaves have accomplished if they had totally lacked insurrectionary spirit and if their masters had had no fear of getting their

---

[99] Peasants who demonstrated a rebellious spirit in defense of their customs and culture would be surprised to learn that their actions were either conservative or meaningless. The conception of peasants' conservatism and radicalism generally emerges from modern observers' conception of what these movements ought to have been. Any qualitative judgment on peasants' sociopolitical actions that does not take into consideration their culture and tradition results in a false picture of the peasantry.

throats cut?"[100] Peasants' sociopolitical actions in defense of their subsistence ethic kept the landed upper class's exploitation indirect and the class antagonisms between them in disguise.[101]

To be sure, by emphasizing the crucial impact of the cultural hegemony of the landed upper class, I am not suggesting that eventually the peasants in the Xinjiang region would not have transcended the limits imposed upon them by the existing larger social order by nurturing alternative expectations and challenging that hegemony itself. But in the Xinjiang region, the first challenge to this order came from outside.

[100] Genovese 1974: 595.

[101] Noting the significance of slaves' sociopolitical actions, which is equally true for those of peasants, Genovese (1974: 656) aptly writes: "These actions paralleled strikes by free workers, for they aimed at winning concessions within the system rather than at challenging the system itself. But, like strikes by free workers, they contained a germ of class consciousness and demonstrated the power of collective action. In both respects, they combatted the sense of impotence that the slaveholders worked so hard to instill in their slaves."

Chapter Six

Fang Zhimin: The Rise
of a Revolutionary Peasant Leader

A new era in the history of the peasants' struggle in Jiangxi begins with the origin of the Xinjiang peasant movement in 1924. Unlike earlier movements, this was not aimed at the defense of paternalism. Instead, it challenged the domination of the landed upper class over rural areas and aimed to build a socialist society. Its ideological break from the past originally came less from peasants themselves than from the leadership of a young Communist intellectual, Fang Zhimin.[1]

An outstanding peasant leader, Fang Zhimin stands in line with such illustrious Chinese revolutionaries as Li Dazhao, Peng Pai, and Mao Zedong, who combined Marxism with the forces of peasantry and contributed to the development of a Communist revolution with indigenous Chinese ingredients. Fang was the leading architect of the Xinjiang peasant movement in the mid-1920s and founder of one of the largest and most famous Gandong-

---

[1] Except for Miao Min's (1962), no other biography of Fang Zhimin exists in English. In Japanese, a study by Fujita Masanori (1960: 1–38), provides a shorter but more substantial sketch of Fang's revolutionary career. In Chinese there are numerous short accounts about the role of Fang in the Xinjiang revolutionary movement. In a GMD prison, just before his execution, Fang wrote a number of essays and letters, including a short autobiography, which he managed to smuggle out. During the Sino-Japanese War, these were published under the title *Fang Zhimin zichuan*. In 1952, the book was republished under the title *Keai de Zhongguo*. This provides useful information on Fang's early life, education, and prerevolutionary political activities. However, most of his early writings are still unavailable. Like Peng Pai, Fang was downgraded during the Cultural Revolution. But after the death of Mao, he was restored to his earlier prominent place in the history of the Chinese Communist revolution. In 1977, the *Renmin Ribao* (August 4, 1977, 2) published a laudatory account of Fang's life. See also *Geming Wenwu* 2 (1978): 23–36. The latest and most reliable biography of Fang is *Fang Zhimin chuan* 1982 (*FZM*). For comparative study of Fang as a revolutionary intellectual, see the work on Li Dazhao by Meisner (1970) and on Peng Pai by Marks (1984) and Galbiati (1985). See also Smedley 1934, 1972.

bei [northeastern Jiangxi], or Min-Zhe-Wan-Gan [Fujian-Zhejiang-Anhui-Jiangxi], soviets during the Jiangxi era of the Chinese Communist Party. His successful revolutionary activity was applauded by Mao Zedong. In the article "A Single Spark Can Start a Prairie Fire," Mao proclaimed that policies adopted by Fang Zhimin to establish soviets in rural areas were as accurate as his own and Zhu De's.[2] Extolling Fang's social, political, and economic reforms in the soviet, Mao exhorted party workers to emulate that model.[3] Fang's intelligence and excellent organizational capacity in rural areas were outstanding even in the opinion of the Guomindang (GMD) officials. Hu Guofang, the officer in charge of the GMD Suppression Campaign in the Xinjiang region, commended him as a brighter organizer than Mao Zedong.[4] Not surprisingly, the GMD announced an 80,000-silver-dollar reward for his head, an amount second only to the prize of 100,000 dollars fixed for Mao and Zhu.[5] Honoring him as a great hero, peasants of Jiangxi composed numerous folk songs in praise of him. An inquiry into the rise of Fang Zhimin as a revolutionary peasant leader and an analysis of his revolutionary ideology are thus imperative to an understanding of the Xinjiang peasant movement.

Fang Zhimin was born on August 21, 1899, in Hutang village in Yiyang district.[6] Named Yuanzhen by his grandfather, he was affectionately called Zhenggu by his parents. His formal name at school was Zhimin. The Fang lineage to which he belonged predominated in his native village, and his family had once been one of the richest and largest in the locality. His grandfather, Fang Zhanggeng, reportedly cultivated more than two hundred mu of land, out of which about half was rented from local landlords. He paid approximately two hundred dan of rice just for rent. The whole family then consisted of thirty to forty persons. The male members helped in cultivation and the females raised pigs and chickens and wove clothes. Zhimin's grandfather thus appears to have belonged to that category of the few rich post-Taiping peasants who were able to gain rapidly both landownership and permanent tenancy rights. However, the same socioeconomic forces that brought about the massive decline of post-Taiping small peasant freeholders and permanent tenants also gradually reduced the fortunes of this family after 1900. Moreover, after the death of Fang Zhanggeng in 1913, the divi-

[2] Mao 1965: 1:118.
[3] Ibid., 129–36, 141–46.
[4] Hu Guokang 1967: 20–21.
[5] Fujita 1960: 1.
[6] For a thoughtful discussion of various chronological controversies in biographies of Fang, see Xu 1983.

sion of property between his seven children under the family inheritance system finally resulted in Zhimin's father, Fang Gaozhu, receiving use rights to over only about twenty mu of land.

While his inheritance made Fang Gaozhu a self-sufficient peasant, his financial condition rapidly became unstable. He not only sold off a portion of his land but also incurred a heavy debt of seven to eight hundred dollars to provide for his family. During his youth, he attempted to improve his family's socioeconomic status by cultivating tea and getting into the tea trade. But declining tea prices made it an economically unenviable proposition. He therefore turned back again to subsistence crops. In his autobiography, Fang Zhimin frequently mentions his father's constant worries, which were caused by the lack of financial resources and increasing debts.

Fang Zhimin was the oldest son and the second child in his family. He had an older sister, Fang Rongnian, and a younger brother, Fang Zhihui. His mother, Jin Lianshang, came from a peasant family of the nearby market town of Qigong. Zhimin's relationship with his family appears to have been good. His father encouraged and supported his studies. Later, when the peasant movement developed in this area, all members of his family participated in it. His mother's contribution to the revolutionary movement has received honorable mention by several of Jiangxi's Communist leaders. She became a celebrity in her own right. Zhimin's brother was one of the organizers of the peasant self-defense corps and was later appointed commander of the Red Army's Eighty-first Regiment. In 1934, during the last Communist Suppression Campaign of Jiang Jieshi, he was killed in the battle of Wangang in his native district.[7]

The village of Hutang is located about sixty li east of the district city of Yiyang. From the eastern gate of the city, a narrow and winding road brings a traveler here. Soon after the market town of Qigong, this road turns to the northeast and passes through two thickly wooded hills. The village stands just beyond an old stone bridge over a small stream. Earlier, in the front of the village, there were three small ponds that were used for raising fish and for irrigation purposes. There are small hills in the back.

The village was fairly large and had about eighty families. Like other areas of Jiangxi, most of the land was owned by either a few absentee landlords, who lived in the nearby market town of Qigong, or by self-sufficient rich peasants. Consequently, out of the eighty families, about seventy had

[7] Shao 1959b: 13–14. Chen Mu (1952: 5–15) and Lo Ning (n.d.) discuss the revolutionary struggle of Fang's family, and especially his mother; see also *FZM* 1982: 2–3.

to rent land in order to meet their subsistence needs. The system of fixed rent prevailed and no discounts were made in the event of crop failure. The local rent system was popularly known as *shuangzu shuangding* (double rent, double deposit). According to this scheme, if a tenant rented one mu of land, he was required first to pay two silver dollars as the security deposit and then to pay two shi or dan of grain as the rent. Besides that, a tenant renting more than three mu of land was also required to arrange a feast for the landlord. The local custom of *songli* (presentation of gifts) required presentation of chickens and meat to the landlord four times a year.[8]

The market town of Qigong was closely connected with the village. This town had a pawnshop known as Shao Ding Feng (Shao's Flourishing Harvest Shop), which was operated by the landlord-merchant-moneylender Shao Xiangzhen. Most of the peasants of Hutang and other neighboring villages were in debt to Shao. He charged an interest of 10 percent per month on a silver dollar, which was high even in comparison with the average rate prevalent at that time in other areas. He also reportedly earned more than two thousand dan of rice as rent from about one thousand mu of land he owned. His small force of local musclemen helped him collect rents and interest from tenants and debtors, who were spread through not only Yiyang but also the neighboring Hengfeng and Dexing districts. Like other landlords' local militia forces, Shao's armed men extorted their own agent's fees and a "footwear" levy. Resisting peasants were severely punished. Locally known as "Rich Buddha," he achieved his high status through skillful management of his varied businesses in the first decade of the twentieth century. He was thus characteristic of those small businessmen whose local social and economic status rapidly moved upward during the post-Taiping period.[9]

Qigong also had a police station, which was set up during the period of northern warlord rule. The chief local police official, Yu, was more commonly known as "Big Pock-marked Yu." Basically a corrupt person, he, in league with such prominent local landlords of the area as Zhang Niancheng and Huang Zong, not only extorted various surtaxes and levies but also helped the landlords in collection of their debts, interest payments, and other fees from the peasants. Further, he often instigated trouble in villages by sending local ruffians to extract cash or wine gifts from the people coming to him to complain or file a case. He thus made not less than ten thousand silver dollars annually. Local peasants therefore referred to him with con-

[8] Shanghai renmin chubanshe 1975: 3.
[9] Weida de Fang Zhimin 1953: 3–4; *FZM* 1982: 4–5.

tempt as the "heavenly emperor" of the area, or "an old tiger that after eating human flesh does not even spit out the bones."[10]

Such then were the surroundings in Hutang village where Fang Zhimin grew up. Financially not very secure, most of the boys of the Fang family had only two to three years of education in a local village school. The girls stayed at home and learned weaving and other crafts. Zhimin was sent to the village school for primary education at the age of seven, and he studied there for three years. His first teacher was a very incompetent individual who had had only four years of formal education. However, while Zhimin was in his first year at the school, the teacher left. His position was taken by a learned person who was a Xiucai degree holder, Yan Changxin. Zhimin was a bright student and Yan encouraged him to study. Classes in this school were usually held only during the inactive part of the farming season. At harvest time, students worked on their own or other peasants' family farms. Like other village boys, Zhimin collected animal dung and helped his father in harvesting the rice crop and picking peanuts.

In 1909, there were abnormal rains all over Jiangxi. Most of the province was hit by either a severe drought or a heavy flood. Appalled by the plight of famine-stricken peasants, M. Fatiguet, the French missionary and the chief of the Catholic church of northern Jiangxi, addressed an open letter to the *North China Herald* in December 1910 requesting immediate relief aid for the region near Jiujiang. He wrote that a large region in northern and northeastern Jiangxi had been devastated by successive floods during the last two years. Whatever had been left after the ravages of water was later effaced by the drought.[11] Consequently, between 1909 and 1910, bandit activities increased and rice riots took place all over the province. The districts of Jian, Jianchang, Fuzhou, Xinchang, Xinyu, Yichun, Yiningzhou, Linjiang, Nanan, Boyang, Dean, Wanzai, Wuning, and Yongxiu were scenes of large-scale peasant riots and bandit attacks.[12] Confronted with a critical situation, many peasant families of Hutang left home to earn their living elsewhere in order to survive. The local village school was thus closed and Fang's studies were disrupted.

Fang was soon able to continue his education, however, at a private school in the neighboring Lieqiao village. This school was managed by a famous local landlord, Zhang Niancheng. Unlike Qigong's absentee landlord-merchant-moneylender Shao Xiangzhen, who had rapidly acquired

[10] Fang 1978: 33.
[11] *North China Herald*, December 23, 1910.
[12] See chapter 5 for the general characteristics of these peasant riots and uprisings.

high local status and had no customary ties with local peasants, Zhang Nian-cheng belonged to a traditional village landlord family with a fairly long history of literary activities and service in the imperial bureaucracy. Known as "Beixiang Wang" (the king of northern Yiyang villages), Zhang still maintained such customary paternalistic functions as the arbitration of justice, administration of law, management of local welfare schemes pertaining to charity, repair of roads and dykes, and the organization of local private schools.[13] His pretensions to generosity through such visible paternalistic acts contributed to the perpetuation of his authority and influence in the local area. During the imperial regime, Zhang was closely connected with the imperial bureaucracy and was a loyal supporter of the dynasty. After the collapse of the Qing state, he cut off his queue—a symbol of adherence to the imperial rule—and switched his loyalty to the new regime to maintain his dominant position in the countryside. He opened a preparatory school in Lieqiao, which enhanced his local prestige. The school provided free education to the needy and bright children from peasant families. Zhang thus obligated a large number of local persons to him and gained their support in the locality.

Fang Zhimin was introduced to Zhang by his village school teacher, Yan Changxin. Yan was Zhang's father-in-law and had started teaching in the Lieqiao Preparatory School after the natural disasters necessitated the closure of the Hutang village school. Finding Fang an exceptionally intelligent student, he invited him to Zhang's house to continue his education. Fang studied there for about a year until the age of fourteen. Impressed by his devotion to studies, the landlord Zhang treated him as an "adopted son" of the family. There was another reason for his kindness toward Fang. After preparing him for entrance into the bureaucracy, he wanted to make him his son-in-law.

Meanwhile, in 1911, the Qing state had unceremoniously collapsed. Following the Wuchang Uprising, officers of Jiangxi's New Army and members of the Revolutionary Alliance grabbed the provincial capital, Nanchang, on October 31.[14] In Jiangxi, the violence was brief; the revolutionaries succeeded in about ten days. Starting on October 23 in Jiujiang, the struggle ended on November 4 with complete control by the revolutionaries over the entire province. Although there was some chaos and confusion, the revolutionary accession to power was, on the whole, peaceful.

[13] *FZM* 1982: 6–7.
[14] Kupper 1971: 217–28. For the activities of Chinese bourgeoisie in Jiangxi before the 1911 revolution, see Tang 1985: 57–60.

In fact, the war between pro- and anti-Yuan forces, which began immediately after the overthrow of the Qing state, was more destructive and affected more significantly the masses of northeastern Jiangxi. However, by July 1913, the anti-Yuan forces of Li Liezhun, a militarist and a member of the Revolutionary Alliance, were defeated at Hukou. Yuan Shikai appointed Wang Rukai the civil governor and Li Zhun the military governor of Jiangxi. The province was thus completely taken over by the northern warlord forces. However, the same establishment that had traditionally patronized the rural areas continued to wield power during the northern warlords' control. The Revolution of 1911 therefore brought about no significant change in the rural social and political structure. Consequently, neither the situation in the rural areas nor the condition of the peasants improved.

To be sure, the revolutionaries of 1911 had separated themselves from the peasants in 1906, when their planned rebellion in collaboration with the Hongjianghui failed.[15] The Pingxiang Rebellion, or the Ping Liu Campaign, not only started earlier than planned but also deviated from the original political goals of the Revolutionary Alliance. Starving peasants and unemployed coal miners, who constituted the major force of the rebellion under the leadership of the Hongjianghui, were more interested in compelling the local elite to maintain customary rules of social justice than in the political overthrow of the state. As many of the intellectuals of the Revolutionary Alliance and officers of the New Army came from families of the local gentry, the rebel attack threatened their base of power. The rebellion was, therefore, quickly suppressed. It marked, as Kupper writes, the last attempt of revolutionaries in Jiangxi to organize an alliance with the masses on the basis of the ideas of Sun Yat-sen. Their later attempts were primarily concentrated on conducting political propaganda among the military units and the educated elite.[16]

In Jiangxi, not unlike other provinces of China, the Revolution of 1911 had only symbolic impact. Young men cut off the queues that the Qing rulers had forced Han Chinese to wear. The practice of binding girls' feet was denounced and women's rights were advocated. Other new and radical ideas were introduced. Most significantly, the revolution provided a favorable atmosphere for the beginning of a new political and cultural movement.

[15] For a detailed description of the Pingxiang Rebellion and the Hongjianghui, see Chang Kuo-t'ao 1971: 1–15; Kupper 1971: 78–93; ZNYS 1957, 1:616. This rebellion is also referred to in various GMD sources on the 1911 revolution. A branch of this society, Hui Dang, was active in Leping district and was instrumental in a massive uprising there in 1904.

[16] Kupper 1971: 92.

In the city of Yiyang, a visible impact of the revolution was the change in the name of the local prestigious school, the Dieshan Academy, to the Yiyang Higher Primary School. During the Qing period, this academy had produced many degree holders and, even after the revolution, it remained a major center of education in northeastern Jiangxi. Fang Zhimin joined this school in 1916 after successfully passing the entrance examination. His move from the village to the district city broadened his horizons and exposed him to the problems confronting contemporary China. In the autobiographical essay "Beloved China" (Keai de Zhongguo), he writes that before joining the school in Yiyang city he was perplexed about such prevalent contemporary concepts as patriotism, imperialism, and colonialism. He also failed to comprehend the dynamics and the wider dimensions of the imperialists' invasion of China.[17]

In China, the abolition of the examination system in 1905 and the collapse of the Qing state in 1911 had eliminated the basis for Confucian learning and precipitated the spread of modern education and Western-style schools. New education disseminated new conceptions of society among the youth and provoked them to seek fresh solutions for contemporary ills. It thus initiated an intellectual movement for which the schools became the organizing centers. Like others, the Yiyang Higher Primary School also emerged as a base for radical activities in the city after the Revolution of 1911. Many of the young teachers at this school were influenced by, and propagated, current cultural and political ideologies. Prominent journals, such as *Xin Qingnian* (The new youth), which were enthusiastically read by young students and teachers, presented new visions for China. The real beginning of Fang's intellectual and political development thus can be traced to his experiences in this school.

Deeply influenced by the new currents of thought in Yiyang, Fang organized a Ninth District Youth Society sometime between 1916 and 1917.[18] In the course of his organizational activities among students of the school, he became a close friend of Shao Shiping. Like Fang, Shao was a native of Yiyang district and came from Shaobanjia village, which was not very far from Hutang. The two were introduced to each other by Fang's father, who had known Shao's family. In this district town school, the domination of students from urban rich and gentry families brought the young village students closer. In a memoir, Shao notes that, looking uncouth and "ancient"

[17] Fang 1952: 4.
[18] *FZM* 1982: 8–11.

in their dress, both he and Fang studied together, discussed common issues, and lived like brothers.[19] Shao later became a close associate of Fang's and a famous revolutionary leader of the Xinjiang peasant movement.

The Ninth District Youth Society was an organization of progressive students. It opposed the conservative group in the school, which had continued to maintain and propagate superstitious beliefs; Shao says that many students sincerely believed in gods and ghosts. When members of the Youth Society criticized these beliefs, conservative students attempted to scare them by having one of their number impersonate a ghost. But Fang and his associates caught hold of this so-called ghost and exposed him to the other students. Consequently, the popularity of the Youth Society grew and its membership increased.[20]

Enlightened by the new political and cultural currents in Yiyang city, Fang and other spirited members of the Youth Society naturally found the activities of local landlords like Zhang Niancheng incompatible with their beliefs. Fang made his first attempt at local reform soon after returning to his native village during a holiday. He wrote a letter to landlord Zhang urging him to change his ways. Moreover, he reproached Zhang for ten major crimes against the people in an article that was not only sent to local officials for Zhang's indictment but also pasted on the walls of a popular local restaurant, Huangtianshou Fandien at Huangshaling, for public reading. Infuriated by Fang's and the Youth Society's activities, Zhang complained to the local chief of police, Yu. But before the police could arrest him, Fang escaped from Hutang village to the nearby Lailong Mountains. One of his friends, Huang Zhenzhong, however, was arrested. Huang, who later became one of the organizers of the Xinjiang peasant movement, was kept in a local prison for ten months. He was released only after Fang and his friends collected a considerable sum of money to pay to the local police chief as a bribe. Frightened by this example, other members of the Ninth District Youth Society, especially those from rich peasant and landlord families, stopped participating in political activities and left the organization. The Youth Society thus closed down.[21] In its place, Fang later organized the

[19] *HQPP* 1957–60, 9:13.

[20] *FZM* 1982: 8–11; *Buxiu de geming zhanshi* 1960: 1–2.

[21] There is some confusion about the exact date and other facts of this incident. Some of the biographies mention that during this time Fang opposed the candidacy of Zhang for a seat in the assembly. I have followed the version presented in *FZM*, which is chronologically more structured. It was probably revolutionaries' continuing struggle with Zhang that resulted in some mixing of dates and the confusing versions in biographies prepared by them a long time after actual incidents. See Miao 1962: 4–5; Miao 1958b: 57–60.

Yiyang Revolutionary Youth Society. Active members of this society comprised ten or so students from a poor-peasant family background. They included Shao Shihping, Huang Zhenzhong, Zou Ji, and Peng Nie, all of whom later played an important role in the revolutionary movement.[22]

While the repressive and corrupt rural sociopolitical structure forced Fang to think seriously of an alternative solution to liberate common people from traditional bondage, Japan's expansionist designs on China as presented in its twenty-one demands in 1915 proved to be a crucial factor in Fang's rejection of imperialist ideologies and capitalist models of development. The acceptance of Japan's twenty-one demands was tantamount to the surrender of China's sovereignty. Yuan Shikai's weak resistance to these pressures, and his capitulation in the treaty of May 25, 1915, enraged many intellectuals and exacerbated a strong and widespread anti-Japanese movement in China. At Yiyang, Fang wholeheartedly plunged into this movement. Together with young teachers and students of the school, he participated in mass demonstrations and wrote inflammatory slogans and posters, which he distributed on the streets. During this period, as he later confessed in "Beloved China," impassioned speeches brought tears to the eyes of many students. Everybody was so much seized with fury that if a Japanese had been found, his flesh would have been torn apart.[23] With great zeal and enthusiasm, he and other students burned and smashed all Japanese-made materials. In spite of his relative poverty, he destroyed his Japanese Jingangshih (Diamond) tooth powder, Dongyang (Eastern Ocean) soap, and an umbrella, which he had bought at Yiyang in an effort to be more like an urban educated person.[24]

But, in 1918, Fang's political ideas were still colored by patriotism and idealism. Like Mao, who once emphasized military spirit and heroism to save China, Fang contemplated organizing and leading brave Chinese soldiers to defeat Japan. He also often dreamed, as his "Beloved China" describes, of entering a military school after graduation and amassing money to build a strong navy to fight against China's enemies on the Pacific Ocean. His ideal heroes were great military generals who fought innumerable battles in remote areas and brought honor and glory to their countries.[25]

In Western history, he was particularly fascinated by Napoleon and Washington. His favorite authors were Aldous Huxley, Montesquieu, and

---

[22] *FZM* 1982: 12.
[23] Fang 1952: 5.
[24] Ibid., 6.
[25] Ibid., 7.

Herbert Spencer. Among Chinese heroes, his fascination was for the famous Song general Yue Wumou, popularly known as Yue Fei. To be sure, Yue Fei attracted the imagination of many radical young intellectuals searching for solutions to China's contemporary problems. During his younger days, the prominent Chinese Marxist Chen Duxiu, as Feigon has demonstrated, formed a Warrior Yue Society in an attempt to emulate this traditional heroic figure in reviving the country.[26] Fang's respect for Yue Fei also resulted from the fact that the latter, during the period of the Southern Song, saw no solution to the Jin state's expanding power other than military conquest of the lost territories and elimination of Jin as a state. Yue Fei strongly opposed any compromise with the enemy, considering it treasonous and immoral. Some Song officials, however, feared that his policy would enhance the power of militarists and charged him with conspiracy. Although there was no evidence against him, he and his young son were executed. His body was buried in Hanzhou. Later a temple was built there in his honor that became a famous national shrine. For Fang, the distinction between Yue Fei's loyalty to the emperor and Napoleon's hegemonic despotism were, however, still not clear. His patriotism was rooted in his strong culturalistic beliefs, which he acquired during his early experiences at Yiyang and which colored his nationalism throughout his life. Like most other intellectuals of the May Fourth period, he never abandoned his Chinese nationalism for a Marxist internationalism.

Fang graduated from the Yiyang Higher Primary School in 1918. He thus became the first person in Hutang village to achieve the equivalent of a traditional Xiucai degree. In the eyes of the villagers, it was an attainment that would later assure him a lucrative and powerful official position. Impressed by this and at the urging of his relatives, his father borrowed money to help him pursue studies at the capital of Jiangxi, Nanchang. In spite of his childhood dream of entering a military school, he entered the First Provincial Industrial School after passing an entrance examination in 1919. His growing realization of the significance of Western science and technology in building a strong nation-state perhaps led him to abandon his earlier wish to receive military training. Within a year, he completed preparatory courses for engineering and enrolled himself as a first-year student in mechanical engineering.

During his first year as an engineering student, Fang's financial condition deteriorated to such an extent that he was often unable to pay all his ex-

[26] Ibid., 5; *FZM* 1982: 10. For an illuminating discussion of Chen Duxiu and the Warrior Yue Society, see Feigon 1983: 77–78.

penses for tuition and board. His father frequently borrowed money to support his education. His cousin, Fang Zhichun, also sold the surface rights to five mu of family land to ease the financial burden.[27] In spite of his impoverished state, Fang diligently pursued his studies. He took evening refresher courses in English and mathematics and performed well in these subjects and in applied mechanics in the school examination. But he was unable to complete the engineering degree, for his increasing political activities were soon to make him suspicious to local authorities and force him to leave Nanchang.

In 1919, the year when Fang had joined the Industrial School at Nanchang, rising anti-Japanese sentiments culminated in the famous May Fourth Movement. All of China was shocked and humiliated to learn the verdict of the Versailles Peace Congress, which secretly accepted Japan's claim to the former German concession at Shandong. In spite of China's support during the First World War, the Allied powers betrayed her. Indignant, intellectuals and students organized a mass rally at Beijing on May 4. As the news of the Peace Congress's decision and the demonstrations in Beijing spread, a mass movement of students, workers, and merchants began in major cities throughout China. The May Fourth demonstration, which started as a protest against Japanese aggression, soon developed into a wider anti-imperialist nationalist movement. It marked the beginning of a political and intellectual movement that questioned the very basis of Chinese society.

At that time, as an engineering student at Nanchang, Fang's first exposure to the foreign imperialists' control over key Chinese institutions and their privileged status in the provincial capital exacerbated his antiforeign sentiments. There he saw Westerners for the first time. In "Beloved China," he writes that the city was so full of foreigners that one could encounter them by just walking on the street. The sight of a foreign manager of the Chinese post office being carried in a sedan by native postal workers shocked him. He often wondered why the Chinese could not even manage their own post office. Why should the control of Chinese post offices be handed over to the foreigners?[28] To be sure, Chinese delegates at the Versailles Peace Congress had demanded, unsuccessfully, an end to the foreign control of the Chinese postal services. But the aggressive imperialist powers continued to manage the postal system, even after the Washington Conference of 1921 had passed a resolution against international control of it.

Thus, as the news of the May Fourth Incident reached Nanchang, Fang

[27] Miao 1962: 20.
[28] Fang 1952: 7–9.

vigorously participated in the movement organized by the local student association. This association was an organization of progressive students from all the schools of Nanchang. Among its active participants were Huang Dao, Yuan Yuping, Zou Nu, Cui Hao, Wang Qun, Feng Ren, Xiao Guohua, and Liu Junshan.[29] Together with these like-minded students, Fang went from shop to shop to enforce the boycott of Japanese goods. His increasingly deeper involvement in the anti-Japanese political movement not only turned him into a prominent student leader of the province but also brought him closer to the radical groups of Nanchang. This, in turn, exposed him for the first time to Marxism and other progressive ideologies.

More confident after his political exposure in Nanchang, Fang also attempted to remove the corrupt police chief, Yu, of Qigong market town. Whenever he returned home, local peasants complained to him about Yu's atrocities. Moreover, he wanted to settle a score with Yu for imprisoning one of his friends during his Yiyang school days. He wrote and submitted several petitions against the police chief to the Provincial Police Headquarters. This finally resulted in an inquiry, but Yu bribed the investigating official and was acquitted of all the charges.[30]

Meanwhile, Fang's political activities both outside and inside the industrial school had enraged school authorities. In comparison with the Yiyang Higher Primary School, the atmosphere at the industrial school was conservative. Teachers were unenthusiastic about the growing cultural and political ferment within China and were often incompetent in their subjects. Fang found the environment of the school incompatible with his new thoughts and ideals. Like many other pre-1911 Chinese students, the school's principal, Zhao Baohong, had spent only five to six months in Japan, which was necessary to get a quick unmerited diploma. Despite his lack of qualifications in engineering, his status as a Japan-returned student soon earned him the principalship of the school. He was therefore often unable to answer students' questions satisfactorily. Fang, as Miao Min writes, also hated his English language teacher, Mr. Wu, whose knowledge was too deficient to allow him to teach the language to students.[31]

Dissatisfied with the affairs of the school, Fang in 1921 wrote a satirical play called *Strange Phenomena in a Private School* that derided the incompetence of teachers who wasted students' time. (This was later published in

[29] *FZM* 1982: 18.
[30] Ibid., 18–19.
[31] Miao 1962: 20–21.

the *New Jiangxi Journal*.)[32] When repeated petitions to the principal to reform
the educational pattern failed, he finally organized a Student Self-Government Association at the First Provincial Industrial School. In a meeting, this
association charged the principal with the embezzlement of school funds,
nepotism, and conservatism. Enraged by this, the principal expelled Fang
and two other students from the school in mid-1921. Although students,
together with other radical groups of Nanchang, staged protest marches for
fifteen days, the principal closed down the school early for the summer and
suppressed the movement with the active support of the provincial warlord
police. The expulsion orders were not revoked. Convinced that new science
and technology could not by themselves solve China's contemporary problems, Fang diverted his attention more to the study of politics and new radical ideologies.

FROM THE JIANGXI REORGANIZATION
SOCIETY TO THE NATIONAL
REVOLUTIONARY MOVEMENT

Like that of many other contemporary Chinese intellectuals, the beginning
of Fang Zhimin's involvement in the national revolutionary movement corresponded to the unprecedented political and intellectual ferment sparked by
the May Fourth Movement. In Jiangxi, a prominent center of such political
and intellectual activities was the Jiangxi Reorganization Society. Fang's participation in this society exposed him to a variety of intellectual debates over
China's contemporary problems and drew him finally toward Marxism. It
was to carry him toward his ultimate destiny—the commitment to revolution to emancipate China. It was also to bring him closer to many like-
minded students who would participate along with him in the protracted
revolutionary struggle in Jiangxi.

The Jiangxi Reorganization Society was an outgrowth of the Poyang Lake
Society.[33] The latter was formed by the progressives of the Second Nanchang Middle School soon after the May Fourth Incident in Beijing. As the
intellectual and political activities of the Poyang Lake Society expanded outside the school, the Jiangxi Reorganization Society was set up in December
1920 to bring all radicals in the city into one larger body. Formally established on January 1, 1921, at a students' meeting at the Second Nanchang

[32] This essay appears in *HQPP* 1957–60, 9:5–6.
[33] *WSSQ* 1959, 3:27–40.

Middle School, members and followers of the society included students, intellectuals, merchants, and workers. However, the total number of its core members never exceeded twenty, and it remained small in size. Within two years of its inauguration, it was disbanded by the warlord governor of Jiangxi, Chen Gongyuan. Notwithstanding its short existence and small membership, as the first important modern radical society of Jiangxi, it played a significant role in bringing together radicals from different social groups to discuss the social and political problems of contemporary China. Some of the members of the society, such as Fang Zhimin, Huang Dao, Huang Hongyi, Shi Xiupeng, Wang Qun, Wang Wei, and Yuan Yuping, later became prominent leaders of the Communist movement in Jiangxi.

Fang was introduced to the Jiangxi Reorganization Society in late December 1920 by two of its eight founding members, Yuan Yuping and Huang Dao. Both of them were classmates at the Second Nanchang Middle School; Huang came from Guixi and Yuan, from Xingguo district. Fang, after his expulsion from the First Provincial Industrial School of Nanchang, wholeheartedly devoted his time to expanding the society's activities.

Members of the Jiangxi Reorganization Society published a quarterly journal called *Xin Jiangxi* (New Jiangxi). The aim of this journal, according to the preface to the first issue was to change the "dark and old Jiangxi" into a "bright and new Jiangxi." Editors of the journal announced that its major purpose was not to encourage direct participation in politics but to promote severe criticism of society. To achieve this purpose, they introduced three general guidelines. First, the journal would strive to promote the real spirit of democracy and attack such oppressive social-class relationships as those existing between warlords and the masses, capitalists and workers, and men and women. Second, it would vigorously develop a proletarian spirit to liberate workers in order to lead them toward a brighter future. Third, it would attempt to bridge the gap between the dark and bright elements prevalent within the contemporary society.[34] These aims reflect, on the one hand, the apparent consensus among editors of the journal and members of the Jiangxi Reorganization Society to reject the Confucian past and promote egalitarianism and, on the other, a wide difference of opinion among them on a program to be followed to bring about changes in society.

Consequently, articles in the *New Jiangxi Journal* promoted a mixed bag of ideologies ranging from anarchism to Marxism to various strains of liber-

[34] Ibid. 1:447.

alism.[35] Many contributors stressed the need for the overhaul of the backward educational system, which promoted corruption in society and thus weakened China. Abolition of the repressive examination system, introduction of a more practical and less-textbook-oriented education, and promotion of a uniform coeducational system were emphasized. Viewing the dominance of the military in contemporary Chinese politics, some articles suggested that dedicated young men should enter the army to push for radical social change. They maintained that military dictatorship was the only solution for China's contemporary ills.

But radicals like Yuan Yuping strongly and openly promoted Marxism. Responding to the critique by Hu Shi's adherents, who believed in "more study of problems and less talk of isms," Yuan answered, "We cannot have 'non-ism' beliefs. We should struggle and sacrifice ourselves for an ideology, and eliminate 'superstitions' [against the ideology] existing in literature, philosophy, and science. Learning from Marx, we should become fighters to reorganize society in reality."[36] In another article, he repeated that only by following the scientific social ideology of Marxism could fundamental changes in society be brought about. "We cannot wait for the luxury to conveniently discuss the reorganization of society and then to act, for, by that time, we all might be destroyed by the warlords and foreign imperialists."[37] In the last issue of the journal, which was published on January 15, 1923, Yuan attacked all non-Marxist ideologies prevalent in contemporary China as "empty talk" and "dangerous." This last issue also introduced its readers to works of Marx and Lenin, writings on communism, and the political activities of such progressive student organizations as the Guangdong Socialist Youth Corps.[38] The increasing promotion of Marxist ideology in the last two issues of the journal, which were published during 1922–1923, indicate its editors' and many of the Reorganization Society members' gradual conversion and commitment to Marxism.

Thus in 1921, already introduced to the Jiangxi Reorganization Society and deeply influenced by its promotion of radical thoughts, Fang was getting interested in learning more about the new Western ideas, especially Marxism, that had so overwhelmingly influenced the contemporary intellectual scene. After his expulsion from the Nanchang industrial school, he therefore left the provincial capital to enter the William Nast College (also known as

[35] The contents of these articles have been discussed in *WSSQ* 1959, 1:27–40, 3:552–56.
[36] Ibid. 1:30.
[37] Ibid. 1:31.
[38] Ibid. 1:36–38.

Dong Wen Academy) at Jiujiang in late 1921. Dissatisfied with engineering as well as desirous of learning progressive Western thoughts and Marxism in the original English, he enrolled in advanced courses in this famous Western-style college.[39]

The William Nast College was established by an American Methodist missionary in the late Qing period. Governed by foreign missionaries, it was undoubtedly a popular place to learn modern Western ideas and languages in Jiangxi. The collapse of the imperial examination system had rendered meaningless the learning of old Confucian texts. Hence, the new kind of knowledge provided in the school was considered essential by an ever-increasing number of Chinese students for getting higher positions in the newly emerging modern enterprises in China. However, the primary purpose for which this college was established was to convert Chinese into Christian workers and to prepare them for evangelistic activities. In an annual report of the college, its president, Carl F. Kupfer, candidly remarked:

> If the education alone was the aim of this institution, we could fill our halls with youths who are willing and able to pay for their education; but they are not the class who want to hear religious or moral instruction. A limited number of that class can be safely admitted; but a high moral tone and strong spiritual atmosphere cannot be retained when such make up the majority. The vital need of our collegiate work is the establishment in the adjacent smaller centers of primary and secondary schools with able Christian teachers. The proportion of our students coming from non-Christian homes is too great for a healthy development in the college.[40]

The president noted, however, that the admission of a large number of non-Christian students willing to learn Western ideas provided a wide and fruitful field within the college for evangelistic work.

The city of Jiujiang was then full of foreign business offices. Since it was an important port on the Yangzi River, foreign commercial and military ships frequently cast anchor there. In "Beloved China," Fang writes that standing on the bank of the Yangzi River, he often used to watch innumerable foreign ships sailing with no restraint in Chinese waters and always wondered whether the countries of their origin would allow such free movement of Chinese ships in their own waters. If they did not permit Chinese

[39] Fang Lan 1978: 30.
[40] Methodist Episcopal Church, Annual Report, 1907: 196.

ships, was not the intrusion of these foreign ships an insult to China?[41] The contemporary situation in Jiujiang depressed him even more and forced him to look for a viable ideology of action.

In the William Nast College, Fang also discovered the hollowness of liberal Western thoughts and ideals. He found a wide difference between the theory and practice of foreign missionaries preaching such Christian concepts as the "brotherhood" and the "equality" of all people. As was the common practice, the salaries of the Chinese Christian teachers of the college were considerably lower than those of the foreign missionary teachers. Fang sympathized with his Chinese language teacher who received only a little more than twenty dollars as his remuneration, while foreigners received somewhere between two and three hundred dollars. Moreover, non-Christian Chinese in the college were treated as if they were all fallen sons of God. The predominant atmosphere was not of equality but of superiority and inferiority. Foreigners were the most lovable children of God, and Chinese were the rejected ones who must be taught morality and made civilized.[42] It is, therefore, hardly surprising that Fang's experience with foreign missionaries and imperialists at Jiujiang radically alienated him from the Western liberal doctrines prevalent in contemporary China. His experience also reinforced his beliefs in Marxism as a viable ideology to solve China's deep-rooted problems.

Fang's biographers report that he began to study Marxism seriously in Jiujiang.[43] To be sure, he had already been exposed to Marxist ideology a year earlier at Nanchang. But in the William Nast College, he probably read for the first time *The Communist Manifesto*, *Capital*, and works on the Bolshevik Revolution. Miao Min writes that his favorite place for the study of Marxist works was the college chapel, where every student was required to study the Bible quietly with the pastor. Finding him always engrossed in Marxist literature, friends called him "Mr. Socialism." It thus appears that, initially exposed to Marxism in Nanchang, he fully committed himself to it at Jiujiang. Not unlike many other intellectuals of the period, Fang found confirmation of his earlier political actions against local landlords in Marx's radical critique of society, and confirmation of his anti-imperialist nationalistic beliefs in Lenin's theory of imperialism.

Soon after entering the college in 1921, Fang had formed a small reading society modeled on Nanchang's Jiangxi Reorganization Society. As his com-

[41] Fang 1952: 9.
[42] Ibid., 9–10.
[43] Miao 1962: 24; see also *FZM* 1982: 27–30.

mitment to Marxism grew, this society turned into a Marxist study group. Miao Min mentions that in spite of the strict routine of the college, members of this group often met after the scheduled bedtime for the dormitory and discussed in whispers their preassigned readings.[44] They also established contacts with the members of the Chinese Socialist Youth Corps in Shanghai and received its journal, *Vanguard*. In the spring of 1922, Fang played an active role in organizing students of not only his own college but also of the Sixth Teachers' Training College and the First Middle School of Jiujiang against the outcome of the Washington Conference. Ignoring China's sovereignty, the conference advocated equal opportunities for expansion to all the imperialist countries. During this period, Fang was also drawn to the activities of the Anti-Christian Student Alliance, which was formed in 1922 with the slogan "Love your country sincerely, maintain the spirit of science, use positive methods, and oppose Christianity and the schools governed by them." Although already committed to Marxism, his admiration for this society and its ideology as expounded in the newspaper *Xianqu* indicates his comprehension of the former not in strict theoretical but in broader voluntaristic and populist terms.[45]

These political activities, however, made Fang's further stay at the college extremely difficult. His efforts to build a radical political organization in Jiujiang together with progressive friends annoyed the military chief of the prefectural town, Wu Jinbiao, who demanded their expulsion from the college. Consequently, warned by Wu, college authorities began to place strict limits on the movements of these students. Fang often had to use addresses of his friends outside the college to meet local activists and to receive progressive articles and journals. Under such surveillance, it became impossible for him to maintain in the college a political base for his growing radical activities. Further, during this period the financial condition of Fang's family rapidly deteriorated.

Fang's father had incurred debts of more than seven hundred dollars in providing for his son's education. In the private missionary college, fees for tuition and board were particularly high, and it was becoming increasingly difficult for him to raise money to pay them. As Miao Min writes, "Like a millstone round their necks this debt weighed oppressively on the shoulders of his parents so that there was never a day in the year that his father and mother were not buried in worry. . . . When [Fang] Zhimin was home dur-

[44] Ibid., 25.

[45] For the activities of the Anti-Christian Student Alliance, see *WSSQ* 1959, 3:61–77; see also Chow 1967.

ing summer vacation, the thing he dreaded most was to hear his parents mention the debt."[46]

Torn between his commitment to the family on the one hand and the Chinese nation on the other, Fang was forced to make a crucial decision. Restless and in great mental agony, he fell ill. The flare-up of his lung disease kept him in bed for the whole of the summer of 1922. (Sometime during his childhood, Fang was afflicted with a lung disease that caused him to spit blood. He never fully recovered from it, and under the pressure of work he suffered relapses throughout his life.) He commented on his peculiar situation in a poem written on June 21, 1922:

> Ah! What's this?
> What is this stuff so red?
> Is it blood?
> Or what else could it be?
> But why do I spit blood?
> Is it natural for so young a man as I to be so cursed?
> Yes, it is natural.
> For I'm a poor youth.
> I worry about my family;
> I worry about my education;
> I worry for all my wretched, destitute brethren.
> Thousands of anxieties press on my small heart.
> How can it be that blood be not forced out?[47]

Fang was tormented by his family's concern for him. He was aware of the fact that his growing political involvement had begun to shatter his family's dream of seeing him become a rich official. He finally resolved his personal conflict by completely discontinuing family-supported education and thus dispelling any such hope his family had for him. Instead, he opted to work for his larger family and for his "wretched, destitute brethren." To an already committed Marxist, identification with China's poor as the victims of oppression provided new meaning for action and bright hope for the future. As Edward Friedman has perceptively remarked, inherent in the forward-looking ideologies of Chinese revolutionaries was a backward-looking desire to reknit the family. "What they experienced was the abandonment

---

[46] Miao 1962: 30.

[47] This excellent translation appears in Miao 1962: 28–29. For the original Chinese version, see "Zhuxie" (Spitting blood), in *HQPP* 1957–60, 9:3.

of an already spoiled family relationship seen as a major source of the moth-
erland's tragic plight for service to a new, better, and larger family in which
all China's young men were their children, and the task was as Lu Hsun [Lu
Xun] put it, 'to save the children.' "[48]

Finally, in the summer of 1922, Fang left the William Nast College of his
own volition—less than a year after entering it. This marked the end of his
academic pursuits and the beginning of his deeper involvement in national
politics. In May 1922, Fang wrote in a poem:

> It seems that multitudes are weeping
>   in one strain,
> Crying out their mournful appeal.
> Alas, my heart is broken
> And tears stream down my cheeks!
> Resolutely, courageously I respond:
> "Yes, I will come to your help,
> I will join you . . ."[49]

Within a year, Fang was to join the Chinese Communist Party to help
the multitudes. These early experiences of Fang, which changed the village
youth into a revolutionary, had a crucial bearing on his views about the
course and nature of Chinese revolution.

Between 1922 and 1925, Fang rose from a local revolutionary to a prominent leader of the Xinjiang peasant movement. In the middle of 1922, after
abandoning his family ties with a full resolve to commit himself to political
activities for the emancipation of the larger Chinese family, Fang went to
Shanghai to join the Socialist Youth Corps and also to search for a job. The
city of Shanghai, which was then the center of revolutionary activities of
diverse shades, was also the meeting ground of "rootless intellectuals" like
Fang. Here, in 1920, the prominent Chinese Marxist Chen Duxiu had organized the Socialist Youth Corps as the youth wing of the Chinese Communist Party. Fang had been introduced to this corps through its journal
Vanguard, which he avidly read during his Jiujiang days. In the fall of 1922,
he entered the corps on the recommendation of another radical from Jiangxi,
Zhao Xingnong.

[48] Friedman 1974: 219n.
[49] "Kusheng" (Sound of weeping), in *HQPP* 1957–60, 9:7–8, translated in Miao 1962: 27–
28.

Zhao Xingnong was a native of Nanfeng district, Jiangxi.[50] Belonging to a bankrupt merchant family, he was not able to study beyond middle school. In Shanghai, while working as a newspaper vendor, he become a member of the Communist Party in 1922. Fang was introduced to him by their common friends in Jiangxi. Zhao helped him find a temporary job as a proofreader at a local "left" Guomindang newspaper, *Guomin Ribao*. Natives of a common province, they found many similarities in their ideologies and life-styles and soon became close friends. Miao Min mentions that Fang was deeply influenced by Zhao, who reinforced his commitment to Marxism.[51]

In late 1922, Fang, along with Zhao, returned to Nanchang where together they established the Nanchang Literary Society to organize radical political activities in the province. Most of the student activists of the May Fourth Movement period and members of the Jiangxi Reorganization Society soon joined this. It operated from the premises of the prominent provincial daily newspaper *Dajiangbao* (The great river newspaper). Fang was also provided a temporary part-time job as proofreader by the manager of *Dajiangbao*, Zhang Tianmin. The last two issues of the *New Jiangxi Journal* were published under the auspices of the society and, therefore, displayed a radical outlook. To raise money for their political activities as well as to facilitate their work among local students, members of the Nanchang Literary Society also set up a bookstore by the name of the "Nanchang Poormen's Library" under the managership of Fang. Located near the university, this bookstore kept in stock most of the radical literature published and available in China, besides other materials. It gradually began to attract the attention of many like-minded students of the city, and the membership of the literary society thus grew.

In early 1923, Yuan Yuping, one of the founders of the Jiangxi Reorganization Society, joined Fang and Zhao in Nanchang. Yuan had earlier gone to Beijing University to study philosophy with Li Dazhao, who had introduced him first to the Youth Corps and later to the Communist Party. After his return, he, together with Fang and Zhao, laid the foundation of the Jiangxi branch of the Socialist Youth Corps in January 1923. It appears that after the formation of the Youth Corps, non-Marxist members of the Literary Society, now aware of its increasingly radical activities in Guangdong's countryside under Peng Pai, left the society, which thus dissolved. In place of that, Yuan, Fang, and Zhao formed a "Marxist Study Society" to mobi-

[50] The biography of Zhao, who became one of the most prominent Communist leaders in Jiangxi during the 1920s, appears in *Buxiu de geming zhanshi* 1960: 113–19.

[51] Miao 1962: 41.

lize students, followed in February 1923 by an "Alliance for Democratic Movement" to organize the masses. They also published a small newspaper, *Qingniansheng* (The voice of youth), for the propagation of Marxist revolutionary ideas.[52] For this paper, Fang visited the countryside in southern Jiangxi and prepared an investigative report on rural conditions there. In late March, a large and successful exhibition of new progressive books was organized under the auspices of these Marxist societies. It was at this time in March 1923 that Fang finally joined the Communist Party, once again through the offices of Zhao Xingnong.[53]

Meanwhile, the growing political movement in the province alarmed the warlord military general Zai Chengxun and the governor of Jiangxi, Li Tingyu. They launched an attack on all the radical organizations in Nanchang and forcibly dissolved them. The progressive bookstore was closed down, Yuan Yuping was arrested, and Zhao Xingnong fled to Shanghai. Fang himself escaped arrest only because he was lying ill in a hospital run by foreign missionaries. Shortly thereafter, he too secretly left for Shanghai via Nanjing.

In Shanghai, Fang met with other radical members of the Jiangxi Reorganization Society who had escaped following the suppression campaign by the warlords. Together they revived the *New Jiangxi Journal* under a new format as the *New Jiangxi Bimonthly Journal*. The first issue of the journal appeared on October 1, 1923. Its expressed aim was "to promote criticism of the contemporary political and social situation."[54] Altogether, twelve issues of the journal were published during its lifetime between 1923 and 1924. Unfortunately, most of them are not available now. However, a few of the available issues and the lists of the contents of other issues indicate that this journal severely criticized those beliefs which propounded the necessity of educational reforms, Westernization, or industrialization as the primary goal of the progressive movement to build a new China.

One article promoted a Gandhian type of anarchist "noncooperative movement," but the editors dismissed this idea as "unpractical and empty talk." Instead, they firmly emphasized the imperative of a social revolution. One issue was completely devoted to an introduction and serious discussion of Marxist-Leninist ideology. In others, the concept of exploitation, the rural situation in Jiangxi, movements and activities of progressive organizations, and similar topics were elaborated. Yuan Yuping's release from the warlord

[52] *WSSQ* 1959, 1:37–38; see also *FZM*: 43–45; Zhang 1959.
[53] *FZM* 1982: 47–48.
[54] *WSSQ* 1959, 1:31.

prison in Nanchang was also celebrated by the publication of several articles in praise of his sacrifice.[55] Compared with the intellectual outlook of the earlier journal, the *New Jiangxi Bimonthly Journal* was more political and emphasized a definite ideology, that is, Marxism-Leninism.

In early 1924, both Fang and Zhao once again secretly returned to Nanchang to establish an underground office of the Chinese Communist Party (CCP). By June 1924, the provincial office of the CCP had begun to work under the name of the "Mingxing Bookstore" and the "Liming Middle School." Meanwhile, initial agreements between the CCP and the GMD (Guomindang) for a United Front had been formulated. Thus in early 1924, following the CCP's instructions, Fang and Zhao entered the reorganized GMD as bipartisan members and set up a provincial branch of the GMD.[56]

In the summer of 1924, when Mao was discovering the revolutionary potential of peasants in Hunan, Fang returned to his native village to lay the foundation of the Xinjiang peasant movement. He opened a school there to explain the "New Culture" movement and the necessity of a national revolution to the peasants. During the winter of 1924, he worked among the peasants in the suburbs of Nanchang to mobilize them for the revolutionary movement. His successful organization of the peasantry as well as deep-rooted ties with rural areas earned him the directorship of the GMD's Provincial Peasant Department when the First Jiangxi Provincial GMD Congress was held in July 1925. Zhao Xingnong was elected chairman of the provincial GMD office. With this began the first phase of the revolutionary struggle in Jiangxi, during which Fang very effectively organized peasants for the revolutionary movement and established one of the largest and most famous soviets in the Xinjiang region. Arrested and executed by the GMD in 1935, Fang Zhimin's revolutionary activities during the Jiangxi era of the Chinese Communist Party nonetheless established him as one of the most important Marxist peasant leaders of modern China.

FANG ZHIMIN'S IDEAS
ON REVOLUTION

Like such prominent Marxist leaders of China as Li Dazhao, Peng Pai, and Mao Zedong, Fang Zhimin believed in the revolutionary potential of peasants. According to Marxist-Leninist theory of the time, such a belief consti-

---

[55] Ibid. 1:39–42, 3:555–56.
[56] See *FZM* 1982.

tuted heresy. Moreover, Fang belonged to the class of exploited rural cultivators that traditionally rose in rebellion with a limited scope and defensive
aims. But he combined Marxism with the forces of peasantry and made socialist goals compatible with rural aspirations.

To be sure, Fang was not a revolutionary ideologue, nor did his ideology
play any significant role in molding the character of the Chinese revolution.
He was more a revolutionary activist. As such, Mao praised him for following a correct independent policy for the establishment of soviets in the countryside. Mao's commendation of Fang recently sparked a debate in China on
the nature of the latter's contribution to revolutionary ideology. In this context, Tang demonstrates the distinctiveness of Fang's ideology in the development of an independent style for organizing peasants for a revolution. Another Chinese commentator, Kuang, more convincingly indicates that Mao
found in Fang's style a confirmation of his own views on the revolutionary
potential of the peasants. Chen, on the other hand, finds that Fang developed an independent revolutionary style because his belief in revolution, like
that of many contemporary radical intellectuals, was rooted in his blending
of the Western concept of Marxism with Chinese reality. Guided by scientific Marxism, he not only overcame the limitation imposed by China's past
history and contemporary reality but also charted a revolutionary course
that was characterized by a harmonious unity between revolutionary theory
and practice, enthusiasm for the national essence and a well-defined political
perspective, current and long-term basic political needs and interests, and
patriotism and communism. But the same conclusion was also reached by
other revolutionary intellectuals of the May Fourth generation.[57]

Fang's participation in peasant-based revolutionary activity was a result
of his own comprehension of contemporary reality and his belief in Marxism-Leninism. An analysis of his works will forward an understanding,
probably in more realistic terms, of how the concept of an urban-based
Communist revolution was applied in rural areas by a large number of revolutionary activists. Fang's writings are few and those available are still
fewer. His execution at the young age of thirty-six and his role as a revolutionary activist denied him an opportunity to reflect on and elaborate his
ideas in a systematic way. His works are therefore usually devoid of rigorous
discussions of theoretical issues. During his lifetime, he wrote frequently
only during two periods: first, when he was associated with the Jiangxi Re-

[57] For a discussion of Fang's revolutionary ideology and strategy see Tang 1982; Kuang
1983; Li 1983; Chen 1984(a).

organization Society and its journals and, second, shortly before his execution in 1935, when he was in a GMD prison. Although his writings are few in number, they nevertheless delineate his ideas about the imperative of a peasant-based Communist revolution in China.

Like many other contemporary radical intellectuals, Fang's belief in revolution was the result of his realization of the inability of Confucian China to maintain the integrity of Chinese society. The failure of Confucianism to protect and defend the masses of China from the oppression of the landed upper classes and the invasion of foreign imperialists proved its illegitimacy. For Fang, Confucianism provided no solution to the miserable conditions of the masses and instilled no hope for a brighter future for China. In his earlier writings, he thus attacks the Confucian past that legitimized and perpetuated the exploitation of man by man.

Fang's first essay for the *New Jiangxi Journal*, "The Private School," appeared in its second issue.[58] Written as a short story and probably based on his first experience at the local village school, it portrays the village students' indignation over the forced teaching of Confucian classics, by a schoolteacher who is also a bean merchant. Unable to understand, and uninterested in Confucian classics, these students often make mistakes in recognizing ancient characters that are strange and meaningless to them and consequently are often punished by the teacher. They therefore call their teacher, who believes himself to be a master of Confucian thought and learning, uncultured and barbaric. Fang writes that once a village student, Huang Hai, failed to read classical excerpts fluently and was severely beaten. Later, he indignantly remarked to other students that he did not know what crimes he had committed to be forced to attend this school. Such study could not be compared in any way with the happiness of herding cattle in the village. All the village students agreed with Huang Hai's remarks. Through such disavowal of contemporary Confucians and culture and exaltation of the village life-styles, Fang not only demonstrates the futility of the former in contemporary rural society, but also projects his concern at the cultural domination of the peasantry by the ruling elites and landed upper class.

Certainly, during this period, the crisis of paternalism had begun to disintegrate linkages between the so-called high and low cultures. Sensing this, Fang expresses Gramscian anxiety over the limitations imposed by the cultural hegemony of the ruling elite on the full growth of consciousness of the masses. Like Gramsci, he finds that the power of ruling elites was not only

[58] "Sishu" (The private school), in *HQPP* 1957–60, 9:5–6.

based on their political and economic domination but also on their cultural domination of the society. In his preface to an unfinished article, "The History of the Establishment of the Northeast Jiangxi Soviet," he writes that one of the main reasons for the successful exploitation of the Chinese masses by the "parasitic class" was its promotion of an "educational system to keep the masses ignorant." This parasitic class, he continues,

> to firmly establish its rule, does not desire our intellectual awakening, but instead wants us to sleep stupidly. It does not wish us to understand truth, and employs all its efforts to deceive truth. Its newspapers, books, schools, opera houses, churches, temples, lecture halls, public reading places, and the like, are all means to keep masses ignorant. It has all along taught us to believe in gods, ghosts, geomancy [*feng shui*], eight characters, fate [that is, everything is predestined and cannot be changed], the ideology of suffering in this life for a beautiful future in the next life, four cardinal virtues of the people-propriety, justice, honesty, and a sense of shame—and the invincibility of the sacred right to private property. Employing this poisonous spiritual opiate, it has thus doped the minds of us—the workers and the peasants. . . . It has forced us to behave as obedient and peaceful "good" masses and to suppress the courage to stand up and struggle.[59]

Again, like Gramsci, Fang finds law to be the tool that enabled the "parasitic class" to maintain its hegemony and exploit the people. Gramsci writes that "if . . . the state tends to create and maintain a certain type of civilization and of citizen (and hence of collective life and of individual relations), and to eliminate certain customs and attitudes and to disseminate others, then the law will be its instrument for this purpose (together with the school system, and other institutions and activities)."[60] Similarly, Fang remarked that the reason for perpetual exploitation and the failure to "fanshen" (to remake oneself) lies in the parasitic class's control of the government, army, police, and law courts. If workers demonstrate against oppression, the police beat them and the law court punishes their leaders as criminals. If peasants do not pay rents or debts, warrants are issued for their arrest. The parasitic class's control over the repressive state apparatus thus perpetuates its own hegemonic rule.[61] To Fang, members of this parasitic class, that is, the upholders of Confucian ideology, are "evil satans," "cannibals," and "man-eaters."

[59] Fang 1957: 61.
[60] Gramsci 1971: 246.
[61] Fang 1957: 61.

In his writings, Fang frequently uses these metaphors, originally employed by Lu Xun, to describe the exploiters within Chinese society not only because he was deeply inspired by the author but also because these terms belonged to the vocabulary of the peasants. Peasants viewed larger social forces not in abstract but in real human terms on the basis of their performance in maintaining the paternal-deference equilibrium. A bad landlord was thus equated with the most hated and feared object that peasants could imagine. In Fang's village, peasants called the local police chief, Yu, "an old tiger that after eating men does not even spit out the bones."[62] Employing similar terms from the peasants' vocabulary, Fang warns his fellow countrymen in an article, "Happy God," that "surrounding you, there are many atrociously evil Satans. They are killing and eating people with their fangs. Look at the dim traces of blood everywhere. Listen to the pathetic cries everywhere."[63] In "Beloved China," he writes that "among ourselves exists a small minority of traitors, puppets, and betrayers. They are like man-eating tigers." Later he asks his countrymen to examine the evil-looking ghosts of imperialism, "whose faces are worse than any of the ghosts described in so many Chinese stories. Their whole body is full of hair, their bloody mouth is very deep, their teeth are long and protrude from the mouth, and their hands have iron paws. Among human beings, they are man-eating chimpanzees. There are five such evil-looking ghosts in China."[64]

Fang's harsh, vigorous, and imaginative descriptions of the exploiters, the landlord-capitalists and the imperialists, may seem exaggerated and laughable. But, as Franz Fanon explains, "sometimes this literature of just-before-the-battle is dominated by humor and by allegory; but often it is symptomatic of a period of distress and difficulty, where death is experienced, and disgust too. We spew ourselves up; but already underneath laughter can be heard."[65] Moreover, if Fang's village students call their Confucian teacher barbaric and uncultured and exalt the happiness found in cattle herding in the village, and if Fang vigorously employs folk metaphors to describe exploiters, it reflects his attempt to use the thoughts and feelings of the Chinese people, the peasants and workers, to raise their dignity and consciousness.

Concerned by the exploitation of man by man, Fang divides contempo-

---

[62] Fang Lan 1978: 31.

[63] *WSSQ* 1959, 1:33.

[64] Fang 1952: 23.

[65] Fanon 1968: 222. Fanon's chapter "National Culture" is perhaps one of the best analyses of the impact of culture on the ideology of native intellectuals. He finds revolution a cultural manifestation of the oppressed masses. Unfortunately, in spite of their relevance in the study of revolution, Fanon's theories are no longer discussed as much as they should be.

rary society into two classes, the exploiters and the exploited. As a Marxist, he believes that the exploited are those producers of materials who are alienated from their products, never able to enjoy the fruits of these products themselves, and forced to live a dehumanized life. His essay, "Blood . . . Flesh," published in the third issue of the *New Jiangxi Journal*, asks, "Of what construction materials were those grandiose and beautiful buildings built? Blood and flesh. What is written under the big and small porcelain bowls and plates arranged on a white-cloth-covered table? Blood and flesh." [66] In a later work, Fang again writes that every useful and beautiful object in the world is created by the workers and the peasants, but none belongs to them. It has been snatched by "a nonworking, nonproducing, idle, and parasitic class." Commenting on the plight of China's poor, he writes:

> We have built high and massive buildings, but we ourselves live in a small room together with pigs and dogs. We have woven clothes, but we do not have enough of that to cover ourselves and we suffer during cold winters. We have cooked good-smelling delicious foods, but we do not have enough to fill our bellies and we live with hunger. . . . Besides that, we have made guns that we ourselves give them to shoot us. We have manufactured hand grenades that we ourselves give them to scatter and tear apart our blood and flesh. We have created all material riches, which have been forcefully snatched by them, but we ourselves are the ones who have nothing. We have brought good fortune, but our own fortunes have been destabilized by them and we live in poverty. [67]

Fang identified himself with all of China's poor, whom he, employing the current Chinese translation of the Marxist term "proletariat," called *wuchan jieji* (propertyless class). In his description of the exploited "propertyless class" of China, he always used the term "we," that is, the workers, peasants, and intellectuals. Like Gramsci's "organic intellectual" or Fanon's "native intellectual," he considered himself to be the victim of the same oppressive social system that had prevented the social, cultural, and economic growth of the majority of the Chinese people. In a poem, he equates his chronic lung disease with the problem of poor people and refers to it as tantamount to a social wound inflicted by the oppressive social system:

Oh yes, it's for the poor man to spit blood,
Any poor man is liable to spit blood—

[66] *WSSQ* 1959, 1:33.
[67] Fang 1952: 30.

Certainly I must with my weak body.
For if the poor do not spit blood,
Can it be the rich that do?
Still, two things I fail to understand:
Why should I be propertyless?
And why should I spit blood?[68]

Attracted by the humanizing and liberating aspects of Marxism, Fang finds the revolutionary overthrow of the exploiters the only way to save China. He thus appeals to contemporary intellectuals to abandon writing academic essays, delivering eloquent lectures, and crying in protest over the encroachment of foreign imperialists and the exploitation of their collaborators. "Can we ask imperialism not to invade China? Is it not like asking the old tiger to stop eating meat?"[69] Instead, we must call "masses of the entire nation to struggle, to take arms in hands, and to wage a sacred people's revolution against imperialism."[70] Fang owes this belief in revolution to the guidance of Marxism-Leninism and the Communist Party of China. These, he writes, have raised the status and dignity of the propertyless class and have demonstrated to it the importance of unity, struggle, and armed revolution to gain power.[71]

Fang could simultaneously combine his Marxism with a belief in the Chinese people because the theory of Marxism conveyed to him by its original Chinese mediators, as Maurice Meisner has argued, was itself laden with strong nationalism, populist impulses, and voluntaristic strains. Meisner has demonstrated that a strong populist impulse appeared and grew more or less simultaneously with the introduction and spread of Marxist ideas in China. "This non-anarchist populism is apparent in the ideas and action of such activist groups as the Mass Education Speech Corps in 1918, the Marxist oriented students in Shanghai and elsewhere who went to the countryside to work with peasants and advocated destroying the very concept 'intelligentsia', and in the activities of P'eng P'ai [Peng Pai] and members of the Socialist Youth Corps who went to the villages in the early 1920's."[72] Belonging to, and influenced by, the same group of student activists, Fang, as a Marxist, believed in the imperative of revolution, but as a populist, the lack of social and economic prerequisites in China did not lead him to think

[68] *HQPP* 1957–60, 9:3, translated in Miao 1962: 29.
[69] Fang 1952: 27.
[70] Ibid., 27.
[71] Fang 1957: 63–64.
[72] Meisner 1971: 337.

that without such necessary forces of history, socialism and communism could not be achieved.

Like many other contemporary Marxist intellectuals, Fang's nationalistic beliefs also reinforced his populist faith in the enormous revolutionary energies of the Chinese people. He writes, "Does China really not have strength to save herself? I can never think that. I consider that China has enough strength to save herself. Have not Chinese people demonstrated their unsurpassed energy in recent events?"[73] The belief in the basic unity of the Chinese people leads him to write that "the majority [of the population in China] comprises the strong patriotic Chinese people who still desire to save their nation."[74] In other writings, too, he emphasizes the numerical majority of the exploited revolutionary Chinese people as against the small minority of landlords, capitalists, and foreign imperialists. He writes that "innumerable fists of workers and peasants are strong and tough enough to, even without actually killing, scare the exploiters to death."[75]

But Fang never resolved the central contradiction of the populist world view that, as Meisner notes, rested on a voluntaristic belief in the decisive revolutionary role of the consciousness of the intelligentsia, and simultaneously on the basic faith that the truly creative forces of revolution reside in the people themselves.[76] Like other Chinese Marxist intellectuals, he remained ambivalent about the relationship between the intellectuals and the masses. He never clearly specified who among them should provide leadership. Perhaps this question never seriously arose in the mind of Fang, who was less a Marxist theoretician and more a revolutionary activist. He sincerely believed in the Communist Party and its leaders but never separated them from the masses. His exaltation of and identification with the exploited Chinese people and village life suggest that he, perhaps, believed in an organic link between the revolutionary intelligentsia and the people—a link in which both learned from each other and struggled together for a national revolution.

Marc Bloch has remarked that "to the great despair of the historian, men fail to change their vocabulary every time they change their customs."[77] This is also true of the vocabulary of revolution. If in Fang's writings one finds an appeal for sacred as opposed to secular revolution, the concept of China

[73] Fang 1952: 30; see also Fang 1957: 60–71.
[74] Fang 1952: 34.
[75] Fang 1957: 60.
[76] Meisner 1971.
[77] Bloch 1954: 35.

as a mother as opposed to a nation, a dialogue with God, and an invocation of traditional norms of justice, one must also consider the culturalism or backward-looking beliefs that underlie his progressive ideology. It has been noted that in the history of the Chinese Communist movement, the most nationalistic Communists either had or sought to acquire the deepest roots in Chinese culture.[78] Edward Friedman also demonstrates in the activities of revolutionaries an effort to reknit the larger family and in revolution the fulfillment of the religious and moral needs of the masses.[79]

These cultural yearnings of revolutionary intellectuals cannot be ignored. The claim to a past national culture and the fervent desire to reknit the larger family, which frequently appear in the intellectuals' vocabulary of revolution, provide a new meaning to struggle and revolution. Fanon, in his excellent discussion of the native intellectual and national culture, writes: "The claim to a national culture in the past does not only rehabilitate that nation and serve as a justification for the hope of a future national culture. In the sphere of psycho-affective equilibrium it is responsible for an important change in the native."[80] It is not a luxury but a necessity in any coherent program. "The native intellectual," he writes, "who takes up arms to defend his nation's legitimacy and who wants to bring proofs to bear out that legitimacy, who is willing to strip himself naked to study the history of his body, is obliged to dissect the heart of his people."[81]

It is thus hardly surprising that Fang should have frequently referred to China, the nation, as a mother, and all the Chinese people as sons of her larger family. The historical necessity to reaffirm his own humanity and that of the Chinese people against general ostracism led Fang to glorify the physical beauty and potential of Mother China. He therefore writes that there is no other mother in the world who is endowed with so many children, vast lands, long rivers, and large tracts of fertile land, or such a good climate, beautiful scenery, and rich art. But "our mother is crying at the inability of Chinese people to rise and defend her. Some of her own children, influenced by the foreign imperialists, are using knives to cut her flesh and kill her. Do all of you want that? Do all of you like to live without a mother? . . . Friends and Brothers! rise quickly, save Mother, no matter what. Do not let her die."[82] In the same essay, he further writes that Mother China was originally

[78] Meisner 1970: 48.
[79] Friedman 1974: 146–48, 218–20.
[80] Fanon 1968: 210.
[81] Ibid., 211.
[82] Fang 1952: 26.

the most beautiful lady in the world. She was much prettier than European, American, and shorter Japanese women. But she now appears ugly because she does not have money to buy either nice clothes to dress herself or aromatic soaps to clean her body. Oppressed by the evil people, she is really in a wretched condition.[83] Fang's "Beloved China" is full of such emotional phrases about the past glory of Mother China, her present miserable condition, and the physical injuries caused to her beautiful body by both Chinese and foreign exploiters. Fang thus reflects a great enthusiasm for the national essence. He glorifies China's remembered past and inherited tradition and blames her contemporary weakness on the emergence of new exploitative forces, both foreign and native.

Consequently, in his writings, Fang invokes the remembered peasant norm of justice against the evil sons of Mother China. He appeals to them to be sympathetic to the exploited and thus reminds them of their paternalistic obligations toward the peasants. In a poem about "man-eaters" within Chinese society, he writes:

This bunch grabs food from the mouth of
    starving children
To feed the dogs and horses on.
It dashes the tatters of poor men shivering
    in the snow
To the ground and stamps on them.
People's very lives are its delicate fare,
The people's blood is savoury broth to it,
But eating and drinking, it is still not satisfied—
looking upon its life as dull and monotonous.
Ah, if only these people had sympathy,
They could never be like this!
Oh, God, beloved and divine,
When you created man
Why didn't you endow him with sympathy?[84]

If these exploiters fail to be sympathetic to the problems of the people, Fang finds the only solution in the "*sacred* people's revolution [emphasis mine]." He thus appears to be out of date, his ideas obsolete and a negation of reality. His invocation of symbols from the historically unspecified past

[83] Ibid., 21–22.
[84] "Tongqing xin," in *HQPP* 1957–60, 9:4.

seems to contradict his own belief in Marxism and the Communist revolution.

Perhaps, most of the intellectuals who venture into a mythical or remembered past, as opposed to the historical past, run the risk of being out of date. But such a venture is often necessary to raise hope and invite action. Indicating the importance of remembrance and imagination in social protest, Frank Hearn argues that "the remembered past supplies the standard which enables people to discredit the legitimacy of, legitimate opposition against, and anticipate future alternatives to, the present order. Accordingly, the category of remembrance . . . is necessary to the formation of progressively oriented social protest movements."[85] It is, therefore, not surprising that Gandhi should have called the most downtrodden caste in India *harijana* (people of God), a term that provided it with a new impetus to struggle for equal social status with other castes. It is also not surprising that, in most of the popular wars, leaders are seen as prophets, messiahs, or supernatural human beings. When the remembered past is injected with revolutionary ideologies, a new framework for the future is created.

Thus, in early-twentieth-century China, the sudden burgeoning of the "mother" metaphor and other symbols and norms from the remembered past is evident not only in the writings of Fang but also in those of many other contemporary intellectuals. In the wake of failure of hegemonic Confucian culture to maintain and defend the integrity of Chinese society, they indicate many intellectuals' conscious or unconscious attempts to go beyond the immediate Confucian past to a mythical past where every Chinese was a dignified son of the larger family and protected by a loving mother. Such an attempt was necessary to create a New China.

With the development of the crisis of paternalism and the disruption of the equilibrium between the hegemonic culture and peasant culture, traditional social relationships and values had begun to break. The invasion of foreign imperialists and the overwhelming force of the foreign ideology and culture had not only exposed the weakness of the hegemonic culture but had also contributed to the decline of the traditional social and moral order. The new foreign ideology and culture were unable to satisfy the social and cultural needs of the Chinese masses and intellectuals. Thus, neither the existing hegemonic culture nor the new foreign ideology provided a solution to China's moral problems. The immediate past could not be restored and the new ideology could not be introduced in toto. In such a situation, to reaffirm

[85] Hearn 1975: 222.

the totality of the nation, intellectuals like Fang, who had deeper ties with rural areas, went backward to a mythical past and vigorously pursued the well-remembered folk notions for their revolutionary cause.[86]

Fang prevented himself from being out of date and becoming a traditional peasant leader or a conservative intellectual. He did so by synthesizing those artifacts of indigenous culture which belonged to the remembered past and those elements of the Marxist ideology which were relevant to the Chinese situation. His vision of the future Chinese society was, therefore, devoid of any concept of the restoration of the actual historical past. The aims envisioned by him were Communist goals derived from the utopian promises of Marxism. He writes that in the future Chinese society, "everywhere there will be an active leap in creativity, everywhere there will be continuous improvement, happiness will be substituted for sorrow, cheering faces for crying faces, plenty for poverty, health for weakness, enlightenment for ignorance, profusion for desolation, love and friendship for hatred and hostility, joyous living for misery and death. . . . Be assured, friends, that this glorious day is not far off but is ours tomorrow."[87] He thus proclaimed: "I hate and detest to the utmost the landlords, capitalists, and traitorous warlords; I sincerely love my brethren of the working class, the Party and the Chinese people . . . I can give up all—all but the Party, the working class and the revolutionary cause, for which I will work till my last breath."[88]

Thus, agreeing with Chen's comment referred to earlier,[89] one may argue that the significance of Fang Zhimin's revolutionary ideas lies in his creative synthesis of traditional folk cultural values with modern Marxist thoughts. Like other contemporary revolutionary intellectuals, Fang believed that all that was evil in China was rooted in the oppressive domination of the hegemonic Confucian culture and foreign imperialism, which divided Chinese society into two classes—the exploiters and the exploited. Attracted by the liberating and humanizing character as well as antifeudal and anti-imperialist

[86] Fanon 1968: 224–33. He writes: "The desire to attach oneself to tradition or bring abandoned traditions to life again does not only mean going against the current of history but also opposing one's own people. When a people undertakes an armed struggle or even a political struggle against a relentless colonialism, the significance of tradition changes" (p. 224), and therefore, he "who writes for his people ought to use the past with the invitation of opening the future, as an invitation to action and a basis for hope. . . . All those men and women who are fighting with their bare hands against French colonialism in Algeria are not by any means stranger to the national culture of Algeria" (pp. 232–33).
[87] Fang 1952: 36.
[88] See Miao Min 1962: title page.
[89] See note 57 above.

features of Marxism, he found the solution to China's contemporary problems in a Communist revolution. This revolution was to be carried out by the exploited, that is, the peasants, the workers, and the intellectuals. They were the real "proletariat" of China. But, unlike most others, Fang, as an activist, more forcefully employed the peasant vocabulary to justify the need for a Communist revolution on cultural grounds. A revolution, he suggested, would restructure the Chinese familial society in a morally cohesive fashion; society would then derive its strength not from the historical Confucian but the inherited mythical past. It would also restore the peasants' remembered cultural values. The sacred task for all the Chinese people, therefore, was to participate actively in the revolution in order to save the children of "Mother China" from the exploiters. It is Fang's commitment to such revolutionary ideas that distinguishes him from both the conservative and "culturalist" right-wing GMD ideologues as well as most other urban-biased contemporary radical intellectuals.

Fang thus made revolution meaningful and attractive to peasants. He united Marxist utopian goals and traditional aspirations of the peasantry. This led to Fang's popularity among peasants and his emergence as one of the most significant Marxist peasant leaders of modern China. In the course of the revolutionary struggle in Xinjiang region, Fang's cult developed, and numerous hill songs were composed in praise of him. After his execution in 1935, he was elevated to the position of a revolutionary god in rural areas. A hill song goes:

> South fighting star, East fighting star,
> Fang Zhimin is a liberating star.
> Heaven's dragon king, Hell's dragon king,
> Fang Zhimin is a liberating king.[90]

[90] Lo Ning 1958: 16. This is a collection of fifty-three hill songs composed by the peasants during and after the revolutionary struggle for the soviets. They are, perhaps, the best expression of peasants' love and respect for Fang and the popularity of his cult. As described in the next chapter, this cult did not develop because of Fang's charisma but because of his deeper involvement with peasants' traditional problems in the countryside. For a description of the significance of the cult in rural society, see Worsley 1968. For the variety of folk songs compiled during the soviet period, see Jia 1963.

Chapter Seven

The United Front in Jiangxi: Urban Forces and the Organization of the Peasant Association Movement, 1924–1927

On January 24, 1924, the day Lenin died, the First National Congress of the Guomindang and its ally, the Chinese Communist Party, included peasants in its strategy for the national liberation movement. The road to alliance between the GMD and the CCP was paved by the famous Sun-Joffe declaration, which categorically stated that China was not ready for communism and that priority had to be given to the struggle for reunification of the nation and its full independence. The declaration brought both parties to a common platform for a National United Front program under the guidance of a Russian adviser, Borodin. Sent by Stalin in the fall of 1923, he played a significant role in the reorganization of the GMD according to the Leninist principles of democratic centralism, and in the formulation of the United Front's political programs.

To achieve reunification and the full independence of the nation, the United Front proposed a militant anti-imperialist mass struggle, which was to be carried out with the support of both workers and peasants. Moreover, in order to bring these forces from "below" to the forefront of its national struggle, it promised a labor code for workers and suggested a 25-percent reduction in land rents for peasants in accordance with Sun's concepts of "restriction on capital" and "equalization of rights in land." Officially approved at the First National Congress of the GMD, the rural strategy of the United Front precipitated the first initiatives by both Marxist and non-Marxist intellectuals to expand their political movement to the countryside.

ORGANIZING PEASANTS FOR A REVOLUTIONARY MOVEMENT

Dissipated by the crackdown of the warlord government in mid-1923, revolutionary intellectuals of Jiangxi's Marxist Study Society began to return one by one to Nanchang in early 1924. As their senior leader Yuan Yuping was in the Soviet Union, the task of reorganizing the political activities in the province was entrusted to another veteran local activist, Zhao Xingnong. Already a member of the CCP, Zhao was advised by the Party to immediately establish a provisional office in Nanchang, probably to avoid GMD dominance over local politics under the United Front program. Zhao was to be assisted by three other members of the Party from Jiangxi—Deng Heming, Zeng Tianyu, and Fang Zhimin. Unlike Zhao and Fang, Deng and Zeng were new to the local political scene and had become members of the Party while studying in Beijing. Sometime between late February and early March 1924, a secret office of the Party had thus started functioning from a printing shop in Nanchang. Most of the members of the old local Marxist Study Society now formally joined the Party. Their activities soon expanded under cover of the Mingxing Bookstore and Liming Middle School established and operated by them.[1]

In the absence of any effective political organization of the GMD in the province, it was hardly surprising that members of an already active local branch of the CCP were entrusted with the task of building a nucleus of the provincial GMD on the principles of the United Front. Entering the reorganized GMD as bipartisan members, Zhao Xingnong and others also established a secret office for the Provincial GMD Party, on the premises of Liming Middle School, sometime in mid-1924. Within a year, branch offices of the GMD had started to function in seventeen towns and districts of the province and had enrolled more than a thousand active members.

In July 1925, the First Congress of the Provincial GMD officially announced the opening of the Jiangxi party office and elected its Jiangxi officials. Out of the seven members of the office's Executive Committee, five—namely, Zhao Xingnong, Fang Zhimin, Zhang Chaobian, Zhu Dazhen, and Deng Hewu—belonged to the CCP. Among other Communists elected were Tu Chengnong, who became one of the four supplementary members of the Executive Committee; Zeng Tianyu, who joined the three-member body of the Investigation Committee; and Wang Lisheng, who became one of the Investigation Committee's two supplementary members.[2] The Second Congress of the Provincial GMD, held in March 1926, was similarly dominated by the Communists and leftist GMD members. Thus, until the victory of the Northern Expedition in Jiangxi, the provincial GMD displayed a radical outlook under the chairmanship of Zhao Xingnong. While Zhao and Deng took

[1] *FZM* 1982: 51–56.
[2] Wen 1983: 73.

responsibility for the party activities in, respectively, southern and northern Jiangxi, the organizational task in the northeast region and Wannian district was left in the hands of Fang and Zeng.[3]

In June 1924, the GMD had proposed establishment of self-governing peasant associations in all the provinces in order to expand political work in the countryside. The preface to the Agreement of the Peasant Association stated that it was "organized for gathering together the oppressed and poor peasants on the basis of the spirit of the Three Principles of the People. Its purpose is to aim at the self-defense of the peasantry and also to realize the improvement of rural organization and the betterment of peasant life."[4] According to the first article of the agreement, its membership was to include only independent or semi-independent poor peasants, tenants, agricultural laborers, handicraftsmen, and rural workers. Excluded were opium smokers, gamblers, landlords, usurers, priests, and agents of the imperialists.

Organizationally, these peasant associations were to follow, as Roy Hofheinz notes, the Eastern European model of a hierarchical structure erected in the style of labor unions. Accordingly, fifty or more peasants, by assembling together, could petition to form a provisional district association and could sponsor and promote the establishment of village associations within the district. Three village associations could form a subdistrict association, and three subdistrict associations could organize a formal district association. All the district associations were to be controlled by the provincial peasant association office. Moreover, each provisional district association was to be headed by a preparatory committee consisting of revolutionary intellectuals. The task of the preparatory committee was to be the organization of village associations.[5]

In Jiangxi, in accordance with the GMD's proposal, a temporary Provincial Peasant Department was set up in 1925. Zhao Xingnong appointed fellow Marxist Fang Zhimin as its director. Fang earned this position not only because he was a Marxist but also because he had already gained some experience in organizing peasants, especially in the suburbs of Nanchang and in his native Hutang village. Following the guidelines of the national GMD, he soon began to set up temporary district preparatory committees under the leadership of local radical students and activists, who were to form regular peasant associations in their areas.

Between 1925 and 1926, however, except for some successes in a few

[3] *FZM* 1982: 52.
[4] Nihon Kokusai Modai Kenkyusho 1970, 1:409.
[5] Hofheinz 1977: 95–96.

districts of the province, these preparatory committees on the whole failed to arouse local peasants' enthusiasm significantly for the United Front's political program. In spite of working within an elaborate bureaucratic structure, they fell short of enlisting even the minimum number of peasant participants needed to establish regular peasant associations in several districts. Before the arrival of the Northern Expedition forces in the Xinjiang region, an October 1926 report of the Provincial Peasant Department notes that only eleven districts were able to set up offices for local peasant associations (see table 7.1). But the number of participating peasants varied greatly in these areas.[6]

Radical student activists thus failed to mobilize the local peasants. This was primarily because of their inability to solve, as well as their scant attention to, the most immediate and urgent subsistence problems of rural cultivators, which arose out of a severe famine in 1924–1925. During the latter half of 1924, heavy rains fell in northern and western Jiangxi. In the first week of July alone, these areas received more than ten inches of rain, double the average amount for the month. According to local reports, there had

TABLE 7.1
*Number and Total Membership of Peasant Associations
in Jiangxi, October 1926*

Districts	Number of Subdistrict Peasant Associations	Number of Village Peasant Associations	Total Members
Jian	4	24	1,084
Jishui	0	2	280
Xinjian	0	1	40
Yiyang	3	10	427
Jiujiang	3	12	662
Nankang (Xingze)	2	3	306
Dean	0	1	40
Duchang	5	31	1,200
Wuze	2	4	367
Yongxiu	6	30	1,216
TOTAL	28	128	6,276

Source: Tanaka 1930: 118.

[6] Tanaka 1930: 118.

been nothing like it for the preceding fifteen years. Abnormal rainfall and the consequent flooding completely destroyed the autumn crop.[7] On September 27, 1924, O. J. Todd reported in the *North China Daily News* that the government's neglect of dykes had caused extensive flood damage in the province. It was estimated that about 200,000 peasants seriously suffered in thirty-eight districts of the province.[8]

Before completely recovering from devastation wrought by the massive 1924 flood, several districts of northern and northeastern Jiangxi were also hit by a drought in August 1925. A long spell of dry weather caused a severe famine in Jiujiang, Hukou, Pengze, and other areas of the Xinjiang region.[9] Two continuous years of crop failures made the price of rice soar more than 100 percent, from seven dollars to fourteen and sixteen dollars per picul. Meanwhile, in November 1925, the warlord governor of Jiangxi, Sun Zhuanfang, had imposed many new taxes on the peasantry to support his ambitious military expeditions. But in spite of the new taxes, the revenue collected by the state in 1925 was significantly less than the amount collected in 1924.[10]

In 1925, the warlord government finally organized a Famine Relief Committee at Jiujiang to aid peasants in northern and northeastern Jiangxi. It was headed by Nin Zhanshan and Jiujiang's military commander, General Dong Zuoren. While it granted five hundred dollars to each of the affected districts, this sum was too meager by any standard to mitigate the peasants' plight.[11] Newspapers thus soon reported the mass exodus of famine-stricken peasants to cities. Massive peasant riots took place at Jiujiang, Jian, Yongxiu, Xingzi, and other neighboring districts. In Dean, according to one account, peasant-bandits killed corrupt and oppressive local police officials, then took out and ate their livers and hearts.[12] At some places, rebel peasants became so powerful that local landlords had to call the army to protect their lives and property. In Duchang, according to Tanaka Tadao, about a thousand

[7] *North China Daily News*, July 12, 17, August 16, September 20, 1924.

[8] Ibid., September 27, 1924.

[9] Ibid., August 29, 1925.

[10] Ibid., November 22, 1924, March 17, 1926. It was reported that profits of banks and pawnshops soared to $90,000 in Jiujiang alone. Pawnshop profits were triple those of banks (Ibid., February 27, 1927).

[11] Ibid., October 17, 1925.

[12] Ibid., December 19, 1925. It also reported that in Jiujiang peasant bandits held the son of the famous landlord-merchant Mr. Zhou for a ransom of $12,000. When denied the money, they finally killed him. In Guangfeng district, bandits held and robbed a postal carrier who was carrying money orders.

peasants rebelled because the district magistrate stole funds designated for relief work in the countryside. Infuriated peasants attacked and wrecked the offices and properties of local members of the landed upper class. They also detained the district magistrate, and tore to shreds all tax records. Such riots and uprisings continued in several areas of the province until the beginning of the rice planting season in May 1926.[13]

Thus, in 1925–1926, when peasants were involved in their own sociopolitical struggle to maintain the security of subsistence, student activists failed to bridge the gap between local concerns and their national revolutionary program. To initiate a national revolutionary movement, Fanon remarks, "the activists and their party cannot succeed by just having contacts with masses. They must also be the direct expression of the masses."[14] A revolutionary movement emerges when the party combines peasants' "traditional" aspirations and "backward" and spontaneous actions and connects them to the national social and political program or ideology. Neither vigorous and courageous efforts nor fine slogans of revolutionary intellectuals alone are enough. As Barrington Moore perceptively writes, "the intellectuals as such can do little unless they attach themselves to a massive form of discontent. . . . It is a particularly misleading trick to deny that a revolution stems from peasant grievances because its leaders happen to be professional men or intellectuals."[15] During the first phase of development of the peasant association movement, peasants, not only in Xinjiang but also in other areas of Jiangxi, rejected the larger national revolutionary strategy and ideology of the United Front because they provided no solution to immediate economic needs. Peasant associations thus grew unevenly and failed to enlist the support of a large number of rural cultivators.

It is therefore hardly surprising that the Provincial Peasant Congress of 1926 noted the lack of a contiguous relationship between revolutionary intellectuals and peasants as one of the major mistakes of its political activities in the countryside before the Northern Expedition. It pointed out that before launching their movement, revolutionary activists neither investigated properly the local sociopolitical and economic situation nor paid sufficient attention to work among peasants. Consequently, they failed to follow a coherent strategy. Their propaganda work and slogans remained incompatible with local demands. Local landlords were able to enter the associations and manipulate their work. Further, an excessive emphasis on increasing the

[13] Tanaka 1930: 117.
[14] Fanon 1968: 187.
[15] Moore 1966: 480.

number of association members to the detriment of educating the peasants made the major purpose and goal of these associations meaningless. Among other reasons for the restricted growth of the associations, the Congress cited the organizational weakness of preparatory committees, lack of financial resources, insufficient power to implement the social program of the United Front, the absence of a close relationship between the Provincial Peasant Association and the district associations, and the failure to organize village housewives.[16]

Thus, if revolutionary intellectuals' propagation of the ideology and program of the United Front failed to attract peasants in most of the areas of Jiangxi, their successes in a few districts could be attributed to their support of peasants' "backward" sociopolitical actions. A large number of peasant associations were formed in the areas that experienced spontaneous peasant uprisings. For example, in Duchang, where peasants rebelled against the corrupt practices of the district magistrate, about thirty village peasant associations, with a total of 1,200 members, were established. In the so-called bandit-infested district of Yongxiu, Tanaka Tadao notes that more than a thousand peasants joined the district peasant association within two months of its formation.[17] A similar burgeoning of the peasant association movement, as will be described later, was also evident in Jiujiang and Yiyang districts of the Xinjiang region.

THE NORTHERN EXPEDITION, URBAN POLITICAL TURMOIL, AND THE DEVELOPMENT OF PEASANT ASSOCIATIONS IN JIANGXI

On July 9, 1926, the Northern Expedition to unify China was launched. The First National Congress of the GMD had declared the elimination of the warlords as the immediate goal of the United Front. After consolidating its

[16] Tanaka 1930: 120–21; see also Gan Naikuang cited in McDonald 1975: 191. In December 1926, Gan wrote that the peasant movements in Jiangxi and Jiangsu were remarkable for their lack of success. More than a hundred students had been sent out to work in each of these provinces, but they had not been able to enlist more than 6,000 to 7,000 peasants during several months of effort. The problem, according to Gan, was not that they lacked fervor or determination, but that their leadership had been at fault: they had been sent out to do adult education work among the peasantry (McDonald 1975: 190). It also seems probable, as McDonald suggests, that the emerging peasant associations were in many places structurally not very different from those agricultural societies which were established in the late Qing period as a part of the self-government reform.

[17] Tanaka 1930: 118.

base in Guangdong, the GMD found itself strong enough to move against the powerful northern warlords. Meanwhile, following the death of Sun Yat-sen, Jiang Jieshi's skillful manipulation of the political vacuum, his vague political colorations, and his influence in military circles had facilitated his rise as one of the most important leaders of the GMD. He was appointed chief of staff of the GMD's Northern Expedition armies. Although his stripping of the Communists from the leadership of various departments of the GMD in early 1926 had begun to weaken the United Front, neither he nor the Communists were prepared for a serious confrontation at this time. Both gave higher priority to eliminating warlords and uniting China, believing that victory in the Northern Expedition would establish their influence.

In 1926, the northern warlord camp was full of rivalries and was far from united. Each warlord believed that the defeat of the other would strengthen his position and extend his influence over a wider area. During this period, Jiangxi was governed by a "super warlord," Sun Zhuanfang, whose control extended into four other provinces of the lower Yangzi—Anhui, Zhejiang, Jiangsu, and Fujian. His rival was Wu Beifu, who dominated Hunan and Hubei. Thus, when the Northern Expedition first moved against Wu, Sun did not support him. By September 1926, Wu was completely defeated.

The first offensive of the Northern Expedition in Jiangxi began on September 4, 1926.[18] Sun had earlier rejected Jiang's proposal to join the national revolution. After the defeat of Wu, he was planning to attack Hunan and Guangdong. Jiang, therefore, immediately moved his army along three routes through the north and central border hills into southern Jiangxi. The defection of the Jiangxi Army's Fourth Division commander, Lai Shihuang, facilitated his advance. Within two days, the Northern Expedition forces occupied most of southern Jiangxi and its major city, Ganzhou. On September 11, they seized the provincial capital, Nanchang. Although the arrival of Sun's military reinforcements delayed the advance to northern Jiangxi, the occupation at the end of November of Jiujiang, a major port on the Yangzi, extended the control of Nationalist forces over the entire province.

The victory of the Northern Expedition signified the transfer of political power from the hands of warlords to the revolutionaries of the United Front. With the establishment of the GMD's control over Jiangxi, the United Front government began to restructure its various organizations, which had hitherto operated in a clandestine manner to promote the cause of the national

[18] For a complete account of the military movements of the Northern Expeditionary forces in Jiangxi, see Jordan 1976; see also "Beidai zhanzhengzhong di Jiangxi zhanchang" 1981: 30–33.

revolution. It also moved to reconstitute the provincial and district administrative setup in order to consolidate its control over the whole province. These tasks proved to be difficult.

The United Front's program to unify China and build what Kuhn describes as "a national regime concerned to reassert control over rural China and redress the century old imbalance between bureaucratic and extra-bureaucratic power"[19] threatened the traditional hegemony of the landed upper class. It endangered the social, political, and economic basis of its control over rural areas. No longer could its members unhesitatingly exploit the state machinery for their private benefit. To maintain the status quo, they therefore organized their own powerful local factions and competed with the United Front's revolutionaries for power and authority in local areas. This brought about political disorder and administrative chaos, which ultimately culminated in a bitter struggle between the revolutionaries and members of the landed upper class.

Moreover, revolutionaries within the United Front believed in different ideologies and represented the interests of their distinct political groups. Each political faction was thus interested in strengthening its position by capturing the maximum number of positions in the newly emerging administrative structure. While the national government formally established in Wuhan was dominated by the "left" GMD, Jiangxi had become the headquarters of the Jiang Jieshi–supported "right" GMD. The stay of Jiang's forces in the province for several months after their victory bolstered the strength of his faction.

The main leader of the right wing of the GMD in Jiangxi was Duan Xipeng.[20] A native of Yongxiu district, he was a graduate of Beijing University and had studied in the United States and Europe. Working for the GMD in Guangdong, he was responsible for organizing a secret anti-Communist Youth Activity Corps (*Qingnian gongzuo tuan*), which in early 1926 had changed its name to the Communist-Suppression Corps (*Changong tuan*). He and another staunch anti-Communist, Zhou Lisheng, were dispatched to Jiangxi in September and November 1926, respectively, by Jiang Jieshi to promote the interest of the "right" GMD. Arriving in Nanchang just before the victory of the Northern Expedition troops, Duan formed a secret AB, or Anti-Bolshevik, League to subvert the leftist control of the provincial office

[19] Kuhn 1975: 287.

[20] For a revealing discussion of the AB League in Jiangxi, see Wen 1983: 73–77; Averill 1982: 123–37; *FZM* 1982: 66–74.

of the GMD. (*A* denoted the group involved at the provincial level, and *B*, the group at the lower district level.)

The AB League provided an organizational basis for rallying the support of all conservative and right-wing persons, who were frustrated because of being deprived of any role in the provincial GMD dominated by the leftists and the Communists. Under Duan's leadership, the rightists participated in provincial and local politics as members of the AB League. Among the most prominent were Zhou Lisheng, Cheng Tianfang, Hong Gui, Wu Qisheng, Zeng Huaying, Xiong Yuxi, Wang Lixi, Wang Guanying, Luo Shishi, He Yangling, He Qihuo, Jiang Bozhang, Wang Zhenhuan, Gan Jiaxin, Huang Beiya, Xue Qiuxian, He Renhao, Li Songfeng, and Xu Hongdeng. As soon as the provincial administrative structure began to be reorganized, they planned to take control of it.[21]

In the period immediately after the Northern Expedition, the CCP suddenly found itself too weak to counter effectively the growing strength of the right wing of the GMD. Originally the provincial branch of the GMD was led by Jiangxi's most senior Communist leader, Zhao Xingnong, and all its other organizations were dominated by CCP members. However, Zhao was arrested for leading a demonstration in support of the Northern Expedition and was executed by the warlord government on September 16, 1926, just before the arrival of the Revolutionary Army in the province. Another senior Communist leader, Zeng Tianyu, had left for the Soviet Union.

The head of the Communist-dominated Peasant Department of the provincial GMD, Fang Zhimin, was also away in Guangdong to participate in the Second National Peasant Association Congress. Held on May 1, 1926, it was attended by special representatives of the provincial peasant associations from central and south China. Fang stayed there longer to participate also in the Sixth Session of the Peasant Movement Training Institute, which was organized by Peng Pai and Mao Zedong. While returning, he once again fell ill due to the recurrence of his lung problem. He was hospitalized for two months in Shanghai and Jiujiang. At the time of the victory of the Northern Expedition, he was still in a hospital at Jiujiang.[22] Thus, the absence of all the key leaders had weakened the formidable domination of the CCP over the provincial GMD office.

[21] Wen 1983: 74.

[22] For a discussion of the activities of Marxist leaders and the CCP during this period, see *FZM* 1982: 63–73, Buxiu de geming zhanshi; Fang Zhiqun 1978; *Zhongguo geming genjudi shiliao xianbian 1982*; *Zhongguo gongchandang zai zhongnan diqu lingdao geming douzheng de lishi zeliao* 1951; Averill 1982.

Soon after the establishment of the GMD's control over the province in November 1926, both the right wing and the Communist-supported left wing of the GMD frantically attempted to strengthen their positions in the new administrative structure. The ensuing political struggle resulted in the domination of the "right" GMD and its AB League over the Provincial Political and Financial committees. The CCP and the "left" GMD maintained control over the Governmental Affairs Committee. Their authority over most mass organizations also continued. However, the "right" GMD's influence over the Political Committee, which supervised activities of the Governmental Affairs Committee and the Financial Committee, which collected tax revenue and special levies for the Northern Expedition, naturally made it powerful enough to threaten the growth of revolutionary forces in the province.[23]

This became evident when the Third Provincial GMD Congress was convened in Nanchang on January 1, 1927, to elect members to the Executive and Control committees. This congress was attended by about two hundred delegates from district branches of the GMD. Due to the CCP's domination of the pre–Northern Expedition provincial GMD organization, most of the delegates were either its own or the "left" GMD's activists. Fang Zhimin, who had by now returned to Nanchang, was selected temporary chairman of the congress to preside over the election. In spite of the AB League's effort to bribe the delegates, the "left"-GMD and CCP forces gained a clear majority on all the newly elected committees. Failing in its effort, the AB League, with the support of Chen Guofu, the head of the GMD's National Organization Bureau, declared the voting irregular. A revised procedure for the election was formulated. It entrusted all the power for nominating committee members, on the basis of delegates' votes, to the Organization Bureau. The result was predictable. Only two members of the CCP and one of the "left" GMD were nominated. The right-wing-supported AB League thus gained a clear majority.[24]

Having thus acquired control over the GMD's provincial party apparatus, the AB League swiftly moved to destroy the CCP's domination over the local

[23] See Wen 1983: 73–77; Averill 1982: 126–37.

[24] The Third Provincial GMD Congress in Jiangxi elected an Executive Committee composed of Duan Xipeng, Liu Yipeng, Liu Bolun, Cheng Tianfang, Deng Heming, Zhou Lisheng, Hong Gui, Wang Zhenhuan, and Wang Liyang. Reserve members of the Executive Committee were Zhu Youkeng, He Qishen, and Wang Zhanxin. Elected to the Investigation Committee were Xun Yuyang, Qi Bozhang, and Yang Gengsheng. Reserve members of the Investigation Committee were Huang Jiemin and Kong Shaorao. Dominated by the right wing of the GMD and the AB League members, the congress elected Li Liejun as the governor of Jiangxi (*Geming Wenxian* 1958, 25:5219).

party organizations in the districts. It sent its "special emissaries" there to establish and strengthen its own right-wing organizations, and it received complete support from local members of the landed upper class. Threatened by the growing radical mass movement, they welcomed such endeavors. The AB League appointed members of its own group to key positions in peasant and other mass movement organizations and began to subvert these organizations from within.[25] Betrayal from above significantly retarded the growth of the revolutionary movement in the countryside. Fang Zhimin and his CCP colleagues' strong resistance to the AB League's activities finally prevented total collapse of the peasant association movement in Xinjiang and other regions of the province.

FANG ZHIMIN AND THE DEVELOPMENT OF THE PROVINCIAL PEASANT ASSOCIATION

Fang Zhimin returned to Nanchang in November 1926 on urgent advice from the CCP. He was soon reappointed chairman of the Provincial Peasant Association. This replaced the temporary department that he had headed earlier. Greatly impressed by the activities of the Guangdong Provincial Peasant Association during his recent visit there, Fang began to build a Communist-dominated and self-governed peasant association organization in Jiangxi. He established three separate offices to conduct the activities of the association. The Organizational Office was entrusted with the task of investigating and reporting rural affairs. The Propaganda Office supervised the publication of various educational materials, wrote editorials, printed special pictorial newspapers, and developed propaganda for the countryside. It also published *Xiechaoshe Huabao* (Pictorial newspaper of the Blood-Tide Society), printed five types of small educational volumes for the peasants, and developed twenty slogans to promote the growth of the association in rural areas. The Administrative Office, consisting of one secretary, three clerks, and one accountant, managed the organization of preparatory committees for district peasant associations.[26]

To develop the peasant association movement efficiently, the province

---

[25] *FZM* 1982: 69–70.

[26] Tanaka 1930: 119–20. He perhaps inadvertently omits the name of Ganbei administrative division. As there was already a rudimentary peasant-association structure in northeastern Jiangxi under the leadership of Fang Zhimin, it seems more likely the Ganbei administrative division was also organized during this period. See also *FZM* 1982: 57–62.

was divided into four administrative divisions. The Gandong (east Jiangxi) Administrative Division with its head office in Linchuan controlled Jinxi, Dongxiang, Zixi, Nancheng, Lichuan, Nanfeng, Yihuang, Chongren, and Lean districts. The Ganxi (west Jiangxi) Administrative Division governed Jishui, Taihe, Wanan, Suichuan, Ninggang, Yongxiu, Anfu, Lianhua, Yichun, Pingxiang, Fenyi, Xinyu, Xinjian, Xiajiang, and Yongfeng districts. Its head office was at Jian. The Gannan (south Jiangxi) Administrative Division supervised Nankang, Yudu, Chongyi, Dadou, Xinfeng, Longnan, Quannan, Xunwu, Huichang, Ruijin, Shicheng, Ningdu, Xingguo, and Guangchang, as well as other areas in Ganxian. The Ganbei (north Jiangxi) Administrative Division included Yiyang, Guixi, Hengfeng, Hukou, Leping, Boyang, Jiujiang and other districts of the Xinjiang region.[27]

Fang also defined the aims of the association. They included destruction of oppressive landlords and local strongmen, elimination of local militia in favor of the peasant self-defense corps, and authorization of the district administration to bear the expenses of local peasant associations for expanding revolutionary activities in the countryside. The "right"-GMD-led provincial government, however, rejected them. It also appointed a person known as Mr. Zou to supervise and control the activities of the preparatory committee for the Provincial Peasant Association.

Fully aware of the impending conflict between the "right" GMD and the CCP, Fang put all his energies into developing the association separately from the GMD's Peasant Department. For this purpose, he convened a secret meeting of the Communist members of the preparatory committee in Nanchang. It was decided that the First Provincial Congress of the Peasant Association should be held immediately in order to establish formally the office of a provincial association within the newly organized administrative structure. Fang was authorized to lead an attack against the unreasonable demands and false propaganda of Mr. Zou and the AB League in the congress. Additionally, in order to control the forthcoming Provincial Peasant Association elections, trusted persons were to be sent to districts to select reliable and radical delegates. Thus a strategy was formulated to prevent the AB League's planned takeover of the association.[28]

The First Jiangxi Province Peasant Association Congress was held from February 20 to February 27, 1927, at Nanchang. Organized by Fang Zhimin, it was attended by 141 delegates from forty-five districts of the

[27] Tanaka 1930: 119–20.
[28] *FZM* 1982: 66–74.

province. Ironically, Jiang Jieshi was the guest of honor and the major speaker at the congress. The AB League employed both bribes and threats to lure the delegates away from the CCP. Convened in a politically charged atmosphere, this congress, for the first time, officially elected Central Executive Committee members and Standing Executive Committee members for the Provincial Peasant Association. Fang skillfully managed to get all members of the CCP elected to the executive body of the association. Tanaka Tadao provides the names of those who were elected:

The Executive Committee consisted of Lu Zhixi, Fang Zhimin, Shu Guobo, Qiu Ti, Liu Yipeng, Wang Zhenxin, Tu Guhe, Zhou Jihui, Peng Zhenya, Dai Xikuang, Liu Qingchuan, Yuan Desheng, and Guo Shengbin. The Standing Executive Committee members were Huang Dui, Kong Shaolong, Ma Weiqi, and Ge Guilin.[29] The members of these committees then appointed Fang as the secretary general of the Provincial Peasant Association.

Following Guangdong's pattern, the Jiangxi Provincial Peasant Association also adopted a proposal at this congress entitled "Minimum Political and Economic Demands of the Peasantry," based on the resolution of the Plenum of the CCP in July 1926. It provided peasant associations autonomous power over almost all local social, political, and economic affairs. Aims of this proposal were to develop associations as organizations of, and for, the peasants. Formal adoption of the proposal led to the development of a dual structure of power in local areas and undermined the district government's authority over the countryside. Resolutions on the proposal are noted by Tanaka Tadao.[30]

Politically these resolutions supported the GMD's rural strategy. The development of an alliance between peasants and workers and a link between rural problems and the national revolution were emphasized. District peasant associations, together with the district government, party, and mass organizations, were authorized to investigate the affairs of "local ruffians and oppressive landlord-gentry" and indict them in special courts. To be organized by the Provincial Party Office and the Provincial Peasant Association, these special courts were to invite representatives of local peasant associations as jurors. These local associations were also authorized to exercise judicial rights to arrest people and issue summonses for appearances in court to all those who violated their rules and regulations.

[29] Tanaka 1930: 121.
[30] Ibid., 121–28.

The establishment of a peasant self-defense corps was proposed. Besides requesting the government to send troops to bandit-infested regions, each category of local peasant association was also to organize a self-defense corps and an *yiyong dui* (troop of the village braves) to protect peasants in its area and to strengthen the cause of the national revolution. The government was urged to supply arms and ammunition for this purpose at either a subsidized rate or free of cost. Further, a reduction in the number of policemen at the district government's administrative office was demanded. In each district, the number of policemen was restricted to thirty, and they were prohibited from extorting wine, straw sandals, or court fees from the peasantry. Their salaries were to come from official funds and not from levies on peasants.

An economic proposal adopted at the congress demanded abolition of different types of land rents and surtaxes. Levies, such as security deposits, advance rent, wine rent, salt taxes, and the like, were forbidden. The collection of levies for military expeditions from peasants owning less than ten mu of land was declared illegal. In accordance with the guidelines of the GMD, tenants were granted a 25-percent reduction in land rents beginning in 1927. Moreover, during periods of natural disaster, flood, or drought, tenants were exempted from paying rent. To guarantee the security of subsistence, a consideration largely ignored in the prevalent trend toward shorter tenancy contracts, it was decided that no tenant could be evicted from his land without the permission of the peasant association, and a landlord could not arbitrarily reclaim previously rented land.

Pawn rents (*dianzu*) and the system of "payment of father's debt by son" were abolished. Moneylenders were ordered to lower their interest rates. Tax collectors were now responsible for correctly recording the tax payment of each peasant and ensuring that no fees other than those fixed by the collection bureau were charged. Corrupt tax collectors were to be arrested by the peasant association.

Greater emphasis was now placed upon the repair of dykes and irrigation canals. Local peasant associations were to lead peasants in planting trees to protect dykes. The government was requested to arrange dredging of fallow and muddy spots in rivers. Peasant associations were also to control the reclamation of wasteland and mountain land for farming purposes. Such lands were to be distributed to landless peasants. Moreover, if a landlord failed to develop his wasteland within six months, he was to be forced to hand it over to the associations for distribution among the peasants.

Several resolutions were addressed to social problems of the countryside. The task of organizing village housewives to liberate them from feudal bondage was granted utmost priority. Women were encouraged to participate in schools run by the associations. Equality in wages between men and women for equivalent jobs was decreed. The selling of girls, the dowry system, maltreatment of widows, female infanticide, and customs of foot binding and ear piercing were prohibited. No marriage could now take place without the consent of the woman.

Hired peasants, or agricultural laborers, were assured of fixed wages, which were to be decided according to local living conditions. Working hours were reduced from fourteen or fifteen hours a day to ten. Landlords were ordered to provide laborers with vacations on special occasions and to take care of their needs during illnesses or other periods of crisis.

To be sure, these resolutions constituted something less than a social revolution in the countryside. They did not aim at complete annihilation of the landed upper class and redistribution of land. Instead, they focused attention upon pressing age-old rural problems, the source of many peasant uprisings of the past. They voiced the traditional demands of the peasantry, based more on the latter's vision of a "fair" socioeconomic and political system. Resolutions concerning social liberation of women reflected village housewives' traditional protests against the feudal Confucian bondage. These protests were often expressed in their folk songs: "What does it matter if I have big hands and feet? I can collect manure and break clods for you."[31] But if demands of the peasant association corresponded to the traditional yearnings of peasants, this did not mean they were conservative. They attacked the social basis of the landed upper class and challenged its political, economic, and cultural hegemony over the rural area. Thus, the peasant movement grew into a lot more than a political movement.

These guidelines, which promoted peasants' demands and involved revolutionary intellectuals in local issues, contributed to a massive growth of the peasant movement. Moreover, Marxist activists' struggle, with the support of the Nationalist Army, against the enemies of peasants in the countryside established them as peasant leaders. Once established as peasant leaders, they would have no problem in raising a rural force for revolution. This combined force would expand the peasant movement following the Nationalist Army's suppression of the United Front and its subsequent collapse.

The phenomenal growth of the peasant association movement in Jiangxi during 1927 is reflected in the statistics collected and compiled by the GMD's

[31] Ho 1954: 129.

Ministry of Agricultural Administration. Within less than four months after the First Congress of the Provincial Peasant Association, the number of peasant association members increased from about 50,000 to 382,617. The total number of district, subdistrict, and village peasant associations reached 2,190 as compared with 156 in 1926.[32]

In 1927, however, not all intellectuals were sympathetic to the peasant movement. Deeply concerned with the problem of national revolution and the unification of China under the United Front program, many were not yet ready to confront the problem of agrarian revolution. Powerful forces within both the CCP and the GMD soon realized that the colossal growth of the peasant movement and consequent deepening of struggle on local issues were dangerous.

While recognizing peasants as a tactical ally and their liberation as one of the major tasks of the party, the CCP, under the leadership of Chen Duxiu, was opposed to any further advance of the peasant movement that might disrupt the immediate task of national revolution and the unity of the United Front. "It required Chinese Communists," Harold Isaacs remarks, "to reconcile the irreconcilable, to safeguard the interests of peasants and landlords at the same time when they were openly in conflict, to maintain the unity of 'all strata of the population' when these strata were obviously pulling in opposite directions."[33] Condemning the vigorous promotion of peasant demands by some of its members as "excessive leftism," a CCP report to Moscow on March 17, 1927, noted that their vision of the United Front, pitting good gentry against bad gentry, was essentially a replacement of social categories by moral categories that suspended the revolutionary movement in the villages.[34]

On the other hand, the right wing of the GMD vigorously defended its allies among local militarist-landlords who were the major target of the growing peasant movement. In fact, the power of this faction had further increased because of the support it received from a much respected native hero of the 1913 revolution, Li Liejun. Li arrived in Nanchang sometime in January 1927. Finding it difficult to ignore his strength in his native province, Jiang Jieshi and the right-wing GMD members aligned themselves with him. Thus, when the provincial government was formally established after successfully ousting the Communists in February 1927, Li was made governor of Jiangxi.

[32] *Diyici guonei geming zhanzheng shiqi de nongmin yundong* 1954: 17–19; see also Tanaka 1930: 129.
[33] Isaacs 1968: 122.
[34] Ibid., 115.

With this began the concerted effort from the top to gain control over local areas by defending militarist-landlords and destroying the centers of revolutionary movement at the lower level. Orders were issued to the district magistrates to protect the property of the rural gentry and landlords and to restrain the growth of the peasant movement. The state's support for the peasant self-defense corps was withdrawn, and funds allocated for the development of this corps were diverted to build an extensive network of local police forces.[35] Violating the proposals accepted by the First Provincial Peasant Congress, Li's government turned its back upon the revolutionary movement. It was left at the mercy of the local police forces, which more often than not aligned themselves with those very members of the oppressive landed upper class whom they were supposed to contain. This provided opportunities for local landlords and the AB League to launch a massive suppression campaign toward the end of February 1927 against the peasant associations controlled by the "left" GMD and the CCP. Unarmed or poorly armed peasant forces were no match for their superior and well-organized troops. Members of the peasant associations went into hiding, their movement temporarily suppressed.

COLLAPSE OF THE UNITED FRONT

Threatened by Li Liejun's counterrevolutionary activities, the "left"-GMD-controlled Wuhan government finally decided to replace Li with Zhu Peide. Zhu, an important military general of the Northern Expedition, had manifested his disapproval of Li as he was bypassed in the reorganized provincial power structure. The occasion for the change was provided by Fang Zhimin. Sometime in late March 1927, Fang, who had earlier escaped to Wuhan because of the "right" GMD's suppression campaigns and was elected there to the thirteen-member executive committee of the All-China Peasant Association, returned to Nanchang. On April 2, he led a very large demonstration of workers and peasants in Nanchang to protest against the violence unleashed by Li Lie-zhun's right-wing GMD forces and the murder of a prominent CCP leader, Chen Zanxian, in Ganzhou district. On the same day, on instructions from the Wuhan government, the Nanchang police, led by the Communist military official Zhu De and with the support of local radical workers, began to arrest the right-wing GMD members. Duan Xipeng and several other members of the AB League escaped to Boyang district. Li Lie-

[35] *FZM* 1982: 82–86; Shao 1958: 249.

jun was forced to leave Nanchang. He encamped in Shangrao district of the Xinjiang region.[36]

On April 7, 1927, a new provincial government under the leadership of Zhu Peide was formally established. The Second Conference of the Delegates of the Third Provincial Congress was convened by Fang Zhimin on May 20. This conference expelled all right-wing GMD members from the provincial government. In their place it reelected such prominent members of the "left" GMD as Xiao Bingzhang, Huang Shi, and Wang Qun, and co-opted such veteran activists of the CCP as Fang Zhimin, Shao Shiping, Huang Dao, and Luo Shiping. In the new party apparatus, leftist members of the GMD and the Communists had an absolute majority.[37] They soon repealed the anti–peasant association laws promulgated by Li Liejun's government. The peasant self-defense corps was reinstated, and CCP activists were dispatched to those districts where the "right" GMD had subverted from within the local peasant associations. They were aided by Zhu De and students of Nanchang Military Academy in suppressing the local militia forces. Attempts were made also to revive the provincial CCP organizations, which had suffered a considerable setback in Nanchang and Jiujiang. Fang also established a Peasant Movement Training Institute in Nanchang where Zhu De trained students in military science and Peng Pai taught for some time.[38]

Meanwhile, on April 12, Jiang Jieshi staged a bloody anti-Communist coup at Shanghai that had repercussions in Jiangxi. Fearful of the growing strength of Jiang Jieshi, left-wing members of the GMD and the officers of Zhu Peide's Jiangxi Army demanded the expulsion of Communists. Finally, just before the Wuhan debacle, Zhu raided the offices of the provincial labor union, the peasant association, and other revolutionary mass organizations. All Communists were forced to leave the city. Known as the "courteous send-off" in Communist historical annals, it was marked by Governor Zhu's invitation to a farewell dinner to all twenty-four Communist members of the provincial government, who were presented with cash gifts for travel expenses, escorted to Nanchang Railway Station in the ceremonial state carriage, and given a strict warning never to come back.[39] The Wuhan debacle marked the final collapse of the United Front and the official peasant asso-

---

[36] Shao 1958: 248–53.

[37] *Geming Wenxian* 25:5220; Fujita 1960: 6–7.

[38] *FZM* 1982: 86; Wen 1983: 76.

[39] Miao 1962: 49–50; see also *FZM* 1982: 92–97. Averill (1982: 143–150) provides a good description of overall developments during this period.

ciations in Jiangxi. This did not, however, mean the end of the peasant movement; it was only the beginning of a revolution in the countryside.

Powerless after the breakup of the United Front and before finally moving to the countryside, the Communists launched an uprising at Nanchang on August 1, 1927, to regain their strength in the cities. This uprising was the first of a series of abortive revolutionary attempts that were carried out by the Communists in the latter half of 1927. Led by Zhou Enlai, with the support of such sympathetic and radical leaders of the local Nationalist armies as He Long, Ye Ding, and Zhu De, the Nanchang Uprising failed to establish the Communists in urban areas. Within five days of capturing Nanchang, the Communists were forced to retreat south to join Peng Pai's rural soviet in Hailufeng. In the course of the retreat, the revolutionary troops were severely routed by the Nationalists. Zhu De's troops escaped to Hunan where they were to be joined by Mao's defeated forces after the Autumn Harvest Uprising. Together they would establish their first revolutionary base in the remote Jinggangshan area on the boundaries of Hunan and Jiangxi.

In Jiangxi, the still disunited peasant self-defense corps was unable to launch an uprising in support of the Nanchang insurrectionists. Scattered and hidden in the mountainous regions, possibly they were unaware of the planned uprising. Miao Min mentions that the provincial CCP office had not notified local party organizations about the uprising in time, and the rebel army therefore failed to coordinate its actions with the peasant forces.[40] Fang Zhimin learned about this event only after the Seventh Division of Zhu Peide's army stationed at Jian (where he was secretly working among peasants after the Wuhan debacle) began arresting and executing members of the CCP.[41] Moreover, most of the local CCP leaders were underground, and it was difficult to coordinate them for this very secretly planned insurrection.

Following the abortive Nanchang Uprising, the CCP decided at the August Seventh Emergency Conference held in Jiujiang to launch an armed insurrection in the countryside. The conference noted that

unorganized, sporadic uprisings by the peasants are immediately crushed by the militarists. At the present time, therefore, the preparation by the Party of systematic, planned peasant insurrections, organized on as wide a scale as possible, is one of the main tasks of the Party. We should take advantage of the harvesting period this year to intensify the class struggle in the villages. The

[40] Harrison 1969: 120–23. For a detailed description see Hsiao 1970.
[41] *FZM* 1982: 97–107.

slogan of the peasant insurrections should be the transfer of political power in the villages into the hands of the peasant associations.[42]

Hunan, Hubei, Jiangxi, and Guangdong were the provinces originally selected for the armed insurrections. But in Jiangxi, the provincial CCP organization had gone underground after the Nanchang Uprising, and its leaders had lost contact with higher party authorities. Having not yet recovered from rapid and successive failures, the local CCP organizations and revolutionary intellectuals were still unprepared to join the Autumn Harvest Uprising. Peasants, too, had become increasingly skeptical about the ability of urban-linked peasant associations and other organizations. Thus no uprising was organized in Jiangxi. It was only after independently rebuilding their local organizations that revolutionary intellectuals would be able to launch a vigorous peasant movement and establish a soviet. From urban forces, they would turn into rural forces to re-create the world. It is in this context that I will examine in the next chapter the origin of the Xinjiang peasant movement and its development into a Communist revolution.

[42] Brandt, Schwartz, and Fairbank 1966: 122. For an account of the fateful year 1927, see also Hsiao 1970; Jiang 1957; Isaacs 1968: 272–92.

Chapter Eight

From Peasant Movement to Communist Revolution: Revolutionary Intellectuals and Peasants in the Xinjiang Region

A belief in folk culture, populism, or the revolutionary energies of the masses does not by itself bring about a revolution in the countryside. Intellectuals cannot gain the support of the peasants by simply delving into the past or by finding coherent elements in their culture to correspond to a revolutionary ideology. They must move to the countryside and coalesce with the peasants. They must, as an ideologue of African revolution aptly remarks, "work and fight with the same rhythm as the people to construct the future and to prepare the ground where vigorous shoots are already springing up."[1] To comprehend the growth of a revolutionary movement in the Xinjiang region, it is imperative to analyze the way in which the fusion of revolutionary intellectuals with peasants came about. It is also necessary to determine what stimulated the spread of the movement of "outside" intellectuals into rural areas after the reorganization of the Guomindang and its alliance with the Chinese Communist Party in early 1924.

In Jiangxi, the establishment of a party office of the GMD precipitated organized effort from the above to promote the rural strategy of the United Front. Revolutionary intellectuals moved to the countryside and began a concerted effort to enlist peasants in their associations to prepare them for a national liberation movement. Thus, in the summer of 1924, Fang Zhimin returned to his native district, Yiyang. With the help of his cousins, Fang Zhichun, Fang Yuanjie, and Fang Yuanhui, he set up two small private schools in Hutang village to give political education to village youths and peasants. The school for the village youths was known as Xukuang Yiwu Xiaoxue (Bright and Glorious Duty Primary School), and the adult night school was called Pinmin Qianzi Keben Xuexiao (Poor Men's Thousand

[1] Fanon 1968: 233.

Characters' Textbook School). At his alma mater, the Yiyang Higher Primary School, he also reactivized the Youth Society and its journal *Cuntie* (An inch of iron), which had become defunct after he went to Nanchang for higher studies. Moreover, in late 1925, as a director of the Provincial Peasant Department, he guided twenty-four radical students of this Youth Society in the formation of the nucleus of preparatory committees for the Provisional District Peasant Association and the district branch of the GMD in Yiyang.[2]

By late 1925, similar preparatory committees also surfaced in other areas of the Xinjiang region. They were organized by Fang's close associates Shao Shiping and Huang Dao and by other local student activists. In Shaojiaban village, on the border between the districts of Yiyang and Guixi, Shao formed the Yiyushe (Association of Helpful Friends) to train students for political work in the countryside. In Hengfeng district, Huang Dao, in league with Wu Xianmin, Xiu Shuipeng, and Cheng Boqian, established the Cenyang Xuehui (High Hill and Sun Reading Society). He also launched a monthly journal, *Cenyang Yuekan*, to propagate revolutionary ideology among local youths. In Guixi district, a Guixi Qingnianshe (Guixi Youth Society) and a journal *Xiyin* (Sound of rivulet) was set up by Jiang Zonghai and Wang Qun.[3] As in Yiyang, these reading societies and their radical student members were soon to play a crucial role in expanding the United Front's political movement to the countryside. In early 1926, offices of the provisional peasant associations functioned in seven districts of the Xinjiang region. Names of these districts and their prominent student activists were as follows:[4]

1. Yiyang—Fan Hexiang, Fang Zhichun, Fang Yuansheng, Hu Delan, Huang Tianzhong, Huang Yingzhong, Lei Xia, Peng Nian, Bo Shiqing, Shao Shiping, Shu Yi, and Yu Hanzhao
2. Hengfeng—Chen Bi, Chen Yingfan, Xiang Chunfu, Xiu Shiupeng, Huang Qiu, Huang Ruixi, Huang Dao, Li Mu, and Wu Xianmin
3. Guixi—Jiang Zonghai and Shao Dang
4. Yugan—Dong Siyuan
5. Boyang—Li Xiuhan
6. Duchang—Li Maoshan
7. Dongxiang—Shao Tong

[2] *FZM* 1982: 57–58; *Weida de Fang Zhimin* 1953: 8; Miao 1959: 7.
[3] Lai 1984: 105.
[4] Shao 1958: 243. Much of the discussion about the general development of the CCP organ is based on this as well as Shao, Wang, and Hu 1981; Fang and Miao et al. 1977; Johnson and Taube 1934.

Except for Yiyang, Hengfeng, and Guixi, however, which later developed into the core area of the Xinjiang peasant movement and the Gandongbei (northeastern Jiangxi) soviet, revolutionary intellectuals failed to penetrate the countryside. Even in the above three districts, only in Yiyang were there as many as three subdistricts and ten village peasant associations with a total of 427 members by October 1926.[5] In Hengfeng and Guixi, the growth of peasant associations remained limited. The revolutionary ideology of the United Front and its propagation alone thus proved to be inadequate to induce peasants to join these urban-linked associations. Burdened by subsistence concerns, more so in the agriculturally devastating year of 1925, peasants remained skeptical about new ideas and "outside" associations that gave priority not to the local but to national exigencies. In such a situation, whatever success revolutionary intellectuals achieved was due primarily to their exploitation of traditional kinship ties and identification with local needs.

In Yiyang district, newly established schools initially proved ineffective. They did not even attract enough peasants to provide for day-to-day running expenses. While they mustered support from radical students of Fang Zhimin's Youth Society, strong opposition from the local elite generally kept peasants away from them. In such an unsympathetic rural environment, Fang's vigorous struggle against landlords ultimately broke the ground for the foundation of a local peasant association. Biographers of Fang shed some light on his activities during this period.[6]

What finally instilled hope for the newly established peasant associations was Fang's struggle against the famous local landlord, and his one-time patron, Zhang Niancheng. During his school days in Yiyang, he had alienated Zhang by exposing the landlord's corrupt and oppressive practices in a letter to local authorities. However, he had overlooked close connections between

[5] Tanaka 1930: 118.

[6] See *FZM* 1982: 59–62; Fang and Miao et al. 1977: 1–7; Miao 1958a: 103–8; Miao 1958b: 90–94; Shi 1975: 14–15; Miao 1959: 7–10. Most of these works are based on memories of the revolutionary movement and, therefore, not much attention has been paid to the accurate recording of the dates of these events. Moreover, as struggles with these local landlord figures continued for a long time during the movement, some of the incidents have been referred to in various ways time and again, sometimes creating doubts in the minds of readers about whether these happened earlier or later. For example, Fang Zhimin's fight with Zhang Niancheng began when the former was in a school in Yiyang and continued until 1929 when the latter finally escaped to Shanghai. During his campaign against Zhang, Fang used the same criticism that he had first written and pasted on walls in the local market town during his school days. In the general description, I have, therfore, relied much on *FZM* 1982, which attempts to present history in a more structured fashion.

Zhang and local officials. Consequently, his efforts not only were in vain but brought on the suppression of his Youth Society's activities and the arrest of some of its members. In 1924, Zhang's plan to contest for an assembly seat provided Fang and members of his Youth Society with another opportunity to settle old scores with him. To get himself elected, Zhang attempted to fabricate a list of ten to twenty thousand voters and purchase votes with the assistance of local landlords. Learning of this, radical activists launched a vilification campaign against him.

This campaign received support from the local peasants for another reason. What had infuriated the peasants was not Zhang's flagrant violation of democratic electoral practices but persistent, apparently true reports about his intention of imposing a levy for the collection of election-expense funds. Threatened, peasants sought the help of the Youth Society to forestall such a move. A common enemy thus united them with radical activists. Soon, big posters listing Zhang's "ten heinous crimes" were plastered on the walls of the local Qigong market town. The list had been compiled by Fang during his earlier school days. His article "Piglet Parliament Members," which exposed the corrupt character of the contemporary Chinese parliament and advised peasants to refrain from voting, was also published and widely circulated by the Youth Society's journal, *One Inch of Iron*. The campaign against Zhang thus intensified.

Agitated by all these activities, Zhang and other landlords summoned Fang to the local police station to threaten him. In spite of their intimidation, Fang refused to cancel the campaign against Zhang. Meanwhile, learning the news of his arraignment by Zhang, peasants and members of the Youth Society crowded around the gate of the local police station. This saved him from a possible arrest. Afraid that an action against Fang would not only spark peasant violence but also cause opposition from the burgeoning United Front forces, Zhang set him free. He also told provincial authorities that the intended levy was not for his personal use but for raising funds to introduce an education program for poor peasants in the locality. In any case, Fang's successful resistance to Zhang, whose local power and authority could be judged from the ease with which he and other landlords used the local police office for their private purposes, naturally earned the support of peasants for the association.

During early 1925, the year of widespread natural disasters in Yiyang district, a landlord of Hutang village, Qi, refused to reduce rents and rates of interest. On the advice of Fang, the local peasant association took up this case and chided Qi for unfair practices. Panic-stricken, Qi finally relented and decreased the rents and the interest rates on the unpaid portion of loans. This success of the local peasant association triggered a rent-resistance movement and expanded the association's influence to other areas of the district. Such involvement of revolutionary intellectuals in the local subsistence problem provided a meaning to the work of the peasant association and attracted a larger number of peasants to their activities.

Finally, and probably most important, was Fang's prosecution of his own fifth paternal uncle, Fang Gaoyu. Gaoyu was a moneylender and a landlord of "middle" status, with several long-term agricultural laborers. When the rent-resistance movement spread, he took for granted that the local peasant association, which was organized and led by a member of his own lineage, would offer him protection in the same manner as a lineage-based organization traditionally did. His kinship ties with Zhimin's family and his higher status within the Fang lineage reinforced his belief. He therefore declined to lower his interest rates and provide relief to famine-stricken local cultivators. Rumors about his lineage connections soon spread in the village, and local peasants hesitated in reproaching him. Zhimin finally intervened and denounced Gaoyu's exploitation of lineage ties for personal benefit. To dispel any notion of nepotism, he persuaded the local peasants to march along with him against Gaoyu, who ultimately surrendered the debt receipts and donated money for the schools operated by the peasant association. Several such actions would later make it easier for the association to transcend the traditional narrow lineage base and extend its political activities to a large number of exploited cultivators from different lineages.

To be sure, lineage ties played both a progressive and a retrogressive role in the development of peasant associations. Most of the natural villages in the Xinjiang region, as noted earlier, were dominated by a single lineage group. Lineage ties traditionally not only served to provide security and subsistence to the local peasants but also acted as an organizing base for both peasant riots and uprisings as well as for secret societies and smuggler bands operating in the countryside. It is therefore not surprising to find that the peasant association movement in the Xinjiang region initially developed along lineage lines.

In Yiyang, members of Fang Zhimin's own lineage pervaded the successful Hutang peasant association. Fang's relatives, Fang Zhichun, Fang Yuanhui, and Fang Yuanjie, among others, were its core organizers and significantly contributed to the expansion of a revolutionary movement in the district. Another of Fang's rich relatives, Fang Fuhan, surrendered peasants' debt receipts, which served as an example of his lineage's concern for the peasants, justified its leadership role in the village, and promoted the cause of the local association. Moreover, during the post–Northern Expedition period, before executing his fifth uncle, Fang Gaoyu, Fang Zhimin sought the assistance of two of his relatives, the activists Fang Gaohan and Fang Bingshan, to persuade Gaoyu to accept the association's demands.[7]

In Hengfeng district, Huang Dao launched a local peasant association in his native village, Taojialong. This was a multilineage village where the preponderant surnames were Huang and Tao. Like Fang in Hutang village, Huang Dao first enlisted the support of his kinsmen, such as Huang Qiu, Huang Ruixi, Huang Huairen, and Huang Ligui. Together with them, he challenged the authority of the powerful local landlord and an influential traditional leader of his own lineage, Huang Wenzhong. In 1925, during the period of widespread natural disasters, the local price of rice rapidly rose from less than two silver dollars to five dollars a dan. Huang Wenzhong, in collaboration with another landlord, Lao Caiping, hoarded a large amount of rice to profiteer. Finding him violating the local subsistence needs and not performing his customary paternal duties either as a lineage leader or a landlord, Huang Dao organized indignant peasants to attack him. His house was pulled down and his rice godown was looted. Following this incident, Huang Dao emerged as a new local leader who upheld the traditional village norms. He soon received enthusiastic support from the peasants for his "new kind" of school. A branch of the peasant association was also set up in the village.[8] Thus organized, peasants vigorously resisted the oppressive practices of Huang Wenzhong and other local landlords in the countryside.

Another significant leader of the Xinjiang peasant movement, Shao Shiping, adopted a similar course in the organization of a peasant association in his native village, Shaojiaban.[9] Located on the border of Yiyang and Guixi districts, this village, as the name itself indicates, was dominated by the Shao lineage. Entrusted with the task of setting up an association, Shao too broke the ground in his native area with the help of his kinsmen, Shao Dang, Shao Chong, and others. The legitimacy that clan and lineage relationships provided to the revolutionary intellectuals is noted by a GMD official in a report on the origin of the Communist movement in Jinxi district of the Xinjiang region. Observing that the movement was the handiwork of educated children of the established families, he remarks:

[7] This discussion is based on the sources given in note 6.
[8] See Zhonggong Hengfeng Xianwei 1978: 1–9.
[9] See note 6 above.

These youths have been readily won over to the heterodox notions of the Communist party, which ideas they have reintroduced back into the villages. Being progeny of the established families, once back home again on their native terrain, they possess considerable prestige and influence thanks to their clan connections. Ultimately their goals are in tension with [the interests of] the traditional social forces. But at the *initial stage of their peasant movement recruiting they constantly take advantage of the protection offered by these traditional forces in order to survive and expand [their own influence].* Sometimes, they do this by building a following and then laying in a stock of arms. On other occasions, they infiltrate themselves into a militia. Then, when they have built up a party of adherents, they suddenly execute a volte face and turn against the very same traditional social forces that have sheltered them until then, wiping them out in a blow [emphasis mine].[10]

Such circumstantial evidence abounds in the description of the origin of the Xinjiang peasant movement. It indicates the critical role played by traditional lineage ties in facilitating radical intellectuals' penetration in their native areas and in planting the roots of "modern" peasant associations.

But lineage ties also played a retrogressive role. Traditional animosities between lineages often restricted the growth of single-lineage-dominated peasant associations in other villages. For example, as noted earlier, Majia village in Leping district had a long history of peasant riots and uprisings. In spite of that, peasants of this village opposed the revolutionaries because they came from traditional enemy clan.[11] Often lineages, which were the victims of what Kuhn calls "lineage imperialism"[12] and which traditionally relied upon secret societies and smuggler bands for protection, initially patronized the revolutionary intellectuals. However, peasants' commitment and loyalty to their lineage proved to be advantageous in long run. They joined the revolutionary organization after the peasant movement developed along class lines and demonstrated its sincerity and strength by suppressing the powerful landlord leaders of these lineages. In fact, weaker and non-lineage-based peasant associations quite frequently failed to expand their activities in a lineage-dominated area and succumbed to the pressures of local landlords or leaders of that particular lineage. The relative ease with which

---

[10] Fu Xingeng, in Xiao 1977, 173:86144, as translated in Polachek 1983: 817; see also Polachek 1983: 816–26 for an enlightening analysis of the development of revolution in southern Jiangxi, which was also dependent upon the lineage connection.

[11] *North China Herald*, June 3, 1930. For a description of a peasant riot in this area see chapter 5.

[12] Kuhn 1970: 79.

these powerful persons entered the association and controlled its organization is mentioned in several contemporary reports as one of the most crucial reasons for the failure of the peasant association movement to take off in Jiangxi.[13] Lineage ties thus also had the potential to weaken the revolutionary movement and destroy its original character.

In a study of factional politics in South Asian villages, Hamza Alvi remarks that "primordial loyalties, such as those of kinship, which precede manifestations of class solidarity, do not rule out the latter; rather they mediate complex political processes through which the latter are crystallized."[14] Examples from successful peasant associations of Yiyang and Hengfeng districts indicate that the revolutionary movement expanded to larger areas only after transcending its narrow lineage base and promoting the class solidarity of exploited rural cultivators. The historical ingredients for such transcendence were already present in contemporary rural society.

I have already noted that the strengthening of the force of the landed upper class brought about the crisis of paternalism and morally alienated both peasants and their patron-landlords from each other. This enervated horizontal kinship ties as a binding factor and created the basis for the emergence of vertical class solidarity. As the traditional lineage leaders increasingly trifled with the paternal deference equation, peasants responded with growing hostility to their landlord kinsmen. This created favorable opportunities for revolutionary intellectuals to present themselves as a new alternative to traditional leaders in their own lineages and to organize the association of exploited peasants of their locality. Having thus established themselves, their commitment to organizing a wider movement naturally attracted the exploited peasantry from other areas to their revolutionary organizations. To be sure, their realization of this commitment primarily depended upon the ability to suppress the increasingly stronger resistance of traditional leaders of the local areas. Such situations often required the assistance of a revolutionary army.

Thus, prior to the Northern Expedition, whatever successes peasant associations achieved in a few districts of the Xinjiang region flowed from revolutionary intellectuals' support of the peasants' spontaneous sociopolitical struggle, reliance on traditional lineage ties, and vigorous resistance to the oppressive practices of local landlords. More than their efforts to educate peasants about the United Front's revolutionary program, their deep in-

[13] See chapter 7, note 18.
[14] Alavi 1977: 59.

volvement in local issues advanced the revolutionary movement. However, in a larger area of Xinjiang and of Jiangxi, revolutionary intellectuals failed to enter the rural universe through the exploitation of traditional social ties. They awaited the arrival of the Northern Expedition forces to launch their movement.

POST–NORTHERN EXPEDITION DEVELOPMENTS IN THE XINJIANG PEASANT MOVEMENT

Revolutionary intellectuals, as Lucian Bianco observes, "entered the villagers' universe as rulers—rulers of a different kind, to be sure, but who were, like all other rulers, supported and backed by an army."[15] While this statement is only partially true for the Xinjiang region, it cannot be denied that the arrival of the friendly Northern Expedition troops contributed to a massive upsurge in the peasant movement. This, however, does not mean that peasants spontaneously legitimized and backed their new rulers. Revolutionary intellectuals received positive response from the peasants only when they began to implement their agrarian policies and to participate in local issues.[16] In fact, in the long run, their reliance on the army did more to weaken than strengthen the peasant movement. While the Nationalist Army's attack on peasants' traditional enemies helped revolutionary intellectuals to establish themselves in the countryside and expand the activities of their associations, their overdependence on the army at the expense of building strong local peasant forces was ultimately to prove catastrophic for the peasant movement.

In Jiangxi, disintegration of the warlord regime after the victory of the Northern Expedition forces snapped the mutually dependent relationship between the landed upper class and the state. This also destroyed one of the bases for landlords' traditional unfettered control and authority over the countryside. In the consequent political fragmentation and disorder, local landlords found themselves outcasts and their customary authority threatened by the revolutionary intellectuals' concerted move to expand their own

[15] Bianco 1976: 327–28.

[16] Scott (1979: 127–30) remarks that while outside forces may be essential for revolution from the countryside, they require conditioning to the rural environment in order to play any significant role in its precipitation. There is thus only partial truth in Marx's famous statement that "peasants cannot represent themselves, they must be represented. Their representative at the same time appears as their master."

control in the countryside. Thus left alone, they began to build their own power factions and strong militia forces with the support of local toughs, organized criminals, and bandit bands to resist any attempt to disrupt the status quo. In the Xinjiang region, the absence of any effective political force made their task easier. After the retreat of the defeated warlord army of Liu Zhitao and Sun Bofang toward western Zhejiang, no Nationalist Army immediately arrived to exert power in local areas. In collaboration with local strongmen and militia forces, they established their autonomous control over several districts. In the districts of Yiyang, Hengfeng, and Guixi, they also thwarted the revolutionary intellectuals' effort to set up mass organizations. The latter's plan to organize a widespread peasant movement in support of the Northern Expedition and the United Front was thus frustrated.

Describing the contemporary political situation in the Xinjiang region, Shao Shiping notes that three factional groups were active in the struggle for command of the rural areas. They included, besides the revolutionaries, factions of the local elite and of the strongmen and toughs. During the political vacuum following the collapse of the warlord state, the faction of the elite first secured power by bribing and cajoling people of the area to maintain the status quo. When the provincial United Front government announced the appointment of new district magistrates, members of this faction of traditional powerholders launched a petition campaign opposing subversion of the local power structure. Proclaiming themselves supporters of the old *Tongmeng Hui*, many of them sent their offspring and relatives to join the GMD. The dictum "To protect the local power structure, support the development of revolution" became their motto. Failing to preserve their traditional authority through such means, they finally allied themselves with local strongmen and toughs.[17]

Meanwhile, ranks of the faction of the local strongmen and toughs swelled because many soldier-deserters from the defeated warlord armies joined them. They also acquired a large quantity of arms and ammunition from these armies, which retreated through Yiyang and other districts of the Xinjiang region to western Zhejiang. Thus, several armed forces under the leadership of professional vagabonds of this faction surfaced in Yiyang, Leping, Jingdezhen, and Fouliang districts. Loosely bound, they congregated in Fangjiabo village of Yiyang. After gaining the cooperation of the local elite faction, they extended their influence by appointing officials, promulgating decrees on district and village affairs, and deputing delegates to neighboring

---

[17] Shao 1958: 243–44.

districts to gain assent to their leadership. Over a large area of Xinjiang, they thus set up their own local government structure.[18] So powerful had they become that, in 1928, two years after the establishment of Nationalist control over the province, a GMD official found that each district had its own strongman faction with its own apparatus of local government. New district magistrates, deputed by the provincial government, often succumbed to these powerful local factions.[19] Such a situation frustrated revolutionaries' effort to establish roots in the countryside without first overwhelming powerful local factional forces.

The political tide turned in favor of the revolutionaries after the provincial GMD government finally dispatched several units of the Nationalist Army to assume command over the faction-infested Xinjiang region. The first unit of the Nationalist Army reached Yiyang district at the end of November 1926. It ignored the friendly gesture of faction leaders who had planned a customary "welcome party" for its officers and soldiers. Instead, Shao Shiping notes, it accepted greetings from local revolutionaries who had assembled a large number of peasants from nearby villages to applaud it. Acting on the advice of these revolutionaries, the officer in charge of this unit sent an army contingent to the office of the district government. The ruling district magistrate, who was appointed by a faction of local landlords, was reproached for violating orders of the district GMD office. Impressed by the enhanced authority of revolutionary intellectuals, a faction of militia forces, which had a powerful base at Moshanshuyuan in Yiyang, offered them its support against landlords and the ruling district magistrate. But the alliance did not last long. Soon after the departure of the first unit of the Nationalist Army for northern regions, this factional force not only began to coerce peasants into paying levies but also aligned itself with counterrevolutionary local forces in Fangjiabo.[20]

In early December 1926, another unit of the Nationalist Army was dispatched to Yiyang. The political commissar of this unit was sympathetic to the Communists. His unit defeated the militia forces of local strongmen which, in alliance with landlords, had planned to attack the district GMD office from their base at Moshushanyuan. The unit then marched against militia forces congregating in the neighboring districts of Fouliang, Leping, and Jingdezhen and arrested many of their leaders. In January 1927, a new district magistrate, appointed by the provincial GMD government, assumed

[18] Ibid., 243–45.
[19] Hu 1967: 16–17.
[20] Shao 1958: 245–46.

command. This enhanced the reputation of revolutionary intellectuals and provided legitimacy to the district GMD office in the locality. Revolutionaries were thus finally established as the most powerful group in the district.[21]

With such shifts in the local power structure, the revolutionary movement in the old peasant association areas in the districts of Yiyang, Hengfeng, and Guixi spread like wildfire. In Yiyang district, radical activists of the Hutang village peasant association launched an attack on the Qigong market town's infamous police station—the state's institution of local oppression and violence. Acting under instructions from Fang Zhimin, and under the leadership of Huang Zhenzhong, Fang Yuanhui, and Lei Xia, they ousted the hated and oppressive police chief Yu and captured what were described as two and a half guns (probably either two rifles and one pistol or two intact guns and one broken weapon). They also installed one of their leaders, Lei Xia, in place of Yu. Following this, the peasant forces looted the notorious shop of the rapacious landlord-merchant-moneylender Shao Xiangzhen and tore his debt registers to pieces. Shao, however, slipped through the peasants' hands. Their old enemies, the landlord Zhang Niancheng and the corrupt local-gentry member Huang Zong, were arrested. Both of them were sent to Nanchang to await trial. Famous as the "Two-and-a-Half-Gun Incident" in the annals of the official history of the CCP, this preceded the famous Qigongzhen Uprising and marked the beginning of the peasant revolutionary movement in this area.[22]

The attack on the police station and the arrest of the much-feared traditional landlords proved the legitimacy of peasant associations to rural cultivators. In order to embolden peasants' political action for the revolutionary cause, Fang Zhimin found it necessary to destroy the state's instruments of repression and violence after suppressing the factional forces with the support of the Nationalist Army. These acts thus also had a symbolic value. They manifested the beginning of a new political and social order in the countryside and thereby considerably contributed to the revolutionary nature of peasant initiatives in later days. In fact, the growth of the peasant movement in Yiyang district was preceded by similar symbolic attacks on ties of family, kinship, and religion, which had traditionally limited the scope of earlier peasant riots and uprisings. They provided the movement a wider framework and extended its scope to all the exploited rural cultivators. Frequent description of these symbolic acts by peasants and radical activists

[21] Ibid., 246–47.
[22] *FZM* 1982: 74–75; Shao, Wang, and Hu 1981: 69–70; Fang and Miao 1977: 1–7.

in the latter's written memoirs is itself an indication of the tremendous impact they had on the development of the peasant movement.

One such symbolic act was the execution of Fang Gaoyu, a landlord and an elite figure in the Fang lineage, by peasants and his kinsmen. The struggle against Gaoyu was launched by Fang Zhimin during the pre–Northern Expedition phase of the peasant association movement. Gaoyu was then fined and forced to surrender his debt registers. In March 1927, after successfully organizing the First Provincial Peasant Association Congress in Nanchang, Fang Zhimin returned to his native Hutang village to escalate the peasant movement. He found that Gaoyu, backed by powerful local factions, had turned into a bitter enemy of the peasant association. Moreover, Gaoyu's high status within the Fang lineage as well as his close kinship ties with Zhimin's family were the main reasons for the hesitation of the same-lineage-dominated local peasant association in taking any action against him.

Finding that this situation was impeding escalation of the local peasant association movement, Fang Zhimin proposed that all radical activists should follow the traditional redistributive norms by not only personally contributing their excess food grains to needy peasants but also compelling their "rich" lineage members to do the same. He himself set the example by slaughtering pigs raised by his family and distributing the meat among local poor peasants. When Gaoyu was exhorted to donate money to the association and food grains to the poor and needy peasants of the village, he refused. Finally, members of the village peasant association surrounded his house during the night, forcibly entered it, and arrested him. The next day, in spite of the pleas of Zhimin's parents for lenient action against him, he was publicly executed by the peasant victims of his corrupt practices.[23]

Although peasant associations were not authorized by the United Front to execute landlords, and such activities were condemned by the CCP as "excessive leftism," violence encouraged peasants to defy the existing order and to support the revolutionary movement organized by the association. Fanon's argument that organized or symbolic violence by oppressed people liberates them from the traditional dominating bondage is, to a large extent, true.[24] Thus, violence by the Hutang peasants in defense of their value structure itself constituted the act of free men negating the hegemonic function of the existing law of the dominant class in society. It raised the sights of peasants, encouraging them to develop the revolutionary movement beyond narrow kinship lines.

[23] *FZM* 1982: 76–77.
[24] Fanon 1968: 89–95.

At the same time, the attack on the most famous living religious leader of the Xinjiang region, the Taoist Pope Zhang Tianshi, who was also a big landlord, similarly bolstered the strength of the peasant movement. Zhang, as noted earlier, was a descendent of a long line of Taoist Popes from the Eastern Han dynasty (A.D. 25–220). Living at a "heavenly palace" on Longhu Mountain near the border of Yiyang and Guixi, he wielded extraordinary influence over a large area of the province through his band of "heavenly generals" and "heavenly soldiers." Supported by the rural gentry and landlords, he owned land in eight districts around Longhu Mountain. He claimed to possess such Taoist magical powers as the ability to call forth wind and rain and to produce an army by throwing out beans. His tenants were subjected not to the law of the state but to his own rules and regulations, which he framed on the basis of a special power allegedly granted to him by the ancient emperors.

Under the leadership of Shao Shiping, members of various peasant associations, together with Zhang's tenants, scaled Longhu Mountain and attacked his palace with such weapons as swords, spears, sickles, hoes, and clubs. Zhang was arrested. On the advice of Shao, peasants sent him under guard to a prison in Nanchang for punishment. But, before doing that, they held an accusation meeting in his "Hall for the Suppression of Demons" and unanimously decided to distribute his wealth among his tenants.[25] Thus, by humiliating the Taoist Pope, deep faith in whose exceptional religious power kept peasants of this area away from the peasant association, revolutionary intellectuals extended the sphere of the peasant movement.

Another incident that symbolized the end of the traditional order occurred in Qichuanyuan village of Yiyang district. Local peasants there were skeptical of the ability of the peasant association to punish the so far invincible and unchastized landlords. They therefore refused to form any link with the association. Learning that radical activists had failed to gain the support of local peasants to silence overbearing landlords of the area, Fang asked members of his Ninth District Peasant Association to call a meeting of peasants in Qichuanyuan village. In front of all assembled persons, leaders of the association calculated what they considered was the amount of illegally acquired wealth of one of the local landlords and imposed a fine of one thousand dollars on him. The landlord was then assailed and compelled to honor the fine imposed and to surrender the debt register to local peasants.[26]

[25] *FZM* 1982: 77–78; Shao 1958: 250–51; Miao 1962: 48–49.
[26] *FZM* 1982: 75–76.

Between January and April 1927, such selective and symbolic attacks escalated the peasant movement in Yiyang district. Moreover, news of the peasant uprisings in neighboring Hunan province and in other regions of China lent vitality to the peasants' belief in the arrival of the period of liberation. In Dingshan village, located in what was predominantly a paper manufacturing area in the mountainous region of Yiyang district, such news encouraged handicraftsmen to launch an uprising. Local handicraftsmen were probably shed people who belonged to the Yu lineage. Their wrath was not against the master of the paper-manufacturing firm, Yu Peiluo, who came from their own lineage, but against the native landlords Zhu Bingzhang and Huang Zong, whose forces frequently plundered and victimized the local population.

In the winter of 1926, one of the raids by a landlord's gang on this mountainous village probably to search for bandits, left some villagers dead and forced all others to flee to nearby hills to save their lives. Emboldened by the news of uprisings in other areas, local handicraftsmen organized themselves under the leadership of Yu Jie and marched en masse to Landlord Zhu's village. On their way, a large number of peasants joined them. A force of about five hundred, supported by Zhu's bonded tenants, attacked the landlord's house. His stock of grain was taken and distributed among the peasants, and land deeds of tenants were burned.[27] Such spontaneous outbursts evince peasants' defiance of the overbearing exploitative forces in the countryside and the ebullience to rise up against the existing order. Thus, the peasant association movement under the leadership of native revolutionary intellectuals ignited the spark that facilitated bold initiatives by the broad masses of exploited rural cultivators in different areas, transcending parochial considerations.

The rapidly radicalized Yiyang peasants, however, had concluded meanwhile that the United Front government's commitment to revolutionary social and political change was less than enthusiastic. The new district magistrate of Yiyang, appointed by the AB League–controlled provincial GMD, did not bring about any significant shift in the local government apparatus. He continued to rely upon the traditional tax collectors and local police officers, who were a major part of the former warlord regime. In early 1927, when the provincial government needed funds for the Northern Expedition, he authorized these much-hated persons to enter villages for the collection of levies and donations. Their traditional tactics of extorting money infuriated the peasants, who had been assured of the elimination of such practices by

[27] Fang and Miao 1977: 8–14.

the peasant association and the GMD government. Peasants, therefore, demanded an immediate end to the levy collection. Finally the district peasant association sent orders to its local branches to launch a movement to resist such collections of money and to arrest corrupt and greedy officials.[28]

The levy resistance movement soon spread all over the district. In some areas, misinterpreting the association's call to arrest corrupt officials, peasants took over the local administrative structure. Threatened by the growing hostility of the peasants, the district magistrate handed over the task of all such collections to local peasant associations. At the market town of Qigong, under the guidance of the association and following the proposal of the First Provincial Peasant Congress, peasants exempted all the persons owning less than ten mu of land from the payment of levies. Further, they themselves took over the task of ascertaining the financial position of rich peasants and landlords, and fixed the amounts due accordingly. Large landlords were expected to pay more than smaller ones. If any landlord disagreed with the amount demanded, they patiently sat with him for days at his expense to discuss his financial affairs. Those who resisted their authority were arrested and sent to the local peasant association office for trial and punishment. Several landlords consequently fled to the district city for protection.[29] These activities greatly weakened the force of landlords and established the authority of the association over a wider region.

A concerted effort began soon after to organize a peasant self-defense corps to defend the association from retaliation by the forces of landlords, and Fang Yuanhui was appointed its leader. A branch office of the party was established with a Communist, Huang Tianzhong, as its chief. The task of collecting arms and ammunition was assigned to Lei Xia, who was an independent-peasant-turned-Communist and who was probably also a leader of the local secret society. Because of his background, he was ordered to hand over all arms and ammunition only to the local peasant self-defense corps, subserve the peasant movement with Huang Tianzhong and other local Communist leaders, and adhere to the instructions of the district GMD office.[30] Revolutionaries thus attempted to channelize and sustain the district peasant movement, the rapid development of which included the influx of several local forces for their own private benefit. The revolutionaries' efforts, however, failed to curb the subsequent growth of localism, which would ultimately prove to be catastrophic for the movement. Yet, until April 1927,

---

[28] Shao 1958: 247–48.
[29] FZM 1982: 75; Shao 1958: 248.
[30] FZM 1982: 90–91; Miao 1958a, in HSFB 1958, 1:5–8.

the Yiyang peasant movement progressed under a favorable political situation.

In the districts of Hengfeng and Guixi, during the period from the arrival of Northern Expedition troops in late 1926 until the collapse of the United Front in April 1927, the sketchy available information indicates a similar development of the peasant association movement.[31] In Hengfeng, two Communists, Huang Dao and Zou Shuipeng, had established preparatory committees for organizing peasant associations in 1925. But their success in the countryside had remained limited. In late 1926, after establishing its control over Jiangxi, the provincial GMD government appointed a new district magistrate and a chief of the District Public Security Department. They easily suppressed a resisting but comparatively weaker faction of the local landlords. Although these new officials belonged to the right wing of the GMD, they initially adhered to the United Front guidelines and cooperated with the district Communist-dominated party office. Many local landlords subsequently fled to Hukou district, where the faction of the elite had established its independent base. This facilitated the establishment of peasant associations in Taojialong, Qingbanjia, Yunfang, and other neighboring villages.

As the revolutionary movement widened, however, and peasants' "excesses" against the landlords intensified, the "right"-GMD-dominated provincial government began to restrain the activities of the association. Following instructions from the provincial authorities, the Hengfeng district government released several of the landlords arrested and pronounced guilty by the association. Acquitted of the charges, these landlords, in alliance with local officials, launched a massive suppression campaign against peasant associations. The revolutionary movement thus suffered a great setback.[32]

Yet, in April, the leftist takeover of the provincial government after the break between the left wing and the right wing of the GMD made local conditions once again favorable for the revolutionary intellectuals. Shao Shiping, the Communist peasant leader, was appointed to the Special Executive Committee of the new government and was entrusted with the task of organizing the peasant movement in the Xinjiang region. Using his special authority, he dismissed the district magistrate and the local chief of police, both of whom had played a crucial role in subverting the local peasant association in alliance with the right wing of the GMD and landlords. A new

[31] *Buxiu de geming zhanshi* 1960: 151–60; Shao 1958: 248–49.
[32] *FZM* 1982: 102–3; *HSFB* 1958, 1:58–59.

District Political Administration Committee was formed. Two native Communists, Zou Shuipeng and Wu Xianmin, were respectively appointed chairman of the committee and the chief of the local security department. After gaining control over the twenty-man local police force, Wu handed over the fourteen guns possessed by the security department to the peasant self-defense corps. Thus, by the last week of April, just before the beginning of counterattacks by the local landlords and the right wing of the GMD, the district peasant association assumed command over the local administrative structure.[33]

In Guixi district, the struggle between the revolutionary intellectuals and the traditional power-holding elite faction was particularly fierce.[34] In late 1926, the faction of the elite, with the support of militia forces of local strongmen, seized power in the area. They formed their own district administrative structure and expanded their authority to nearby regions. To cope with the situation, the provincial government appointed a district magistrate and sent him to Guixi District with a large contingent of the Nationalist Army. He was, however, unable to smash the independent factional forces, which had temporarily withdrawn to Hekou city.

In early 1927, the city of Hekou had become a stronghold of the factional forces after the suppression of their base at Moshushanyuan in Yiyang district and defeat in other regions. Converging there, they regrouped themselves under the banner of an independent Jiangxi Reorganizing Committee, whose primary aim was to maintain the status quo in districts unconquered by the Nationalist forces. In Li Liezhun's right wing of the GMD, which gained power soon after the Third Provincial Party Congress, they found an eager supporter. Moreover, diffident after the workers and peasants' massive April Second assault on Li's provincial government in Nanchang, conservative members of the district GMD deserted the peasant association movement to find refuge in the factional forces. The district magistrate, who had, meanwhile, become more interested in somehow maintaining his own power with the assistance of his local landlords and gang leaders, also betrayed the movement and did not heed the revolutionaries' plight. Thus, aligned together, counterrevolutionary forces not only disrupted revolutionary intellectuals' efforts to organize a mass movement in the district but also contrived to capture Guixi city. However, as their troops secretly advanced to within ten miles of the city, the plot was exposed. Peasants and district po-

---

[33] Shao 1958: 249–50.
[34] Ibid., 250–51.

lice forces vigorously fought and defeated them. Three local strongmen and rightist members of the district GMD were arrested, and fifteen rifles were captured.

The next day, the district peasant association convened a mass meeting in the city to demonstrate its strength. About ten thousand peasants gathered, carrying swords, spears, and other homemade weapons. Inspired by the defeat of the forces of local landlord factions, they demanded immediate execution of all the arrested persons. Both the district magistrate and the leaders of the peasant association were reluctant to carry out their demands. Not only did executions transcend their authority, but they also violated the principles of the United Front. However, under the persistent pressure of peasants, three arrested persons were killed. In spite of such a demonstration by the peasant forces, the revolutionary movement soon crumbled as the wrath of Li Liezhun's right wing of the GMD soon fell upon it, forcing its leaders to flee. Thus, in Guixi, not until the emergence of independent peasant forces in late 1927 did the revolutionary intellectuals succeed in forging a peasant movement that achieved sustained results.

Between November 1926 and April 1927, in spite of its ups and downs in Yiyang, Hengfeng, and Guixi districts, the peasant movement on the whole was rooted in the region. With the support of the Nationalist Army, revolutionary intellectuals launched campaigns to defy the hegemony of the landed upper class over the rural areas and to set up an alternative social and political order promising the liberation of exploited rural cultivators from traditional bondage. For a large number of peasants, whose family fortunes had rapidly declined because of severe pressures on their living conditions not very long after the Taiping Rebellion, and whose earlier political actions to restore the traditional and weakened paternalistic structure had failed to ameliorate their socioeconomic status, the promise generated by these new developments was tremendously appealing. Once the Nationalist Army and revolutionary intellectuals broke the barriers in their way, post-Taiping independent peasants and tenants rose within a very short period of time to support the revolutionary movement actively as a class of rural cultivators against the exploiters, the landed upper class. Seeds of the movement sowed before the arrival of the Northern Expedition forces by the revolutionary intellectuals acted as a fillip to precipitate the revolutionary momentum in the countryside.

In the final analysis, however, dependence of the Xinjiang peasant movement on the sympathetic Nationalist forces as well as the provincial GMD organization, and the rapidity of its development, proved disastrous for local peasant associations. The movement soon transcended the control of revolutionary intellectuals. Many new leaders spontaneously emerged, and peasant localism dominated its character. Shao Shiping notes that the revolutionary intellectuals failed to provide proper guidance to the peasants as the movement expanded. "Each leader independently directed a section of people who were directly influenced by him. Many other leaders guided the movement without entering the party. This was a mistake."[35] Initial emphasis on the selective use of peasant localism to establish and expand the movement made it deviate from its revolutionary course and turned it into a tool of local interests, which had joined it without any prior commitment to its ideology. They therefore betrayed the peasant movement as soon as it began to be confronted with opposition from above and from the local counterrevolutionary forces, especially beginning late April 1927.

Moreover, revolutionary intellectuals were not able to shake off their dependence on the Nationalist Army and the United Front government to build an alternative power structure within a short period through which to mold the spontaneous character of their movement into a revolutionary one. Standing on their shoulders, peasants dictated the route to be followed for a revolution. They retained the initiative and, in order to sustain the movement, revolutionary intellectuals were forced to endorse their acts. But as the Nationalist Army moved northward to continue its expedition and the cracks within the United Front began to appear, the movement lost its momentum. The conflict between different political parties within the United Front manifested itself in a fierce struggle between their respective supporters for control over the local areas. The right wing of the GMD, soon after its success in installing Li Liezhun as the head of the provincial GMD government, allied itself with local factions of landlords to unleash a reign of terror in the countryside. The poorly armed peasant self-defense corps was attacked and destroyed. Peasant associations were liquidated and their leaders were killed. The peasant movement thus began to decline as rapidly as it had surged forward.[36]

Frustrated, the revolutionary intellectuals organized a mammoth demonstration on April 2, 1927, against the "excesses" of the right wing of the GMD, and engineered the dismissal of Li Liezhun's provincial GMD government. After Li's replacement by Zhu Peide, dominated by the left wing of the GMD and CCP, they attempted to revive the peasant movement by expelling the

[35] Ibid., 253.
[36] The following discussion is based on Shao 1958: 251–53 and *FZM* 1982: 82–86.

counterrevolutionary local officials. In Hengfeng district, the district magistrate and the police chief were dismissed and replaced by CCP members. The Guixi district magistrate was forced to resist the attack of factional and local militia forces. Their successes were, however, very short-lived.

After their expulsion from Nanchang, Li Liezhun and his forces escaped to Shangrao district of the Xinjiang region. Supported by the militia forces of landlords already congregated there, they began to prepare a base from which to resume their authority over the local areas. Their task was made easier when Zhu Peide, after Jiang's coup on April 12 and the consequent collapse of the United Front, shifted his stand. Zhu released all the corrupt and oppressive members of the landed upper class who had been arrested by local peasant associations in different regions and sent to Nanchang for trial and punishment. He also expelled the CCP members from Nanchang. This was followed by the Wuhan debacle and the abortive Nanchang Uprising, which completely snapped the revolutionary intellectuals' link to, and support from, an established authority and turned them into fugitives.

In this period of extraordinary political chaos, Zhang Niancheng and other landlords of the Xinjiang region, after being released by Zhu, returned to their respective areas. Filled with rage, they joined Li Liezhun's forces to wage a final battle against the poorly defended peasant associations. In Guixi, soon after the execution of three rightist GMD members, a well-armed force of two to three hundred men of Li Liezhun's army, supported by local militia troops of landlords, attacked and captured the city. The prominent peasant leader Jiang Dinghai was arrested and executed. Peasant rebels and revolutionary intellectuals were forced to retreat and take shelter in the remote mountainous regions. The local peasant movement was temporarily suppressed.

After occupying Guixi, Li Liezhun's troops moved to neighboring districts of Yiyang and Hengfeng. Unable to confront the superior and well-armed force, one unit of the peasant self-defense corps fled to a mountainous region near the market town of Qigong to wage a guerrilla struggle. Another unit headed by Huang Tianzhong, Lei Xia, and Fang Yuanjie soon joined it. When Li Liezhun's army left Yiyang, they together struck back and recaptured the district city. But their victory was brief, as Zhang Niancheng, the infamous local landlord, retaliated with a large force. His militia defeated the peasant self-defense corps and killed a popular peasant leader of Yiyang, Fang Yuanjie. Twenty villages were burned down by the counterrevolutionary militia forces. Finally, the Yiyang peasant corps again fled to its hideout near Qigong. Meanwhile, a section of Jiang Jieshi's army, stationed in the district, mutinied and joined peasant forces. Although this alliance did not prove successful, it provided arms and ammunition needed by the peasant self-defense corps to survive and sustain its banditlike raids on landlords.[37]

In Hengfeng, too, the peasant self-defense corps, headed by Wu Xianmin, Zou Shuipeng, Huang Ruxi, and Huang Qiu, was routed by Li Liezhun's army. It finally found shelter in the hills between Qingbanjia and Feijialong. From there, it made three successive attempts to recapture the city, all of which failed. However, it succeeded in rescuing members of the district peasant association and their dependents from the city.

Thus, by June 1927, Li Liezhun's army had usurped control of several districts of the Xinjiang region. Li established a provisional provincial government in northeastern Jiangxi in alliance with Jiang Jieshi. But the necessity of a rival government ended when Zhu Peide and his forces joined Jiang's GMD soon after the Wuhan debacle on July 15, 1927. Together they reorganized the district governments and the Communist-dominated mass organizations. In Yiyang and Hengfeng, new district magistrates were appointed. District GMD offices, which were controlled by the Communists, were restructured. The old rural gentry and landlords, driven out of their native areas by peasants, were once again reinstated in their original positions. Local police forces were strengthened and provided with more arms and ammunition. A unit of Zhu Peide's army was transferred from Hukou to Hengfeng to aid district magistrates in both Yiyang and Hengfeng in assuming authority and in suppressing the remaining peasant forces.

A "multiple government" was thus created, with the inclusion of hated members of the landed upper class in the district government and in the GMD's local organizations leading to the kind of dual authority that had earlier arisen out of the peasant associations' takeover of the local administration. The GMD's promotion of factional forces virtually transferred local power to them. With the support of the district police, they arrested and punished the peasants at will. In Yiyang, the landlord Zhang Niancheng burned with impunity twenty villages around the market town of Qigong— then the center of the peasant movement. A local gangleader, Huang Baozhen, who was the son of a rich peasant from the village of Huangjiayuan and also an old associate of Fang Zhimin's in the Yiyang Youth Society, formed a local militia force with the support of younger members of local landlord families to wield influence in the local administration.[38] The

[37] *FZM* 1982: 102–4.
[38] Ibid., 103.

former police chief Yu was reinstated. Other landlords and strongmen followed suit. Peasants were pressured to pay those rent and interest charges which had earlier been annulled by the peasant association.[39] The GMD government found it difficult to restrain these traditional powerholding members of the landed upper class, for it needed their active support to pursue its own interests in tax collection and management of local administration. As both the traditional ruling class and the GMD state scrambled for local power, their interests began to collide. Finally, it was their inner struggle that, Shao notes, prevented the annihilation of the surviving forces of the peasant self-defense corps in both Yiyang and Hengfeng districts.

Thus from May to November 1927, or until the end of the autumn harvest season, the rural Xinjiang area was unusually quiet. In the wake of the above-mentioned depressing developments, an uneasy peace prevailed. Most of the revolutionary peasants either retreated to remote regions or returned to their villages to prepare for the coming autumn planting season. Although, in some scattered areas, they continued to launch independent small-scale guerrilla raids on landlords, the revolutionary movement lost much of its earlier vigor. Defeated and considerably weakened troops of the peasant self-defense corps were forced to remain in hiding until November 1927. On the twenty-seventh day of that month, revolutionary intellectuals from different areas of the Xinjiang region met together for the first time since the collapse of their movement to decide to build their own independent army with the support of peasants and launch an armed struggle under the leadership of Fang Zhimin. This would mark the beginning of a revolution from the countryside eventually leading to the establishment of the Xinjiang soviet.

From Peasant Movement to Communist Revolution

In August 1927, the failure of the Nanchang Uprising turned the political tide against the members of the CCP and its peasant leaders. Treated as outlaws, they began to be hunted, and thus they were compelled to leave the areas of their previous activity. Finally, they returned one by one to their native districts in the Xinjiang region for security. Fang Zhimin came back from Jian district, where the ruthless anti-Communist campaign made it dif-

[39] Shao 1959a: 55.

ficult for him to complete the earlier assigned task of organizing the CCP-led peasant association. Shao Shiping and Huang Dao arrived from Nanchang. Meeting for the first time with other participants in the Xinjiang peasant movement after the disastrous events of April and the ensuing suppression by the GMD and local counterrevolutionary forces, they set about establishing contacts with other scattered peasant forces to rekindle revolutionary fire in the countryside.[40]

In Lianjiawu, a mountainous village of Yiyang district, Fang Zhimin and other revolutionary intellectuals established their independent base. Hunted by strong local militia forces, with a price on his head, Fang secretly moved here from his native Hutang village. This hilly village was the abode of aggressive shed people who had traditionally resisted the domination of native landlords over their area and had enthusiastically supported the peasant movement. The battered but still unbroken Yiyang Ninth District Peasant Self-Defense Corps also sought refuge here. The counterrevolutionary forces had not pursued the defeated peasant corps, probably because of this area's traditional hostility and vigorous resistance to the oppressive forces from the plains. Thus, not unlike Mao in the Jingganshan area, Fang, together with remnants of his old peasant association forces and supportive shed people, began secretly to organize the revolutionary movement from his base in Lianjiawu village. Within a short period, revolutionary leaders like Zou Ji (a sympathetic Whampoa-trained military defector) and Peng Gao (trained in the Peasant Movement School in Wuchang and sent to Jiangxi) from the outside, and Fang Yuanhui, Huang Zhenzhong, Lei Xia, Wu Xianmin, Zou Xiupeng, Huang Qiu, Huang Ruixi, Huang Huairen, and others from the old peasant association areas, gathered here. They decided to fan out among natural villages to revive party organizations. Soon, twenty-nine branches of the party were reestablished in this volatile region.[41] In spite of the earlier failure of the peasant association, the persisting ruthless oppression by landlords once again brought about massive support of local people for these revolutionary intellectuals.

In Qigong, landlord Zhang Niancheng's forcible collection of unpaid rent, with the support of his old friend and chief of local police Yu, infuriated local peasants who once more clamored to teach him a lesson. Finding this an opportune moment to rebuild the revolutionary movement, Fang Zhimin led about two hundred peasants armed with makeshift weapons in

[40] This section is based on Shao 1959a and Miao 1962.
[41] *FZM* 1982: 104.

an attack on the local police station. In spite of the feeble strength of the peasant self-defense corps, it was hoped that a successful raid would enhance revolutionaries' credentials among peasants. The surprise onslaught forced the police chief Yu and his men to flee the station leaving behind their fire-arms, which were captured by the peasants.[42] The news of this attack quickly spread to neighboring villages and signaled the arrival of revolution-ary intellectuals.

In September 1927, however, the month fixed for the Autumn Harvest Uprising by the CCP's Central Committee, leaders of the Xinjiang peasant movement were not yet fully prepared. Fang learned of the proposed upris-ing very late when he was in Boyang to purchase arms for the peasant corps. After returning to Hutang, Fang called a meeting of peasant representatives from neighboring villages to make plans for the uprising. But while they were in session, the combined forces of Zhang Niancheng and the district government attacked and burned the village to retaliate for the peasants' ear-lier raid on the police station. The meeting was therefore adjourned without taking any decision. Fang escaped to Dengshan village in the Moban hills. This was an active revolutionary village, also of shed people, whose main source of income was from a rapidly declining paper-making handicraft in-dustry.[43]

Following this, the return of Fang's old lung problem shelved schemes to launch a large-scale peasant movement soon after the autumn harvest. Ill, Fang was forced to rest. To avoid detection by the counterrevolutionary forces, he moved to his sister's house in Dexing district. But on learning about his stay there, a militia force came after him. He was protected by local peasants, who paid the customary money to the force to move out of the area. But he had to leave the village. He finally found a sanctuary in Huangwu village in Leping district where he could rest to recuperate from his illness. Scared by the growth of revolutionary activities, landlords of this village had already fled. The village population comprised sixty to seventy families, and all of them belonged to the Wang lineage.[44] It was probably because of the conversion of all the members of this lineage into radical ac-tivists that local militia forces usually avoided any engagement here.

After recuperating from his illness, Fang again went to Boyang to seek advice from the district CCP office about plans for peasant insurrections. The Boyang party branch was already involved in a peasant uprising in the

[42] Zhang 1958: 57–60.
[43] *FZM* 1982: 105–6.
[44] Ibid., 106–7.

northern area of the district. Fang was therefore urged to launch immediately a peasant movement in the districts of Yiyang and Hengfeng. He was persuaded to move to Hengfeng to initiate a Yiyang-like reorganization of the peasant association. However, while still in Boyang, Fang learned of a peasant offensive in Yiyang. He then put off his departure to Hengfeng and returned immediately to his native Yiyang district sometime in late October or early November 1927.

In Yiyang, finding the peasant movement quiescent, the government troops stationed there had returned to Hekou. The powerful landlord Zhang Niancheng had also finally gone back to his native Lieqiao village. This provided an opportunity to peasants to settle scores with their old enemy Zhang. Fang Yunhui and Huang Zhenzhong, with about three hundred men of the local peasant self-defense corps, raided Zhang's house. On their way to Lieqiao, they were joined by about a thousand peasants from the neighboring areas. Zhang and his militia troops were no match for this formidable force. He fled from the village and went first to Nanchang and then to Shanghai, where he finally committed suicide.[45] This victory against their most hated local enemy naturally emboldened the peasants. Although the government forces soon arrived, forcing them to retreat, peasant forces retaliated by burning the houses of several local landlords. They also resisted both the landlords' and the state's tax collection activities after the autumn harvest. Their successes once again began to expand the revolutionary movement.

Taking advantage of this spurt in the peasant movement, Fang Zhimin convened a conference of peasant leaders at Jiaotou village in Yiyang district on November 27, 1927.[46] Held after the end of the autumn harvest season, it was attended by the following persons from each of five districts:

Yiyang—Fang Zhimin, Shao Shiping, Zou Ji, Peng Nie, Fang Zhichun, Huang Tianzhong, Fang Yuanhui, and others
Hengfeng—Huang Dao, Wu Xianmin, Zou Xiupeng, and others
Guixi—Shao Dang and others
Shangrao—Comrade Wang (who arrived after the conference)
Yanshan—Que Xi

At the conference, Fang conveyed the decisions of the August Seventh Emergency Conference of the CCP to the delegates, who adopted their own resolutions as well.

[45] Ibid., 109.
[46] Ibid., 110–12.

First, since the GMD had become reactionary, it could no longer promote the revolutionary movement. It was thus the task of the CCP to overthrow the countervailing forces of the GMD and to seize political power by means of armed uprisings. To achieve this, the local revolutionary movement should be widened. As the CCP represented 95 percent of the population, the final victory belonged to it.

Second, during the armed uprising, the following slogans should be employed:

Topple Imperialism, Overthrow the Guomindang.
Eliminate Corrupt and Greedy Officials, Annihilate Oppressive Landlords and the Rural Gentry.
Reduce Interest and Distribute Land, Establish the Government of Workers and Peasants.
If in the Middle of the Action One Changes His Mind, There Would Be No Regrets at His Death.

Third, armed uprisings would be launched by the peasant self-defense corps. The corps would be secretly organized in each natural village. One unit would consist of several *pai* (lines) and *ban* (sections). When thirty or more persons joined the corps, a unit would be formed. Each member of the unit would have to publicly take an oath to protect secrets, refrain from hasty action, secretly promote the development of the unit by means of familial or kinship connections, collect weapons on the pretext of hunting, work hard, and obey orders from higher authorities.

The conference also selected members for its executive committee. These included Fang Zhimin, Shao Shiping, Huang Dao, Fang Zhichun, Wu Xianmin, Shao Dang, and Fang Yuanhui. Fang Zhimin was unanimously chosen to be the general secretary of the committee. Moreover, it was decided that until the establishment of contacts with the CCP's central organization, this committee would serve as the highest administrative organization. Finally the conference proposed to launch the revolutionary movement during the tax collection period just before the lunar year, which was the time of exacerbated hostility between landlords and peasants.

Thus, the foundation for the growth of a revolutionary movement in the Xinjiang region was laid. Organizationally, the revolutionary intellectuals followed those traditional practices for enlisting members for the movement which, throughout the ages, had served to bind peasants to such antiestablishment forces as secret societies, bandit gangs, and smuggler bands and had kept them together in their riots and uprisings. The Jiaotou Conference particularly emphasized natural villages as opposed to administrative villages in order to form close-knit revolutionary units based on the special characteristics of each area. As most of the natural villages were organized along lineage lines, emphasis was placed on the greater exploitation of kinship ties.

I earlier noted that the role played by lineage ties in the development of peasant associations was so critical that the latter had initially, to a large extent, assumed the character of traditional lineage associations with revolutionary intellectuals replacing the landlords as leaders. Moreover, as Miao Min notes, the secret formation of a revolutionary unit was always followed by an elaborate ceremony in which "incense was burned, obeisance made, and chicken's blood drunk, [with] the members swearing to stand by each other until death."[47] Decent funeral ceremonies for the betrayers of the revolutionary movement were denied. Soon after the conference, when the enlistment (*shangmingze*) campaign was launched by Fang Zhimin, these rituals were religiously practiced. Each peasant whose name was registered in the revolutionary book had to undergo a public oath taking and a secret initiation ceremony that marked his ordination into the "sacred" revolutionary group. Thus, an attempt was made not only to prevent the enlistment of opportunists, who had earlier destroyed the peasant association movement, but also to generate among peasants passionate commitments to the revolutionary cause.

Writing from his experiences of the peasant revolutionary movement in Algeria, Fanon remarks that the establishment of a mutual current of enlightenment and enrichment between intellectuals and peasants is necessary for the success of an outside revolutionary organization. During the course of a revolution, therefore, traditional institutions are often reinforced, deepened, and sometimes literally transformed. The tribunals that settle disputes, or *djemmas*, and the village assemblies turn into revolutionary tribunals and political and military committees.[48] No doubt, the reliance on traditional customs and practices for a revolutionary purpose generated a religious fervor among Chinese peasants, who believed, as Shao notes, that "a Pusa (Buddha) had appeared to turn their misfortune."[49]

Furthermore, at a time when landlords were forcibly collecting the overdue rent and interest charges, revolutionary intellectuals' promises to annihilate the oppressive class in rural areas, divide the land equally, and abolish debts raised exploited rural cultivators' hope for a decent life. Traditional

[47] Miao 1962: 56.
[48] Fanon 1968: 107–47.
[49] Shao 1959a: 60.

images of a cohesive and harmonious society were projected through revolutionaries' efforts to tackle the contemporary socioeconomic crisis in the countryside. Peasants' found that their strong antilandlord feelings had much in common with Marxists' antifeudalism and anticapitalism.

After the Jiaotou Conference, Fang moved to the district of Hengfeng. He once again intelligently employed lineage connections and the antilandlordism of peasants to organize peasants for a revolution. In the twin villages of Luoti and Lanjia (also known as Luoti-Lanjia) of the old peasant association base area, Fang relied on Hua Qunshan, and also on the support of two persons of the dominant Lan lineage, Lan Changjin and Lan Gaomao, to expand revolutionary activities. Through their local lineage connections, he convened a meeting of all those cultivators who owed large debts or overdue rent payments. He invoked the traditional images of a decent society and laid before them the imperative of punishing landlords who exploited them through a command over wealth and land. He called on them to launch a campaign to abolish debts and divide land equally. Such an explanation of revolution proved compatible with peasants' traditional solutions for their socioeconomic crises. A large number of peasants, therefore, soon agreed to place their names in the "sacred" revolutionary register. They took the public oath and were initiated into the revolutionary unit, named the Village Huntsmen Society, after performing the earlier mentioned secret society–like rituals.[50] Such a name allowed the society to collect arms ostensibly for hunting purposes.

Similarly, in the Zhang-lineage-dominated Guanshan area, Fang enlisted the support of Zhang Songmao, Zhang Zhixiang, Zhang Deyuan, Zhang Dali, Zhang Xiangmu, and forty others of the same lineage. In the villages of nearby Taojialong and Heyuan, the same pattern of mobilizing peasants was followed. After having been initiated into a revolutionary unit, each peasant was implored to mobilize peasants independently and secretly for its activities in nearby areas. Thus, within a month after the Jiaotou Conference, more than hundred units were set up in Yiyang and Hengfeng districts alone.[51]

As the number of peasant revolutionary units swelled rapidly, demands for an early launch of the peasant movement increased. Thus, the first shots of the revolution were fired a few weeks earlier than planned. It burst forth sometime in mid-December 1927 in the twin villages of Luoti and Lanjia of

[50] *FZM* 1982: 112–15.
[51] Ibid., 116.

Hengfeng district. In these twin villages, out of a total population of about a hundred families, four households were those of landlords and about seventy were those of poor peasants and tenants. The other families were either rich or middle peasants. Landlords owned more than four hundred mu of land in this area; each thus had an average of over a hundred mu. On the outskirts of the villages was a small coal mine. During the Qing period, it was abandoned by the government. Since then, local peasants customarily collected coal for personal use and for sale to other villagers. This often significantly supplemented their income. Local authorities traditionally respected the peasants' customary right to the coal mine.

Detecting peasants' extra income from this officially abandoned mine, the new district magistrate of Hengfeng imposed a coal tax of five dollars per month in late 1927. On December 9, he sent an official with some men of the district police force to collect the tax from mining peasants. What made peasants indignant was not only the tax on what was considered to be their traditional entitlement, but also its imposition and collection at a time different from the pre-fixed tax-collection period in the spring season. In view of this, the peasants expressed their inability to pay on the present occasion and requested the official to collect the tax during the fixed period after the spring harvest. Their petition was rejected and some of them were beaten by henchmen of the official. Infuriated, they sought the support of Fang Zhimin and the local revolutionary unit to resist the tax collection, while keeping the tax official and his retinue in the house of a landlord, Luo Kuangshan, where they indulged in the customary feast. Before Fang could reach Luoti village, members of the local peasant corps arrived, surrounded the village, smashed the sedan chair of the official, and chased him and the members of the police force out.

Meanwhile, Fang rushed to the village. Expecting reprisals from the forces of the district magistrate, he held an emergency meeting of all nearby units of the peasant revolutionary corps. They decided to launch their planned uprising immediately. Messages to this effect were secretly sent to other areas by circulating the picture of a *qunniu* (clay ox) and by beating the gong. It was a traditional village custom to carry a clay ox at the ceremony to welcome the spring. The circulation of the clay ox at this time symbolized the early beginning of the spring and therefore also of the armed uprising to be launched after the winter harvest.

At the same time, sensing the trouble ahead, the landlord Luo Kuangshan, had also called a secret meeting of other landlords, rich peasants, and local notables to formulate a strategy to suppress the peasants. Learning the

news of this meeting, the angry peasants, under the leadership of their revolutionary units, attacked the Luo's house and burned it. They then moved
to assault other landlords of the twin villages. Peasants confiscated the landlords' four hundred mu of land and fifteen hundred dan of hoarded grains.
Three hundred land deeds were discovered and set on fire. Landlords were
forced to surrender all their gold, silver, and other precious items as well as
their agricultural tools. The confiscated items were later distributed by Fang
to the seventy poor families of the villages.[52] Thus began the Xinjiang revolutionary movement.

Within three days of the incident at Luoti and Lanjia villages, the revolutionary movement spread to other areas of Yiyang and Hengfeng districts.
Together with local members of the Village Huntsmen Society, peasants
and Marxist intellectuals took control of a large area. They attacked landlords and burned land deeds and debt receipts. If a landlord was counterrevolutionary or considered exploitative and oppressive by the peasants, all his
property was confiscated. Half of it was redistributed among the poor and
landless peasants of the village, and the other half was given to the local units
of the peasant revolutionary corps for their expenses. If, however, a landlord
was "neutral" in politics and had a good reputation among the peasants, only
that portion of his property was forfeited which was in excess of the cultivating capacity of the total number of his family.[53]

Not unlike earlier riots and uprisings, peasants' political action began in
defense of traditional practices and customary entitlements that were violated by the state in league with oppressive members of the landed upper
class. But as the movement expanded under the guidance of revolutionary
intellectuals, its scope widened. It did not remain limited only to an onslaught on corrupt and oppressive landlords but moved to establish its own
sociopolitical apparatus by demolishing the repressive hegemonic structure
itself—which, more than anything else, had traditionally restricted the spontaneous development of peasants' socioeconomic status.

Thus, with the success of the revolutionary movement in Yiyang and
Hengfeng, Fang united all the units of the local peasant self-defense corps
and reorganized them as an independent Revolutionary Army, or Red
Army, of peasants. This armed force was divided into five units. Each unit
was to strike independently in the areas where the revolutionary movement
was resisted. In the event of armed attacks by counterrevolutionary forces

[52] Ibid., 119–22; *HSFB* 1958, 12:141–42; *HQPP* 1957–60, 5:74–78.
[53] Shao 1959a: 61ff.; *FZM* 1982: 120–21.

or the GMD's army, all units were to unite and fight. Each of these consisted of three to four hundred persons and possessed forty to fifty guns. By January–February 1928, the Red Army successfully set up the Yiyang-Hengfeng Guerrilla District.[54]

Shao Shiping summarizes the location of all five units of the Red Army and their initial victories, which finally led to the establishment of a guerrilla district.[55] The first unit was stationed in the twin villages of Luoti and Lanjia. It was headed by Hua Qunshan, Zou Xuipeng, Huang Ruixi, and Lan Kuangping. It defeated a section of the GMD army that was sent to suppress the peasant uprising caused by the imposition of the coal tax. Peasants surrounded this contigent of the GMD army near a mountainous region and attacked it from four sides. Taken by surprise and unprepared to retaliate, it soon fled to Hengfeng city. A large area between Yiyang and Hengfeng cities thus came under the control of the peasants.

The second unit was based at Qingbanqiao. It was under the leadership of Wu Xianmin, Huang Qiu, Qian Bi, Xiang Chunfu, and Wu Xianxi. Carrying the fight to areas untouched by the peasant association movement, it succeeded in establishing peasant government in several villages near Hengfeng and Loufang cities.

Cheng Boqian, Qiu Jinhui, Hu Cuifang, Yu Quancai, Huang Ligui, and Li Mu led the third unit at Fengshuwu, which was active in Geyuan, Huangcun, and other neighboring villages. Their decisive victory at Geyuan rapidly spread the revolutionary movement in that region. Surrounded by the four districts of Yiyang, Hengfeng, Dexing, and Shangrao, Geyuan was an important market town consisting of about three thousand families, with about eight hundred belonging to the Yu lineage. Utilizing his connections with this lineage, Cheng Boqian had earlier organized a peasant movement here. Fang Zhimin, too, had secretly worked here as a merchant to promote revolutionary activities. When the Gandongbei soviet was established, this market town became its headquarters.[56]

Lingongzhen was the base of the fourth unit. Huang Tianzhong, Fang Yuanhui, Fang Huari, Shao Boping, Hung Shenyuan, and Fang Shenxi carried the torch of revolution to the region around Huban, Fangjiabo, and Taojiaban villages. In this area, Shao notes, there were some large-lineage villages that first resisted the revolutionary movement. Revolutionaries, however, received support from smaller villages, which surrounded the large

[54] *FZM* 1982: 122.
[55] Shao 1959a: 61–62.
[56] Zhonggong Hengfeng Xianwei 1978: 23–30, 57; see also Averill 1982.

ones. Alliance with them finally enabled the fourth unit of the Red Army to form a local government.

The domination and exploitation by the large-lineage villages, termed by Kuhn "inter-lineage imperialism," perhaps contributed to the smaller-lineage villages' vigorous support for the revolutionary movement. The peasant army's attack on the large-lineage villages provided the smaller villages a favorable opportunity to settle traditional scores. However, as the revolutionary movement developed, lineage rivalries gave way to an alliance of exploited rural cultivators from both small and large lineages, all of whom suffered from similar oppressive conditions arising out of the replacement of lineage ties by economic ties under the influence of the crisis of paternalism. Thus, as the revolutionary movement transcended interlineage rivalries, a lineage war gradually turned into a class war.

The fifth unit of the peasants' Red Army was located at Zhangshudun. Its leaders were Lei Xia, She Hanchao, Shu Yi, Gan Yunlin, and Fang Xugen. This unit was the most successful in expanding the revolutionary movement. As mentioned earlier, one of its leaders, Lei Xia, had linkages with a local secret society. Enjoying extraordinary fame and special status in the countryside, he utilized his earlier connections to assume command over a large area. Peasants often remarked, "As soon as Lei Xia arrives, the red flag unfurls and our revolution in each village succeeds."[57]

These five units of the Red Army moved as roving bandit forces in the countryside and made possible the success of the peasants' spontaneous uprising. As the revolutionary movement escalated, they helped to lay the foundation of a guerrilla district government in the Yiyang-Hengfeng area in January–February 1928. With the transfer of local power over several villages into the peasants' and Marxist intellectuals' hands, various laws were promulgated to uphold the cause of the exploited rural cultivators. Within the next two months, their strength increased to the extent that they raided the city of Yiyang and successfully defeated two companies of a GMD battalion. Finally in May 1928, a revolutionary base was established in an area comprising fifty villages in Yiyang and Hengfeng districts. It was the first soviet in the Xinjiang region.[58]

Composed of local people and led mostly by the native revolutionary intellectuals, the Red Army was considered by the peasants as their own force. Miao Min notes that "wherever the guerillas went, there was sure to be some

[57] Shao 1959a: 61.
[58] See Shao 1959a; Averill 1982.

one who would supply what they needed. If they had money, they paid; if their pockets were empty they would accept the provisions with thanks and there was never any quarrel about it, for the guerillas were considered by all as part of one big family."[59] As the Red Army consisted primarily of local peasant self-defense corps and members of the Village Huntsmen Society, voluntarism prevailed. Moreover, they brought to it their localism and spontaneity. Miao writes, "When a battle was fought, one could participate or not as he chose, willingness being expressed by signature or hand raising, those refusing to fight not being obliged to."[60] Untrained in organized armed warfare, revolutionary intellectuals also promoted spontaneity, or "excessive democracy," and failed to train members for their units according to military discipline. Although after defeating the GMD's army they hired some arrested officers to instruct their units, peasants resisted flogging and other punishments employed in the course of instruction. Spontaneity and localism, which characterized the Red Army, restricted its move beyond local areas to the regions previously untouched by uprisings.[61]

Peasant spontaneity contributed to both the strength and weakness of the revolutionary movement. As peasants sprang to political action in their native places to defend their socioeconomic existence, it characterized solidarity for the revolution among the peasants themselves and between them and their revolutionary leaders at the local level. It thus played a crucial role in the triumph of revolution in a locality. But solidarity at the local level is not the same as on a national level. Confronted by the state's wide reach and massive machinery of repression, a local movement required attachment to national issues transcending parochial problems. It needed to create a larger solidarity by raising the consciousness of masses to make them a part of a wider and sustained movement. Failing that, the danger of suppression from powerful counterrevolutionary forces loomed large. The first Soviet in the Xinjiang region suffered from this weakness. In the wake of growing spontaneity and localism, peasants and Marxist intellectuals' efforts proved to be only temporarily dynamic.

In Yiyang and Hengfeng districts, peasants held out in their first soviet for about two months. In the summer of 1928, the GMD army launched a massive suppression campaign in the region after reinforcing itself. Revolutionary intellectuals and peasants of the units of the Red Army failed to break through the encirclement of the GMD army and the landlords' "pacification corps." Finally, once again, they were forced to seek shelter in the

---

[59] Miao 1962: 70.
[60] Ibid., 75.
[61] Ibid., 78.

hills of Moban near the borders of Yiyang, Hengfeng, and Dexing districts. Lei Xia was killed in the battle and Wu Xianmin and Huang Qiu were arrested. With their bases destroyed and their food supply dwindling, the morale of both leaders and members of the Red Army reached its lowest ebb.[62]

It was not so much the peasants' lack of revolutionary initiatives but their military unpreparedness that ultimately led to their defeat in most of the areas. The revolutionary movement was launched earlier than planned, and its leaders did not have enough time to build up a strong and disciplined peasant force. The ill-trained and badly equipped revolutionary army was no match for the superior and professional Nationalist Army. Thus, in spite of the frustration and low morale experienced by both peasants and their leaders after the failure of their uprising, Fang's belief in the revolutionary potential of peasantry remained intact. He correctly realized that in order to win a revolutionary war, it was necessary to develop a strong and well-trained army as well as a military strategy. He therefore pleaded with all the leaders of the Xinjiang revolutionary movement to continue the rural revolution, when they gathered together to discuss the future course of their action in the wake of their recent failures.[63]

The meeting of about twenty leaders of the revolutionary movement took place sometime in June 1928 in an old temple on the peak of Fangsheng Mountain.[64] Some CCP members from Hubei, who had escaped to Jiangxi after the similar failure of their rural uprisings, also participated. Dissatisfied with the "peasantist" and localist character of their movement and concerned about its overwhelming dependence on peasants' spontaneity, most of the revolutionary intellectuals favored dissolving their guerrilla units, burying their arms, and fleeing to urban areas. For Fang, such an action was inconceivable. Wholeheartedly committed to rural revolution with unshaken faith in the immense revolutionary energies of the peasants, he finally convinced other leaders to continue the movement. They came to realize that the present setback resulted from the failure to assess properly the contemporary political situation and to follow a coherent military strategy.

The Fangsheng Conference emphasized the necessity for the establishment of a permanent base, or soviet. To achieve this aim, a military strategy was formulated. It was decided that, instead of fighting the formidable regular government troops that attacked their main revolutionary bases, utmost effort should be made to first defeat irregular local militia forces of landlords scattered elsewhere in the region. Familiar with the local terrain, these forces

[62] Shao 1959a: 64.
[63] Fanon 1968: 136.
[64] *FZM* 1982: 128–35.

were the major stumbling block to the growth of the revolutionary movement in the countryside. And their small size and the lack of unity among
them made it easier for the peasant forces to tackle them first. Conference
participants also expected that the annihilation of these hated militia forces
of landlords would enhance the reputation of revolutionaries among the
peasants and would facilitate wider growth of the movement. The revolutionary army had a total of forty-six guns at that time. It was resolved that:
(1) Shao Shiping would take forty guns and launch an attack on local militia
with the combined force of all the units of revolutionary army; (2) Fang
Zhimin would be provided the six remaining rifles to suppress counterrevo-
lutionaries and expand the movement in neighboring districts; and (3)
Huang Dao would return to his old peasant association area in Guixi district
to establish a new revolutionary base.[65]

The military strategy thus formulated proved successful. Laying the basis
for unified action by vagrant and autonomous local revolutionary forces, it
considerably subdued proclivities for spontaneity and localism that marked
peasants' earlier activities. Within a year, the revolutionary movement had
expanded to a larger area and the Xinjiang soviet was established in February 1929. The Fangsheng Conference, as Miao Min remarks, was therefore
"an important event in the history of the whole revolutionary movement to
establish Soviets in the Northeastern Jiangxi."[66]

Between late 1928 and mid-1930, the Red Army systematically suppressed major local militia forces one by one. It also successfully defended
itself from counterattacks by GMD troops in the autumn of 1928 and in the
last half of 1929. In fact, as a large contingent of the GMD troops was shifted
to the Central soviet area in southern Jiangxi to launch an encirclement campaign, the pressure on the Red Army in the Xinjiang region was somewhat
eased. The Xinjiang soviet thus rapidly expanded, leading to the establishment of a highly effective revolutionary government. In July 1930, after extending its control over several districts along the banks of the Xin River,
the Xinjiang soviet area was enlarged and renamed the Gandongbei soviet.
Its government laid the organizational base on which the Min-Zhe-Wan-Gan
soviet was finally formed in 1932 with its headquarters in the large market
town of Geyuan in Hengfeng district. At the height of its power, this soviet
controlled the following districts in the border regions of Jiangxi, Anhui,
Zhejiang, and Fujian:[67]

[65] Ibid., 128–33; see also Hu 1984.

[66] Miao 1962: 74.

[67] *Zhongguo gongchandang zai Jiangxi diqu lingdao geming douzheng de lishi ziliao*, 1958: 262. For

Jiangxi—Yiyang, Hengfeng, Shangrao, Guixi, Yushan, Guangfeng, Yan-
shan, Dexing, Leping, Wannian, Fouliang, Boyang, Yugan, Yujiang,
Doujiang, Hukou, Pengze, Dongxiang, and Jinxi
Anhui—Wuyuan, Qimen, Dongliu, Qiubo, Xiuning, Taiping, and Jingxian
Zhejiang—Jiangshan, Kaihua, Quxian, Pingyang, Yunshan, Zhujiang,
Yunhe, Taishun, Yingcha Qingtian, Ruian, Qingyuan, and Jingning
Fujian—Chongan, Jianyang, Jianou, Shaowu, Guangze, Pucheng, Fuding,
Fuan, Shouning, Pingnan, Duyuan, and Zhenghe

In terms of size, the northeastern Jiangxi soviet was among the largest
during the Jiangxi period of the CCP. A plan was once mooted to combine it
with the Central soviet region, thus establishing Communist control over
almost three-fourths of the province. Organizationally also, it was among the
best soviets and earned praise from Mao Zedong for its brisk and fruitful
activities in developing the countryside. The area, in fact, prospered during
the soviet period. Between 1932 and 1933, there was a 20-percent increase
in agricultural production, which surpassed even that of the Central soviet
region. Rural handicraft industries, for which this area was traditionally famous, also flourished. Massive demands for the native product in the white
region kept the local economy dynamic and allowed it to procure essential
supplies during the GMD-blockade period. Moreover, many small-scale industries were set up to produce items necessary to sustain the red area.

After the suppression of the Central soviet region by the GMD armies in
1934 and employment of all the major Red Army forces to make possible
the Long March, this region was rendered defenseless. By late 1934, the GMD
armies defeated the remnants of the illustrious Tenth Red Army, which had
been painstakingly raised by Fang Zhimin through combining local units of
the peasant self-defense corps. His soviet destroyed and his revolutionary
movement in shambles, Fang moved from one area to another to avoid detection and to rebuild a base. He was, however, arrested by a GMD army
contingent on January 29, 1935, in Jinjukeng near the Nanhua hills while he
was on his way to the old soviet region in Huawude. Brought immediately
to Nanchang, he was executed there on August 6, 1935, after spending more
than six months in prison.

One may thus conclude that the Xinjiang revolutionary movement successfully developed by basing itself on local issues and problems. Leadership

the economic reconstruction in the Gandongbei Soviet, see Chen 1985: 97–101; Johnson and
Taube 1934. For the political developments leading to the fall of the soviet, see *Jiangxi wenshi
ziliao xuanji*, 1980, 1:84–103; Cao 1961.

was provided by a small group of Marxist intellectuals who were mostly natives with a strong rural background. What made them different from peasants was their education in the cities as well as their prior commitment to Marxism and revolution. Moreover, it was their sensitivity to and comprehension of rural problems, acquired through their own or their family's experiences, that facilitated their fusion of local issues with revolutionary concerns. They penetrated rural areas with relative ease by utilizing their kinship and lineage ties. It was thus that the foundation of their revolutionary organization was laid. Starting from mostly the Marxist intellectuals' native natural villages, the movement gradually expanded to the larger administrative villages, then to market towns, and finally to cities.

To be sure, the initial development of the movement along traditional lines posed the danger of its retrogression and its assumption of the conservative and defensive characteristics of traditional peasant riots and uprisings. The barrier of peasants' traditional localism was removed by systematic and symbolic destruction of oppressive leaders of the lineages. This provided the movement a wider scope and shifted it from a single-lineage, or village, boundary to a larger arena. This also facilitated the unity of the exploited rural cultivators under the umbrella of a revolutionary party. The movement thus gradually turned into class war between, on the one hand, the exploited rural cultivators and the exploiters, and, on the other, the landed upper class and the state. The antilandlord beliefs of peasants merged with the antifeudalism of the Marxist intellectuals and formed the basis for a close alliance between them.

Peasants' spontaneity kept the movement weak for a long time. Before the final phase of the movement, it was not lack of revolutionary initiatives from the peasants but failure to organize them into a disciplined force that led to the movement's temporary suppression by the landed upper class and the state. Organization of a disciplined Red Army and development of a military strategy to outwit the strong militia and superior state forces ultimately enabled the Marxist intellectuals to wage a protracted war to establish their own soviet government in the region. However, neither the comprehension of the wider Communist ideology nor the dependence upon a particular environment can solely explain the phenomenon of the rise and fall of this revolutionary movement. Its origin and growth in the Xinjiang region demonstrate the independent manner in which local peasants and Marxist intellectuals coalesced and mobilized their own local resources to turn the world upside down.

Chapter Nine

Conclusion

Summing up the prerevolutionary situation in the Yiyang-Hengfeng area, Fang Zhimin once remarked that this birthplace of the Xinjiang peasant movement "was . . . a powder keg and, frankly speaking, I was the one who ignited the fuse setting off an immediate revolutionary uprising."[1] This metaphor captures the major issues addressed and the broad conclusion reached in this study, which has analyzed the historical development of those socioeconomic conditions in the countryside which afforded opportunities to Marxist intellectuals to regenerate the rural world through a revolution. This process has confirmed the material basis for the growth of this region, to continue Fang's metaphor, into a powder keg and the significant role of native urban-educated leadership as the detonator.

The present study denies any assumption that seeks the root of the Chinese revolution solely in either the manipulative or coercive strategy of the Marxist intellectuals. It instead traces the historical origin of the Xinjiang peasant movement to disruptions in the post-Taiping rural social structure. This region was the site of reorganization of the land tenure pattern after the bloodletting and enormous devastation wrought by a decade-long civil war between the Taipings and the monarchists. A major consequence of this was the predomination of the small rural cultivators and the resurgence of the small-peasant economy in the Xinjiang countryside. However, during the early twentieth century and within a short span of a little more than fifty years after the Taiping Rebellion, these rural cultivators suffered from serious disruptions in the material basis of their production. Experiencing a rapid decline in their socioeconomic status, they became a major force of the revolutionary movement in the late 1920s.

[1] Miao 1962: 83.

The term "small rural cultivators" has been preferred mainly because of the difficulty in differentiating the Xinjiang rural structure on the basis of absolute socioeconomic categories of poor, middle, and rich peasants. In fact, such categories overlap to such an extent that the drawing of any standard demarcation line between each and the demonstration of greater vulnerability of any one of them to agrarian radicalism becomes onerous. Macroregional studies of rural China and revolution by both Perry and Marks therefore dispense with such notions.[2] Works of Moore, Scott, and Migdal also de-emphasize linkages between structural differentiation and rural revolutions as stipulated by Wolf and Alvi and further developed by Zagoria and Paige.[3] Instead of delineating and dwelling upon the task of differentiation of the peasantry, the study has presented the small rural cultivators as a class that predominated in the countryside immediately after the Taiping Rebellion. This class, however, soon became the victim of the shift in the landed upper class's exercise of power and felt exploited because of the rapid decline in its socioeconomic status. It eventually became the harbinger of the rural revolution. The sources and nature of the exploitation that made it receptive to the appeals of revolution by Marxist intellectuals are traced to the instability of the small-peasant economy and the deterioration in rural class relations.

Disruption in the small-peasant economy resulted from the growing weakness of the state and the increasing aggressiveness of world market forces.[4] After the massive mid-nineteenth-century rebellions, and more so after the fall of the Qing dynasty, the politically and financially weakened state had become incapable of maintaining by itself social, political, and economic stability in the countryside. Moreover, in order to meet newer demands as well as to survive, it needed greater mobilization of national resources. Unable to pursue these tasks alone, the state found a willing partner in the landed upper class. The coincidence of their interests promoted a symbiotic relationship between them. Its consequences were felt in the siphoning off of rural surpluses through fresh taxes and levies. The expansion of the world capitalist economy in China, characterized in Jiangxi by the forced opening of Jiujiang as a foreign commercial port and the beginning of the steamship cargo traffic on the Yangzi River, contributed to the decline of traditional business towns and trade routes. The closer integration of the

---

[2] See Perry 1980; Marks 1984.

[3] Moore 1966; Scott 1976; Migdal 1974; Zagoria, in Lewis 1974: 29–60; Paige 1975.

[4] On linkages of revolution to the breakdown in the state, see Skocpol 1979; Moore 1966; Wolf 1969; for the origin of revolution in relation to the forces of the world economy, see Wallerstein 1974, 1979; Moulder 1977; Bagchi 1982.

world market with the local small-peasant economy disrupted the traditional agrarian sector.

The traditional agrarian sector in China was, of course, already exposed to active markets and the commodity economy and had been considerably influenced by them, especially from the late seventeenth century onward. But during the late nineteenth and early twentieth centuries, greater reliance on the market, which responded to the tunes of busts and booms in world trade, added new disruptive factors of risk to the existing agrarian sector. In the Xinjiang region, this becomes evident in the crash of the tea trade as well as in the growing pressures on indigo-, tobacco-, and cotton-producing cultivators and rural handicraft industries. These developments forced a large number of small rural cultivators and handicraftsmen to meet their subsistence needs by switching from one cash crop to another, by planting subsistence intercrops at the cost of diminishing returns from their market crops— or by abandoning cultivation and the independent base of their handicraft production to become part of the surplus labor force that worked in the newly emerging specialized centers of production at low wages. When their fate was interwoven with outside market forces, and also affected by the highly noncompetitive nature of their production, the small rural cultivators experienced greater constraints on their socioeconomic growth.

But new pressures arising out of the demands of the state and the world capitalist economy by themselves did not bring impoverishment and misery to rural areas. "Outside threats," Perry writes, "were nothing new to many rural inhabitants. . . . Peasants responded to crises, not as atomized individuals set suddenly adrift from the anchor of ancient securities, but rather as participants in organized survival strategies that antedated and outlasted any particular crisis."[5] Such crisis situations demanded activization of protective strategies inherent in the traditional rural institution.

Survival strategies were part of peasants' social relations of production. Embedded within the structure of rural society, these were traditionally organized by the landlord as the leader of the clan, manager of granaries and other local charity organizations, overseer of dykes and other waterworks, and, most important, as the representative of local interests to the state and outside world. Performance of these tasks provided the moral basis for the legitimacy of social hierarchy within or, as Gramsci terms it, for the hegemony of the dominant class over, the rural society.[6] But it was the decreasing effectiveness of organized survival strategies, or traditional leveling

[5] Perry 1980: 253.
[6] Gramsci 1971; see also chapter 4 above.

mechanisms, that characterized the rural society and consequently affected the living conditions of the masses.

Threatened by the massive peasant uprisings and the weakness of the state, especially from the mid–nineteenth century onward, the dominant landed upper class was itself in crisis. Its loss of confidence in maintaining hegemony solely through the organization of traditional survival strategies brought about, to use Thompson's term, the crisis of paternalism.[7] It therefore increasingly sought to legitimize its socioeconomic power and authority by controlling public and private means of coercion and violence. Organization of local militia forces, purchase of official bureaucratic degrees, and usurpation of control over formal institutions of local authority strengthened its coercive force in the countryside. With formal legtimization of its force by the state, the landed upper class became less dependent upon local sanctions and support to maintain its authority. It became the supervisor—instead of the leader—of the peasant community. This was a unique development that characterized the early-twentieth-century rural society not only in the Xinjiang region but also in other parts of China.

References to the growth of these tendencies abound in the studies of various peasant-based movements in the early twentieth century. For example, Peng Pai, the leader of the Hailufeng peasant movement, noted: "Formerly when an argument arose between peasant and landlord, the landlord merely asked officials to handle it. But now the new landlord class uses direct action, mercilessly beating, arresting, and imprisoning peasants. The landlord also directly seizes goods in default of rent or forcibly imposes military tax."[8] In his study of the Southeast Asian rural society, Scott finds similar occurrences marking transformation in the basis of the landed upper class's dominantion. He writes:

> Their control, which was embedded in the primary dependencies of production relations, is now based far more on law, property, coercion, market forces, and political patronage. They have themselves become much more dependent upon the state. . . . It is ironic but entirely logical that this class has been so securely wedded to the state at precisely the moment when its own autonomous control over subordinate classes is fast eroding.[9]

Increasing dependence of the landed upper class on coercive forces to maintain its domination progressively unbalanced the paternal-deference

---

[7] See chapter 4 above for full elaboration.

[8] Cited in Galbiati 1985: 52.

[9] Scott 1985: 312.

equilibrium that formed the basis for cohesiveness within the exploitative rural structure. The paternalistic ganqing relationship turned tenuous, permitting sprouts of antagonistic class relationships. Beginning with the early twentieth century, there is evidence from novels and folk songs for the crisis of paternalism and qualitative changes in the nature of rural social relationships. Fang emphasizes in his writings the lack of sympathy on the part of the landed upper class. The sudden burgeoning of such novels and folk songs is itself a strong indicator of the breaking point in the traditional paternalistic relationship. Thus, it was not a growing consensus but conflict that characterized the rural society in the early twentieth century.

More than the existing characteristic environment of the region, the deteriorating rural class relationship and concomitant changes disrupting traditional adaptive strategies—whether of a protective or predatory nature—brought forth the new crisis. In fact, in the case of the Xinjiang region, assumptions based on linkages of a particular environment to rural radicalism do not adequately explain the origin of a revolutionary movement. Xinjiang is an example of the rapid deterioration of an economically vibrant and flourishing region and not of an outer periphery with diluted resources and weak commercial linkages, as detailed by Skinner. Its vulnerability to revolutionary uprisings cannot, therefore, be solely attributed to environmental features. It is in this sense that it is difficult to endorse Perry's environment-based assumptions about the Huaibei region for the Xinjiang region also.[10] Without denying that an unstable environment or ecological crisis create conditions for rural misery and often protests, it cannot be negated that the breakdown of the customary relationship between the dominant and dominated class acted as fuel to kindle revolutionary fire. To be sure, peasants' protests were directed against those forces whose basis of power, prestige, or wealth created conditions that not only inhibited peasants' socioeconomic development but also curtailed their rights and entitlements, won over a long period of time to facilitate adaptation to a particular environment for the security of subsistence. A focus on these forces therefore enables this study to project the characteristic feature of the rural crisis of the early twentieth century and reasons for peasants' translation of their discontent into a new kind of political action, that is, revolution.

The massive transformation of production relations brought home to the small rural cultivators the reality of exploitation. Charity granaries became high-interest-charging food-lending organizations. Permanent tenancy, in which the tenants enjoyed almost as many rights as did the freeholders on

[10] Perry 1980: 259–62.

the land, began to be replaced by shorter tenancy assignments that ignored the tenants' security of and right to subsistence. In several places, the landlords refused to sign any written contracts, making it possible for them to evict tenants and increase rents at will. The shift from sharecropping to the fixed-rent system forced the tenants to assume the risks of agricultural enterprises. Such everyday services by the landlords as the provision of agricultural tools, seeds, and fertilizers decreased significantly. Customary feasts at the time of the beginning of the harvest or the renewal of tenancy contracts were commuted to their cash value and turned into new levies. Traditional entitlements providing the right, for example, to collect lime for fertilization of the field from nearby mountains or coal from abandoned mines for personal use as well as for sale required cash payments either to the state or landlords. What peasants hated most was the custom of attending on the landlord by waiting for him on the stone benches outside his house. It was in the increasing monetization of customary entitlements, in landlords' maximization of their profits by violating normative practices, and in the general attack on traditional values, customs, and economic security that the exploitation was most strongly perceived by the peasants. It marked the abandonment of those facets of earlier relations of production which restricted the advancement of material interests of the landed upper class.

As the landlords shunned their paternalistic responsibilities, the peasants refused to comply with their deferential obligations. Thus, a rebellious attempt to defend customs, a feeling of moral outrage over the violation of the subsistence ethic, and a calculated attack against "bad," "corrupt," and "unpaternal" landlords are evident in the peasants' sociopolitical actions of the twentieth century. Growing antitax riots reflect peasants' defense of their traditional freedom to carry indigo to the market and collect coal and lime, and indignation at the collection of school taxes (for schools that were to be established in the cities) and advance taxes at the time when new outside pressures were already siphoning off their surpluses, and organized survival strategies were losing their strength. Similarly, food riots exemplified peasants' attempts to invoke traditional norms that imposed the priority of local needs at a time of dearth for the state, merchants, and landlords. To be sure, such riots and uprisings, or the "moments of madness," were rare and extreme responses of the distraught peasants to the problems. However, their increasing frequency from the early twentieth century onward is suggestive of growing chaos and disorder in rural society. They were often preceded by such everyday forms of the struggle as petty thievery and cheating of the landlord to keep as much of the product of their labor as possible. What was new in the early twentieth century was the emergence of these practices as standard in rural society, so much so that they were recorded in numerous works as general complaints of the landed elite. All these demonstrated antagonistic class values and general criticism of the landlords' new forms of power. They did not attack the established order per se but its diversion from the customary roles.

By emphasizing the defensive nature of these actions, this study does not suggest that the peasants in the Xinjiang region would not have ultimately transcended the limits imposed by the existing order through nurturing alternative expectations. As Hobsbawm notes, "Revolution may be made *de facto* by peasants who do not deny the legitimacy of the existing power structure, law, the state, or even the landlords."[11] Yet, in Xinjiang, peasants' growing indignation at the crumbling paternalistic order manifested itself in a revolutionary movement organized by a native Marxist intellectual, Fang Zhimin.

Product of the May Fourth era and an active participant in urban political activities inspired by the contemporary dissemination of new radical ideologies, Fang Zhimin found the solution to China's problems in Marxism and committed himself to it. He thus returned to his native village as a Marxist. But the fact that Fang perceived revolutionary potential in the peasantry cannot be explained simply by his Marxist background. In the 1920s, the Chinese Communist Party was still divided on the issue of the peasantry. The peasants were, at best, seen as tactical allies for a national revolution. His writings on revolution display an extraordinary sensitivity to peasant culture and tradition and a vehement rejection of the hegemonic Confucian culture. In voicing an appeal for the sacred as opposed to the secular revolution, in his concept of China as a "mother" as opposed to a "nation," and in his invocation of the traditional norms of justice, Fang viewed revolution as fulfilling the religious and moral needs of the peasantry. He thus considered himself a part and product of the rural social order. As such, he was not different from fellow Marxist intellectuals like Mao and Peng Pai, who never thought of themselves as urbanites. In fact, most of the revolutionary leaders who ventured in the countryside to promote radical activities came from a strong rural background.

Fang could indeed combine his belief in the rural tradition with Marxism, because the theory of Marxism as it took root in China was itself laden with strong populist impulses and voluntaristic strains. It was such a comprehen-

[11] Hobsbawm 1973: 12.

sion of Marxism that inspired Li Dazhao and Mao Zedong to find in peasantry a major force of revolution.[12] If activities of a large number of Marxist intellectuals involved in rural revolution are any guide, there is a strong reason to suggest that the theory of Communist revolution, with its strong urban orientation, had been tamed to the extent that made it compatible with "backward-looking" peasant ideologies.[13]

Yet, in Xinjiang, as in other regions of China, urban ideas and urban-trained revolutionary intellectuals by themselves did not bring about a rural revolution. They required conditioning to the local environment. Revolutionary intellectuals' first attempt to organize peasantry behind the United Front's program for a national revolution failed. So did their attempt to penetrate the rural areas as "educators" as well as through establishment of "local schools" for the peasants. These activities did not earn them local legitimacy as long as they kept themselves away from the local issues and concerns. It indicates that intellectuals cannot make revolutions as they please, but must work together with the peasants who have their own notions of justice and order. They had to shed their urban ideas of organization.

The coalescence of revolutionary intellectuals with peasants was achieved within a traditional framework. In the Xinjiang region, the former placed particular emphasis on the utilization of their own kinship ties and the support of extended family members in building a base for revolutionary activities. A large number of Fang's relatives not only participated in, but provided leadership to, the local organization of the peasant movement. The same was true in case of many other leaders. At the critical juncture of the general waning of the revolutionary tide after the collapse of the United Front, the Jiaotou Conference exhorted local activists to build up the movement through extended kinship connections. Such a policy proved successful, especially in organizing revolutionary activities in single-lineage-dominated smaller villages.

Moreover, within their lineage, revolutionary intellectuals offered alternative leadership by undermining the traditional authority of the prominent landlords. Not unlike Peng Pai who burned land deeds possessed by his family, Fang pressured his uncle to reduce rents in his own lineage-dominated village, and Huang Dao led a movement against the most powerful landlord of his lineage to force him to distribute rice among his poorer kins-

[12] Meisner 1970, 1971.
[13] Friedman 1974; see also Thaxton 1983.

men in the village at the time of dearth. Their ability to shatter discredited symbolic images of the traditional hegemony and provide protection to the local peasants proved crucial in building the base for the rural revolution.

Within the village, revolutionary intellectuals thus became the natural leaders of the peasants. They were seen not as outsiders but as part of the village population. Like traditional clan leaders or paternalistic landlords, peasants expected them to preserve local rights and customs as well as to solve the peasants' public and private problems. Revolutionary leaders' concerns and efforts to deal with peasants' local issues promoted cults. Fang was eulogized as "the liberating king," "the heavenly star," or "the benevolent Buddha," and so were others in their respective areas. This evoked memories of the traditional savior or prophet. Thus, the peasant movement did not develop along the lines prescribed by modern urban ideology but in conformity with several cult figures.[14]

The Northern Expedition forces played a significant supportive role in establishing the wider legitimacy of revolutionary intellectuals in the countryside. Soon after their arrival in the area, their acceptance of greetings from the radical activists, and not from the welcome party organized by the local landlords, signified change to peasants. The Northern Expedition's attack on powerful local forces signaled the emergence of a new order and liberation of rural areas from oppressive bondage. Consequently, revolutionary intellectuals received wider support in the countryside; and local peasant associations and their movement greatly expanded. Peasants displayed much enthusiasm in implementing the proposals of the peasant associations, which, to a large extent, mirrored their own visions. But this soon brought reprisals from above. Threatened by the growing radicalism, conservatives within the United Front as well as the local elite forces temporarily suppressed the movement.

The movement, however, did not fail because of the lack of revolutionary initiatives from the peasantry. On the contrary, peasant localism and spontaneity regenerated and sustained the movement. It failed because these initiatives in different areas were not channelized in a united form to resist the vastly superior forces with equal strength. Greater dependence on the out-

[14] In the context of the movement of the millenarian sects, Worseley writes: "More normally, the sect has to be involved in the world, and its mere existence as a separate entity and its rejection of conventional values (which are usually those of politically dominant groups) ensure for it the ready hostility of those—more numerous, entrenched, and powerful—it rejects. In this situation, the movement that sets out to live in harmony with God ends up by fighting the state (just as Weber's Calvinist set out to worship God, but produced capitalism)" (1968: p. xxxvii).

side forces in the long run proved to be counterproductive. Revolutionary intellectuals remained dependent on the support of the Nationalist Army. But once this support was withdrawn, they and the peasants found themselves without any significant armed force to defend them. Defenseless and unarmed, they were easily hunted down by the organized troops of the elite. This established the need to develop peasant defensive forces to sustain revolution.

Thus, one of Fang Zhimin's major contributions to the Xinjiang peasant movement as well as to the Chinese revolution was his creation of an organized army of peasants drawn from different areas of the region. Such an army gradually rebuilt the revolutionary movement in the region and led to the establishment of a soviet area. As long as this army remained militarily strong enough to ward off the periodic attacks from the GMD armies, the soviet prospered. But this did not last long. During 1934–1935, the peasant army failed to outsmart and outmaneuver the larger GMD forces and was defeated. Fang Zhimin was arrested while reorganizing his shattered soviet region and was executed. The soviet thus collapsed.

Finally, in broader terms, unlike soviet regions established by Mao Zedong in southern Jiangxi and Shenxi provinces, the Xinjiang soviet was in a true sense developed from below. Mao entered the rural area with a defeated but trained and organized outside revolutionary army. The majority of his Red Army soldiers had a mercenary army background, and their outsider character provoked hostilities from the local peasants. Mao wrote in 1928 that the masses were cold and aloof to them.[15] In 1929, in a letter to the Party's Central Committee, Mao gave the outsider backgrounds of the Red Army soldiers as the first reason for their initial failure to arouse the masses and successfully stage a guerrilla war in the Jinggangshan area.[16] A proper political training for the army was constantly emphasized. It was thus not the local forces but an outside army that facilitated the formation of Mao's soviets.

In Xinjiang, however, as in Hailufeng, revolutionary intellectuals established the soviet not with the help of an outside army but by organizing local peasants into an army. These forces were thus composed of that section of the peasants which was already committed to the task of restoration of their world and liberation from oppressive bondage. This, in fact, led to Mao's appreciation of Fang Zhimin's revolutionary strategy and policy in the Xinjiang region.

[15] Mao 1965, 1:81.
[16] Ibid., 1:123.

By demonstrating this difference between Mao's and Fang's soviets, I am not suggesting that peasants in one area had a more revolutionary outlook than in the other. What I would like to emphasize is that the greater and more detailed study of soviets established by Mao has resulted in a distorted emphasis on the role of outside forces, insofar as the origin of soviets is seen primarily from the perspective of the urban intellectuals' manipulative or coercive tactics with the support of the Red Army. Thus the central "peas-antist" character of the revolution is lost. Without denying the necessity of an organized and disciplined force for the success of a rural revolution, I would conclude that this cannot be divorced from the material basis for the Chinese revolution. Mao thus correctly observed that "without the poor peasants there would be no revolution. To deny their role is to deny the revolution."[17] Urban-educated native intellectuals played a significant role in it. But, in the end, if both the periods of revolution and recent developments are any indication, it appears that they were conquered by the peasants. Thus, in the Chinese Communist revolution and after it, peasants emerged as the ultimate winners.

[17] Ibid., 1:33.

References

Abramson, M., et al. 1935. "Tsiansi: Sotsial'no ekonomi choskeii ocherk." *Problemy Kitae* 14:89–157.

Agrarian China. [1938] 1976. Reprint. Arlington.

"Agriculture and Economic Conditions in Kiangsi." 1935. *Chinese Economic Journal and Bulletin* 17 (4).

Alavi, Hamza. 1965. "Peasants and Revolution." In Ralph Miliband and John Saville, eds., *The Socialist Register*. London.

———. 1977. "Peasant Classes and Primordial Loyalties." *Journal of Peasant Studies* 4.

Alley, Rewi. 1962. *Land and Folk in Kiangsi—A Chinese Province in 1961*. Beijing.

Amano, Motonosuke. 1940. *Shina nogyo keizai ron*. Tokyo.

Averill, Stephen C. 1982. "Revolution in the Highlands: The Rise of the Communist Movement in Jiangxi Province." Ph.D. diss., Cornell University.

———. 1983. "The Shed People and the Opening of Yangzi Highlands." *Modern China* 9 (1).

Bagchi, A. K. 1982. *The Political Economy of Underdevelopment*. Cambridge.

Bastid, Marianne. 1976. "The Social Context of Reform." In Cohen and Schrecker, eds., *Reform in Nineteenth Century China*. Cambridge, Mass.

Beattie, Hilary. 1979. *Land and Lineage in China*. Cambridge.

"Beidai zhanzhengzhong de Jiangxi zhanchang." 1981. *Jiangxi Shiyuan xuebao* 4.

Bharadwaj, K., and P. K. Das. 1975. "Tenurial Conditions and Mode of Exploitation: A Study of Some Villages in Orissa." *Economic and Political Weekly*, Annual Number (Feburary).

Bianco, Lucien. 1976. "Peasants and Revolution: The Case of China." *Journal of Peasant Studies* 2 (3).

Billingsley, Phil. 1981. "Bandits, Bosses, and Bare Sticks: Beneath the Surface of Local Control in Early Republican China." *Modern China* 7 (3).

Bloch, Marc. 1954. *The Historian's Craft*. Manchester.

Brandt, C., B. Schwartz, and J. K. Fairbank, eds. 1966. *A Documentary History of Chinese Communism*. New York.

Brandt, Loren. 1985. "Chinese Agriculture and the International Economy, 1870–1930: A Reassessment." *Journal of Economic History* 45.

Brenner, Robert. 1976. "Agrarian Class Structure and Economic Development in Pre-Industrial Europe." *Past and Present* 70.

Brown, Fred. 1922a. "Clan Customs in Kiangsi." *China Recorder* 53 (8).

———. 1922b. "Superstitions Common in Kiangsi." *New China Review* 4 (6).

Buck, John L. 1937a. *Land Utilization in China.* Shanghai.

———. 1937b. *Land Utilization in China: Statistics.* Shanghai.

Buxiu de geming zhanshi. 1960. Jiangxi sheng: Nanchang.

Cao Boyi. 1961. *Jiangxi suweiai zhih jianli jiqi penggui.* Taibei.

Chandra, Bipan. 1966. *The Rise and Growth of Economic Nationalism in India.* New Delhi.

Chang Chung-li. 1955. *The Chinese Gentry: Studies on Their Role in Nineteenth Century Chinese Society.* Seattle.

———. 1962. *The Income of the Chinese Gentry.* Seattle.

Chang Youyi. 1975. "Taiping tianguo geming qianshi Huizhou dizhu tudi guanxi di yiko shilu." *Wen Wu* 6.

Chang Kuo-t'ao. 1971. *The Rise of the Chinese Communist Party, 1921–1927.* Vol. 1. Lawrence, Kans.

Chao, Kang. 1977. *The Development of Cotton Textile Production in China.* Cambridge, Mass.

———. 1981. "New Data on Landownership Patterns in Ming-Qing China." *Journal of Asian Studies* 40 (4).

———. 1982. *Zhongguo tudi zhidushi.* Taibei.

Chen Han-seng. 1936. *Landlord and Peasant in China: A Study of the Agrarian Crisis in South China.* New York.

Chen Gengya. 1936. *Gan-Wan-Xiang-E shichaji.* Shanghai.

Chen Mu, ed. 1952. *Nanfang lao genqudi fangwendi.* Hankou.

Chen Boxian. 1984. "Jiangxi faxian de Taiping tianguo huobao mingwenkao." *Jiangxi Shehui Kexue* 6.

Chen Qunzhe. 1985. "Min-Zhe-Gan suqu de jingji jianshe shuping." *Zhongguo Shehui Jingjishi Yanjiu* 2.

Chen Zhiping. 1983. "Qingdai Jiangxi de liangshi yunxiao." *Jiangxi Shehui Kexue* 3.

Chen Zhong. 1984(a). "Fang Zhimin aiguo zhuyi sixiang de chengyin ji tedian." *Zheng Ming* 3.

Chesneaux, Jean. 1973. *Peasant Revolts in China.* New York.

Chiang Yee. 1963. *A Chinese Childhood.* New York.

Chow Tse-tung. 1967. *The May Fourth Movement.* Stanford.

Chu, T. H. 1936. *Tea Trade in Central China.* Shanghai.

Chuzo Ichiko. 1971. "The Role of the Gentry: An Hypothesis." In Wright, ed., *China in Revolution: The First Phase, 1900–1913.* New Haven.

Clarke, P., and J. S. Gregory. 1982. *Western Reports on the Taipings.* Honolulu.

Clennel, W. J. 1903. "Province of Kiangsi" (Consular Report). British Sessional Papers (House of Commons), vol. 87.

Cobb, Richard C. 1972. *The Police and the People: French Popular Protest, 1789–1820.* Oxford.

Cohen, Paul A., and John E. Schrecker, eds. 1976. *Reform in Nineteenth Century China.* Cambridge, Mass.

Desai, A. R., ed. 1979. *Peasant Struggles in India*. Bombay.

Diyici guonei geming zhanzheng shiqi de nongmin yundong. 1954. Beijing.

Duan Congguang. 1955. "Ganxi pengmin de kangqing douzheng." *Lishi Jiaoxue* 1 (1).

Elvin, Mark. 1970. "Early Communist Land Reforms and the Kiangsi Rural Economy." *Modern Asian Studies* 4 (2).

———. 1973. *The Pattern of China's Past*. Stanford.

Esherick, Joseph W. 1981. "Number Games: A Note on Land Distribution in Pre-Revolutionary China." *Modern China* 7 (4).

Fairbank, John K., and K. C. Liu, eds. 1980. *The Cambridge History of China*. Vol. 11, *Late Ch'ing, 1800–1911*, part 2. Cambridge.

Fang Lan. 1978. "Yanzhe fujin Fang Zhimin de zuzhi qianjin: gandongbei jixing." *Geming Wenwu* 2.

Fang Xing. 1984. "Qingdai qianqi xiaonong jingji de zai shengchan." *Lishi Yanjiu* 5.

Fang Zhimin. 1952. *Keai de Zhongguo*. Beijing.

———. 1957. *Yuzhong jishi*. Beijing.

Fang Zhiqun. 1978. "Fang Zhimin lieshi de shengping han you guan wenwu jieshao." *Geming Wenwu* 2.

Fang Zhiqun and Miao Min et al., eds. 1977. *Gandongbei Hongqu de douzheng*. Nanchang.

Fanon, Frantz. 1968. *The Wretched of the Earth*. New York.

Faure, David. 1978. "The Rural Economy of Kiangsu Province, 1870–1911." *Journal of the Institute of Chinese Studies of the Chinese University of Hong Kong*.

———. 1985. "The Plight of the Farmers: A Study of the Rural Economy of Jiangnan and the Pearl River Delta, 1870–1937." *Modern China* 2 (1).

Fei Hsiao-t'ung. 1939. *Peasant Life in China*. New York.

Feigon, Lee. 1983. *Chen Duxiu: Founder of the Chinese Communist Party*. Princeton.

Femia, Joseph. 1975. "Hegemony and Consciousness in the Thought of Antonio Gramsci." *Political Studies* 23 (1).

Feng Fengzhu. 1984. "Lun Hukou zhi zhanhou Taipingjun de zhanlue shice." *Jiangxi Taxue Xuebao* 4.

Feuerwerker, Albert. 1969. *The Chinese Economy, ca. 1870–1911*. Michigan Paper in Chinese Studies no. 5. Ann Arbor.

Fortune, Robert. 1852. *A Journey to the Tea Counties of China*. London.

Freedman, Maurice. 1966. *Chinese Lineage and Society: Fukien and Kwangtung*. London.

———. 1974. "On the Sociological Study of Chinese Religion." In Arthur Wolf, ed., *Religion and Ritual in Chinese Society*. Stanford.

Fried, Morton. 1953. *Fabric of Chinese Society*. New York.

Friedman, Edward. 1974. *Backward toward Revolution: The Chinese Revolutionary Party*. Berkeley.

Fu Ruqi. 1929. *Jiangxi teshui jiyao*. Nanchang.

Fu Yiling. 1961. *Ming Qing nongcun shehui jingji*. Beijing.

———. 1977. "Qingdai nongye zibenzhuyi mengya wenti de yige tansuo: Jiangxi xincheng yibian shiliao de fenxi." *Lishi Yanjiu* 5.

———. 1983. "Ming chenghong jian Jiangxi shehui jingjishiliao zhaichao." *Jiangxi Shehui Kexue* 3.

Fujita Masanori. 1960. "Ho Shibin to Bin-Setsu-Ko sobieto ku." *Ajia Kenkyu* 6 (4).

FZM. Fang Zhimin chuan. 1982. Nanchang.

Galbiati, Fernando. 1985. *P'eng P'ai and the Hai-Lu-feng Soviet.* Stanford.

"Gandongbei Nongcun Kaikuang." 1933. *Nonglin Xuebao* 10.

Geertz, Clifford. 1973. *The Interpretation of Culture.* New York.

Geming Wenxian. 1958–. 72 vols. to date. Prepared under the auspices of Zhongguo Guomindang, Dangshi Shiliao Bianzuan Weiyuanhui. Taibei.

Genovese, Eugene D. 1974. *Roll Jordan Roll: The World the Slaves Made.* New York.

———. 1976–77. "A Reply." *Radical History Review* 3 and 5.

Gramsci, A. 1971. *Selections from the Prison Notebook.* Ed. and trans. Q. Hoare and G. N. Smith. New York.

Grove, Linda, and Joseph Esherick, 1980. "From Feudalism to Capitalism: Japanese Scholarship and the Transformation of Chinese Rural Society." *Modern China* 6 (4).

Harrison, James P. 1969. *The Long March to Power: A History of the Chinese Communist Party, 1921–72.* New York.

Hearn, Frank. 1975. "Remembrance and Critique: The Use of the Past for Discrediting the Present and Anticipating the Future." *Politics and Society* 5 (2).

Ho Chi-fang. 1954. "Chinese Folk Songs." *Chinese Literature* 1.

Ho Ping-ti. 1962. *The Ladder of Success in Imperial China: Aspects of Social Mobility, 1368–1911.* New York.

———. 1967. *Studies in the Population of China, 1368–1953.* Cambridge.

Hoang, Le P. P. 1920. *Notions techniques sur la propriete en China.* Shanghai.

Hobsbawm, Eric. 1959. *Primitive Rebels.* New York.

———. 1973. "Peasant and Politics." *Journal of Peasant Studies* 1.

Hobsbawm, Eric, and George Rude. 1968. *Captain Swing: A Social History of the Great English Agricultural Uprisings of 1830.* New York.

Hofheinz, Roy. 1977. *The Broken Wave: The Chinese Communist Peasant Movement, 1922–28.* Cambridge, Mass.

HQPP. Hongqi piao piao. 1957–60. 16 vols. Prepared under the auspices of Zhongguo Qingnian Chubanshe. Beijing.

HSFB. Hongse fengbao 1958–61. 12 vols. Prepared under the auspices of Jiangxi Renmin Chubanshe. Nanchang.

Hsiao, K. C. 1972. *Rural China: Imperial Control in the Nineteenth Century.* Seattle.

Hsiao Tso-liang. 1969. *The Land Revolution in China, 1930–1934: A Study of Documents.* Seattle.

———. 1970. *Chinese Communism in 1927: City vs. Countryside.* Hong Kong.

Hu Delan. 1984. "Fangsheng huiyi qianhou de Shao Shiping." *Zheng Ming* 3.

Hu Guokang. 1967. "Gandong diqu zaifei huiyilu." *Jiangxi Wenxian* 2 (13) and subsequent issues.

Hu Hsien-chin. 1948. *The Common Descent Group in China and its Functions.* New York.

Hu Tingfeng. 1983. "Taiping tianguo Jiujiang baoweizhan de yingxiung—Lin Qirong." *Jiangxi Shehui Kexue* 3.

Huang, Philip C., Lynda Bell, and Kathy LeMons Walker. 1978. *Chinese Communists and Rural Society, 1927–34.* Monograph no. 13. Berkeley.

Huang, Philip C. 1985. *The Peasant Economy and Social Change in North China*. Stanford.

Imperial Maritime Customs. 1892–1901, 1911–1921. *Decennial Reports on Trade, Navigation, Industry . . . of the Ports Open to Foreign Commerce in China and on the Condition and Development of Treaty Port Provinces*. Shanghai.

Isaacs, Harold R. 1968. *The Tragedy of the Chinese Revolution*. New York.

———. 1974. *Straw Sanadals: Chinese Short Stories, 1927–1934*. Cambridge.

Jamieson, George. 1888. "Notes on the Conditions of the Peasantry in Kiangsi. Made in the Course of Travels in 1883–84." In "Tenure of Land in China and the Condition of Rural Population," *Journal of Royal Asiatic Society* (New Series), China Branch 23.

Jen Yu-wen. 1973. *The Taiping Rebellion*. New Haven.

"Ji Jiangxi diaocha hukou zhi fengchao." 1909. *Dongfang Zazhi* 6 (8, 9, 10) (September, October, November).

Jia Zhi. 1963. "Lao suqu de minge." *Minjian Wenxue Lunji*. Beijing.

Jiang Boshi. 1957. *Dierze Guonei geming zhanzheng shiqi de Nongcun geming genzhudi*. Beijing.

Jiang Taixin. 1980. "Qingdai qianqi yazuzhi de fazhan." *Lishi Yanjiu* 3.

Jiangxi shiyuan xuebao. 1981–. Nanchang.

Jiangxi wenshi ziliao xuanji. 1980. Vol. 1. Nanchang.

Jiangxi wenxian. 1966–. Taibei.

JJWT. *Jiangxi jingji wenti mulu*. 1934. Prepared under the auspices of Jiangxi Shengzhengfu Jingji Weiyuanhui. Nanchang.

JN. *Jiangxi Nianjian*. 1936. Nanchang.

Johnson, J., and O. Taube, 1934. *Rate China: Dokumente du chinesischen Revolution*. Berlin.

Joll, James. 1978. *Antonio Gramsci*. Middlesex.

Jordan, Donald A. 1976. *The Northern Expedition: China's National Revolution of 1926–1928*. Honolulu.

Kim, Ilpyong J. 1973. *The Politics of Chinese Communism: Jiangxi under the Soviets*. Berkeley.

Kopsch, Henry. 1878. "Geographical Notes on the Province of Kiangsi." *China Review* 6.

Kraus, Richard A. 1980. *Cotton and Cotton Goods in China, 1918–1936*. New York.

Kuang Cuijian. 1983. "Hewei Fang Zhimin shi?" *Zheng Ming* 2.

Kuhn, Philip. 1970. *Rebellion and Its Enemies in Late Imperial China: Militarization and Social Structure, 1796–1864*. Cambridge, Mass.

———. 1975. "Local Self-Government under the Republic: Problems of Control, Autonomy, and Mobilization." In Wakeman and Grant, eds. *Conflict and Control in Late Imperial China*. Berkeley.

Kupper, Samuel. 1971. "Revolution in China: Kiangsi Province." Ph.D. diss., University of Michigan.

KYKTL. *Kang Yong Gan shiqi chengxiang renmin fankang douzheng ziliao*. 1979. Beijing.

Lai Renguang. 1984. "Gandongbei geming genjudi dangde jianshe." *Jiangxi Shehui Kexue* 1.

Leong, S. T. 1984. "The P'eng Min: The Ch'ing Administration and Internal Migration." Paper presented at the Fifth National Conference of the Asian Studies Association of Australia. Adelaide.

Lewis, John W., ed. 1974. *Peasant Rebellion and Communist Revolution in Asia.* Stanford.

Li Huang. [1931] 1966. *Jiangxi Jiyu.* Reprint. Taibei.

Li Qun. 1982. *Taiping tianguo junshi shigai shi.* Beijing.

———. 1983. "Cong Yi-Heng baodong kan Fang Zhiminshi gongnong wuzhuang geju daolu de xingcheng." In Zhu Chengjia, ed., *Zhonggong Dangshi yanjiu lunwenxuan,* vol. 2. Hunan.

Li Shiyue. 1972. "Qingmo nongcun jingji de benghui yu nongmin yundong." In *Zhongguo jin sanbainian shehui jingji shilun,* vol. 1. Hong Kong.

Li Wenzhi. 1961. "Taiping tianguo geming dui bianhe fengqian shengchan guanxi de zuoyung." *Guangming Ribao* (January 16).

———. 1972. "Lun Qingdai qianqi de tudi zhanyou guanxi." In *Zhongguo jin sanbainian shehui jingji shilun,* vol.1. Hong Kong.

———. 1981a. "Lun Qingdai houqi Jiang-Zhe-Wan sansheng yuan Taiping tianguo zhanlingchu tudi guanxi de bianhua." *Lishi Yanjiu* 6.

———. 1981b. "China's Landlord Economy and the Sprouts of Capitalism in Agriculture." *Social Science in China* 2 (1).

Liang Fangzhong. 1980. *Zhongguo lidai Hukou tiandi tianfu tongji.* Shanghai.

Liang Pu. 1949. "Fang Zhimin tongzhi geming shilie." In Hua Yingshan, ed., *Zhongguo gongchandang lieshiquan.* Hong Kong.

Liew, D. K. 1928. "Land Tenure Systems in China." *Chinese Economic Review* 2 (6).

Lin Zengping. 1979. "Taiping tianguo geming tuidong zhongguo ziben zhuyi fazhan de wenti youtai jinyibu tansuo." *Lishi Yanjiu* 10.

Lippit, Victor. 1978. "The Development of Underdevelopment in China." *Modern China* 4 (3).

Liu, T. C., and K. C. Yeh. 1965. *The Economy of the Chinese Mainland: National Income and Economic Development, 1933–1959.* Princeton.

Liu Shiji. 1978. "Taiping tianguo luanhou jiangnan shizhen de fazhan." *Shihuo Yuekan* 7 (4).

Liu Yao. 1981. "Cong Changjiang xiayu dizhu nongcun jingji de bianhua kan Taiping tianguo de lishi zuoyung." *Lishi Yanjiu* 2.

———. 1982. "Taiping tianguo shibai hou Jiangnan nongcun jingji bianhua de zai shenlun." *Lishi Yanjiu* 3.

Lo Ning, comp. 1958. *Liang tao pan qiangnao geming.* Nanchang.

———. n.d. *Fang Zhimin bobo zai luyangcun.* N.p. (in Hoover Collection).

Lotveit, T. 1973. *Chinese Communism, 1931–1934: Experiences in Civil Government.* Lund.

Luo Bingmian. 1979. "Jindai Zhongguo diandangye de fenbu chushi he tongye zuzhi." *Shihuo Yuekan* 8 (2).

McDonald, Angus. 1975. "Hunan Peasant Movement: Its Urban Origins." *Modern China* 1 (2).

———. 1978. *The Urban Origins of Rural Revolution.* Berkeley.

Mao Jiaqi. 1961. "Taiping tianguo geminghou Jiangnan nongcun guanxi shishen." *Xin Jianshe* 12 (November 12).

Mao Zedong. 1965. *Selected Works of Mao Tse-tung.* 4 vols. Beijing.

Marks, Robert B. 1978. "Peasant Society and Peasant Uprisings in South China: Social Change in Haifeng County, 1630–1930." Ph.D. diss., University of Wisconsin.

———. 1984. *Rural Revolution in South China: Peasants and the Making of History in Haifeng County, 1570–1930.* Madison, Wis.

Marx, K. 1969. *Selected Works.* New York.

Meisner, Maurice. 1970. *Li Ta-chao and the Origin of Chinese Marxism.* New York.

———. 1971. "Leninism and Maoism: Some Populist Perspectives on Marxism-Leninism in China." *China Quarterly* 45.

Miao Min. 1958a. "Fang Zhimin tongzhi er-san shi." In *HSFB* 1958–61, vol. 1.

———. 1958b. "Zhu zai yi yuan." In *HSFB* 1958–61, vol. 1.

———. 1959. *Fang Zhimin de gushi.* Beijing.

———. 1962. *Fang Zhimin: Revolutionary Fighter.* Beijing.

Michael, Franz. 1966. *The Taiping Rebellion: History and Documents.* Seattle.

Migdal, Joel S. 1974. *Peasants, Politics, and Revolution: Pressures towards Political and Social Change in the Third World.* Princeton.

Min Sheng. 1920. "Guangfeng de shehui diaocha." *Shaonian Shijie* 1 (9).

Moise, Edwin. 1977. "Downward Social Mobility in Pre-Revolutionary China." *Modern China* 3 (1).

Moore, Barrington. 1966. *Social Origins of Dictatorship and Democracy: Lord and Peasant in the Making of the Modern World.* Boston.

Mori Masao. 1975. "18–20 seiki no Koseisho noson ni okeru shaso giso ni tsuite no ichi kento." *Toyoshi Kenkyu* 33 (4).

Moulder, Frances. 1977. *Japan, China, and the Modern World Economy.* Cambridge.

Muramatsu, Yuji. 1966. "A Documentary Study of Chinese Landlords in Late Ch'ing and Early Republican Kiangnan." *Bulletin of the School of Oriental and African Studies* 29.

Myers, Ramon. 1967. "Theories of Modern China's Agrarian Problem." *Chungchi Journal* 6 (2).

———. 1970. *The Chinese Peasant Economy: Agricultural Development in Hopei and Shantung, 1890–1949.* Cambridge, Mass.

———. 1972. "The Commercialization of Agriculture in Modern China." In Willmott, *Economic Organization in Chinese Society.* Stanford.

Nan Pingfang. 1937. "A Practical Study of Rural Credits in Four Provinces of Central China." Ph.D. diss., University of Pennsylvania.

Natrajan, L. 1953. *Peasant Uprisings in India, 1850–1900.* Bombay.

Nihon Kokusai Modai Kenkyusho Chugoku Bukai. 1970. *Chugoku kyosantoshi shiryoshu.* Vol. 1. Tokyo.

Paige, Jeffery. 1975. *Agrarian Revolution: Social Movements and Export Agriculture in the the Underdeveloped World.* New York.

Peng Xinwei. 1965. *Zhongguo huobi shi.* Shanghai.

Perkins, Dwight H. 1969. *Agricultural Development in China, 1368–1968.* Chicago.

Perry, Elizabeth. 1980. *Rebels and Revolutionaries in North China, 1845–1945.* Stanford.

Polachek, James M. 1975. "Gentry Hegemony: Soochow in the T'ung Chih Restoration." In Wakeman and Grant, eds., *Conflict and Control in Late Imperial China*. Berkeley.

————. 1983. "The Moral Economy of the Kiangsi Soviet (1928–1934)." *Journal of Asian Studies* 42 (4).

Pong, David. 1966. "The Income and Military Expenditures in Kiangsi Province in the Last Years of the Taiping Rebellion." *Journal of Asian Studies* 26 (1).

"Qianze yundong." 1920. *Cunzhi Banyuekan* 1 (6).

Rawski, Evelyn. 1972. *Agricultural Change and the Peasant Economy of South China*. Cambridge, Mass.

Richthofen, Baron F. Von. 1903. *Baron Richthofen's Letters, 1870–72*. Shanghai.

Rue, John E. 1966. *Mao Tse-tung in Opposition: 1927–35*. Stanford.

Saul, John, and Roger Wood. 1971. "African Peasantries." In T. Shanin, ed., *Peasant and Peasant Societies*. Middlesex.

Schram, Stuart R. 1969. *The Political Thought of Mao Tse-tung*. New York.

Schwartz, Benjamin. 1958. *Chinese Communism and the Rise of Mao*. Cambridge.

Scott, James C. 1976. *The Moral Economy of the Peasant: Rebellion and Subsistence in South-east Asia*. New Haven.

————. 1977. "Hegemony and the Peasantry." *Politics and Society* 7 (3).

————. 1979. "Revolution in the Revolution: Peasants and Commissars." *Theory and Society* 6.

————. 1985. *Weapons of the Weak: Everyday Forms of Peasant Resistance*. New Haven.

Shanghai renmin chubanshe. 1975. *Fang Zhimin*. Shanghai.

Shanin, T, ed. 1971. *Peasant and Peasant Societies*. Middlesex.

————. 1973. "The Nature and Logic of the Peasant Economy." *Journal of Peasant Studies* 1 (1, 2).

Shao Shiping. 1958. "Zhongguo gongnong hongjun dishi juntuan dansheng qian gandongbei chu chi nongmin yundong de gaikuang." In *Zhongguo gongchandang zai Jiangxi diqu lingdao geming douzheng de lishi ziliao*. Nanchang.

————. 1959a. "Zhongguo Gongnong Hongjun Dishi Juntuan de Yansheng." In *HQPP* 1957–60, 12:55–64.

————. 1959b. "Daonian Fang laotaitai." In *HQPP* 1957–60, 9:13–14.

Shao Shiping, Wang Jinxiang, and Hu Delan, eds. 1981. "Min-Zhe-Wan-Gan (Gandongbei) dangshi." In *Jiangxi wenshi ziliao xuanji*, vol. 7.

Shao Xunzheng. 1961. "Taiping tianguo geminghou Jiangnan de tudi guanxi han jieji guanxi." *Guangming Ribao* 205 (Feburary 2).

Shi Feng. 1975. *Fang Zhimin*. Shanghai.

Shi Zhaobin. 1962. *Zhongguo fengqian shehui nongmin zhanzheng wenti taolun*. Beijing.

Skocpol, Theda. 1979. *State and Social Revolutions: A Comparative Analysis of France, Russia, and China*. Cambridge.

Skinner, G. W. 1971. "Chinese Peasants and the Closed Community: An Open and Shut Case." *Comparative Studies in Society and History* 13.

————. 1977. *Cities in Late Imperial China*. Stanford.

Smedley, Agnes. 1934. *China's Red Army Marches*. New York.

————. 1972. *The Great Road: The Life and Times of Chu Teh*. New York.

Sun Jingzhi. 1958. *Huazhong diqu jingji dili*. Beijing. (Translated as *An Economic Ge-*

ography of Central China by the Joint Publications Research Service. No. 2227-N. Washington, D.C., 1960.)

Swarup, Shanti. 1966. *A Study of the Chinese Communist Movement, 1927–1934*. Oxford.

Tan Chung. 1973. "The Triangular Trade between China and India: A Case of Commercial Imperialism." *Proceedings of the Indian History Congress*. Chandigarh.

Tanaka Tadao. 1930. *Kakumei shina noson jisshoteki*. Tokyo. (Translated in Chinese as *Guomin geming yu nongcun wenti*.)

Tang Youqing. 1985. "Xinhai geming qianqi zichan jieji gemingpai zai jiangxi de huodong ji qi yingxiang." *Jiangxi Taxue Xuebao* 2.

Tang Zhiquan. 1982. " 'Fang Zhiminshi' de geming genjudi tedian zhi wojian." *Zhengming* 4.

Tawney, R. H. [1932] 1966. *Land and Labor in China*. Reprint. Boston.

Thaxton, Ralph. 1983. *China Turned Rightside Up: Revolutionary Legitimacy in the Peasant World*. New Haven.

Thompson, E. P. 1971. "The Moral Economy of the English Crowd in the Eighteenth Century." *Past and Present* 50.

———. 1974. "Patrician Society and Plebian Culture." *Journal of Social History* 7 (4).

———. 1978a. "Eighteenth Century English Society: Class Struggle Without Class." *Social History* 3 (2).

———. 1978b. "Folklore, Anthropology, and Social History." *Indian Historical Review* 1.

Tilly, Charles. 1975. "Food Supply and Public Order in Modern Europe." In Charles Tilly, ed., *The Formation of National States in Western Europe*. Princeton.

———. 1978. *From Mobilization to Revolution*. Reading, Mass.

Toa Dobunkai. 1920. *Shina shobetsu zenshi [11], Koseisho*. Tokyo.

Torgasheff, Boris P. 1926. *China as a Tea Producer*. Shanghai.

Wakeman, Frederick. 1973. *The Fall of Imperial China*. New York.

———. 1977. "Rebellion and Revolution: The Study of Popular Movements in Chinese History." *Journal of Asian Studies* 36 (2).

Wakeman, Frederick, and Grant Carolyn, eds. 1975. *Conflict and Control in Late Imperial China*. Berkeley.

Wallerstein, Immanuel. 1974. *The Modern World System: Capitalist Agriculture and the Origins of the European World Economy in the Sixteenth Century*. Cambridge.

———. 1979. *The Capitalist World Economy*. Cambridge.

Wan Fangzhen. 1985. "Qing qianqi Jiangxi pengmin de ruji ji tudi keji de ronghe han maodun." *Jiangxi Daxue Xuebao* (Zhexue Shehui Kexueban), 2.

Wang Hao. 1935. *Shoufu feichuzhih tudi wenti*. Graduate School of Land Economics, Central Political Institute. Nanking.

Wang Tianjing. 1983. "Qing Dong Guang shiqi kemin yiken." *Jindaishi Yanjiu* 2.

Wang Yeh-chien. 1965. "The Impact of the Taiping Rebellion on the Population in Southern Kiangsu." *Papers on China* 19.

Wathe, Henry. 1926. *La Chine qui s'eville; nouvelle edition des fleures et epines du Kiangsi*. Vichy.

Watson, James. 1977. "Hereditary Tenancy and Corporate Landlordism in Traditional China: A Case Study." *Modern Asian Studies* 2 (2).

Watt, John R. 1972. *The District Magistrate in Late Imperial China*. New York.

Wei Jinyu. 1972. "Ming Qing shidai tiannong de nongnu diwei." In *Zhongguo jin sanbainian shehui jingji shilunji*, vol. 1. Hong Kong.

Weida de Fang Zhimin. 1953. Nanchang.

Wen Zongdiao and Wang Ta. 1985. "Wanqing shiqi woguo nongye de xinbianhua." *Zhongguo Shehui Jingjishi Yanjiu* 4.

Wen Yaokui. 1983. "Guanyu AB tuan jige wenti de tantao." *Jiangxi Shehui Kexue* 2.

Wiens, Mi-chu. 1976. *The Origins of Modern Landlordism*. Taipei.

———. 1980. "Lord and Peasant: The Sixteenth to Eighteenth Century." *Modern China* 6 (1).

Williams, Gwyn. 1960. "Egemonia in the Thought of Antonio Gramsci: Some Notes on Interpretation." *Journal of the History of Ideas* 21 (4).

Wolf, Arthur, ed. 1974. *Religion and Ritual in Chinese Society*. Stanford.

Wolf, Eric R. 1969. *Peasant Wars of the Twentieth Century*. New York.

———. 1982. *Europe and the People without History*. Berkeley.

Wong, R. Bin. 1982. "Food Riots in the Qing Dynasty." *Journal of Asian Studies* 41 (4).

Worsley, Peter. 1968. *The Trumpet Shall Sound: A Study of Cargo Cults in Melanesia*. New York.

Wright, Mary C. 1957. *The Last Stand of Chinese Conservatism: The T'ung-chih Restoration, 1862–1874*. Stanford.

———. ed. 1968. *China in Revolution, The First Phase, 1900–1913*. New Haven.

Wright, Stanley. 1920. *Kiangsi's Native Trade and Its Taxation*. Shanghai.

WSSQ. Wusi shiqi qigan jieshao. 1959. 3 vols. Beijing.

Wu Xunyu. 1935. "Jiangxizhi nongtian gaikuang." *Wenhua Bipan* 2: 2–3.

Xia Qunhua. 1983. "Tiyizi guonei gemingzhanzheng shiqi de tudi gaige wenti." *Jiangxi Shiyuan Xuebao* 3.

Xiao Zheng. 1977. *Minguo ershi niandai Zhongguo dalu tudi wenti zeliao*. Taibei.

Xu Huailin. 1984. "Jiangxi lishi renkou zhuangkuang chutan." *Jiangxi Shehui Kexue* 2.

Xu Xiantao. 1983. Fang Zhimin tongzhi shengping ruoganshi jibuwei." *Jiangxi Shifan Xuebao* 1.

Yan Zhongping. 1955. *Zhongguo jindai jingjishi tongji zeliao xuanji*. Beijing.

Yang, C. K. 1967. *Religion in Chinese Society*. Berkeley.

———. 1975. "Statistical Patterns of Mass Actions." In Wakeman and Grant, eds., *Conflict and Control in Late Imperial China*. Berkeley.

Yang, Martin. 1945. *A Chinese Village: Taitou, Shantung Province*. New York.

YEWG. Yu-E-Wan-Gan si shengzhi zutian zhidu. 1936. Prepared by the Jinlong Daxue Nongye Jingjixi. Nanjing.

Youkehua Jiangxi. 1937. Prepared under the auspices of Gesheng Shigan Zhengzhi Yanjiuhui. Shanghai.

Young, Ernest P. 1970. "Nationalism, Reform, and Republican Revolution: China in the Early Twentieth Century." In James B. Crowley, ed., *Modern East Asia: Essays in Interpretation*. New York.

Zagoria, Donald S. 1974. "Asian Tenancy Systems and Communist Mobilization of the Peasantry." In John W. Lewis, ed., *Peasant Rebellion and Communist Revolution in Asia*. Stanford.

Zhang Lung. 1923. "Jiangxi Majiacun nongmin kangshui yundong." *Xiangdao Zhou-bao* 41 (September 23).

Zhang Jinglu. 1959. *Zhongguo xiandai chuban shiliao*. 3 vols. Shanghai.

Zhang Rixin. 1984. "Yetan zhongyang suzhu de chatian yundong." *Zheng Ming* 3.

Zhang Shiguang. 1958. "Luodi Lanjia cun qiyi" and "Qigongzhen baodong." In *HSFB* 1958–61, vol. 1.

Zhang Youyi. 1975. "Taiping Tionguo geming qianxi Huizhou dizhu tudi quanxi de yige shihlu." *Wenwu* 6.

Zhang Zhenhe. 1954. "Yijiulingse nian Jiangxi Leping qunzhong kangzhuan yundong." *Zhongguo Kexueyuan Lishi Yanjiuso Disanso Jikan* 1.

Zheng Xifu. 1978. "Youzheng yuannian Jiangxi Wancai [Pengmin] kangqing shijian chutan." *Taiwan Wenxian*. 29 (4).

Zheng Zhenman. 1984. "Qing zhi minguo minbei liujian 'fenguan' de fenxi." *Zhongguo Shehui Jingjishi Yanjiu* 3.

———. 1985. "Shilun Minbei xiangzu dizhu jingji de xingtai yu jiegou." *Zhongguo Shehui Jingjishi Yanjiu* 4.

Zhonggong Hengfeng Xianwei. 1978. *Gandongbei hongqu de douzheng*. Nanchang.

Zhongguo geming genjudi shiliao xianbian. 1982. Vol. 2. Nanchang.

Zhongguo gongchandang zai Jiangxi diqu lingdao geming douzheng de lishi zeliao. 1958. Nanchang.

Zhongguo gongchandang zai zhongnan diqu lingdao geming douzheng de lishi zeliao. 1951. Wuhan.

Zhongguo jingji nianqian. 1934. Nanjing.

Zhongguo geming genjudi shiliao xianbian. 1982. 3 vols. Nanchang.

Zhou Jie. 1928. *Jiangxisheng yibieh*. Shanghai.

ZNMT. Zhongguo jindai nongye shengcan zhi maoyi tongji ziliao. 1983. Shanghai.

ZNYS. Zhongguo jindai nongyeshi ziliao. 1957. Ed. Li Wenzhi and Zhang Youyi. 3 vols. Beijing.

ZSGYS. Zhongguo jindai shougongyeshi ziliao. 1957. Ed. Peng Zeyi. 2 vols. Beijing.

Index

Chen Zanxin, 189
Chen Zhong, 160, 170
Cheng Boqian, 194, 224
Cheng Tianfang, 181–82
Chesneaux, Jean, 40
Chi Min-chiu, 111
Chiang Yee, 109
Chinese Communist Party, 26, 137, 156–58,
  165–66, 185, 199, 205, 216–17, 219, 227,
  229–30, 237; control over peasant move-
  ment, 209–10; in Jiangxi, 172–74, 180–84;
  and peasants, 188; and United Front, 172–
  73, 188–93; and Wuhan Debacle, 190–93,
  213
Chinese Economic Journal, 56
Chongan, 229
Chongren, 184
Chongyi, 184
Chu, T. H., 48, 51, 55
Chuzo Ichiko, 72, 75
clan. *See* lineages
Communist Manifesto, 153
Communist Revolution, 39, 160–61, 169–71,
  198, 238, 240–41
Communist Suppression Corps, 180
Confucianism, 132, 143, 152, 161, 165, 169–
  70, 173, 237; Fang's rejection of, 161–62
cotton, 51; areas of, 32, 53; import of, 53–54;
  middleman-merchant in, 55–57; pattern of
  trade, 56–57; plight of weavers, 59; pro-
  duction of, 9; and spinning industry, 58;
  and weaving industry, 58–59
Cui Hao, 148

Dadangpan village, 113
Dadou, 184
Dai Xikuang, 185
Daidou village, 133
Danicourt, Monsignor, 26
Daoguang, 5, 82
Daoism, 4
Daoist Pope. *See* Zhang Tianshi
Dean, 7, 10, 140, 176
Dehua, 53
Deng Heming, 182
Dengshan village, 217
Dexing, 7, 10, 45, 47, 139, 217, 224, 227
Deng Heming, 173
Deng Hewu, 173
Dieshan Academy, 143. *See also* Yiyang
  Higher Primary School

Dingguo, 30
Dingshan Village, 207
Dong river, 3
Dong Siyuan, 194
Dong Wen Academy, 152. *See also* William
  Nast College
Dong Zuoren, 176
Dongfang zazhi, 62
Dongliu, 229
Dongxiang village, 124
Dongxiang district, 184, 194
Dongzhi festival, 11
Doujiang, 229
Dragon and Tiger mountains. *See* Longhu
  mountains
Duan Xipeng, 180, 182, 189
Duchang, 176, 178, 194
dyeing industry, 10. *See also* indigo

East India Co., 45
Eastern Han Dynasty, 206
Economic Year Book, China (1934), 38
Elvin, Mark, 33–34, 69, 95
England, 52
enlistment (shangmingze) campaign, 220
Europe, 18, 45, 168, 180
exploitation, nature of, 82–83, 92–93, 100

Fan Hexiang, 194
Fan Village, 88
Fang Bingshan, 198
Fang Fuhan, 197
Fang Gaohan, 198
Fang Gaoyu, 197–98, 205
Fang Gaozhu, 138
Fang Huari, 224
Fang lineage, 197, 205
Fang Rongnian, 138
Fang Rugui, 61
Fang Shenxi, 224
Fang Xugen, 225
Fang Yuanhui, 193, 197, 204, 208, 216, 218–
  19, 224
Fang Yuanjie, 193, 197, 213
Fang Yuansheng, 194
Fang Zhanggeng, 137
Fang Zhichun, 147, 193–94, 197, 218–19
Fang Zhihui, 138
Fang Zhimin, 3, 23, 80–81, 83, 136, 173–74,
  181–82, 189–91, 205–6, 235, 237–41;
  against AB League, 184–85; against Confu-